WOMEN, POWER, AND AT&T

WOMEN, POWER, AND AT&T

Winning Rights in the Workplace

LOIS KATHRYN HERR

NORTHEASTERN UNIVERSITY PRESS • BOSTON

Northeastern University Press

Library of Congress Cataloging-in-Publication Data
Herr, Lois Kathryn, 1941–
    Women, power, and AT&T : winning rights in the workplace /
Lois Kathryn Herr.
      p. cm.
Includes index.
      ISBN 1-55553-536-4 (pbk. : alk. paper)—ISBN 1-55553-537-2 (cloth : alk. paper)
      1. American Telephone and Telegraph Company—Trials, litigation, etc.
2. Sex discrimination against women—Law and legislation—United States.
3. Sex discrimination in employment—Law and legislation—United States.
I. Title.
KF2849.A4 .H47 2003
331.4'133'0973—dc21   2002010868

Designed by Joanna Bodenweber

Composed in Electra by Creative Graphics, Inc., Allentown, Pennsylvania. Printed and bound by Thomson-Shore, Inc., Dexter, Michigan. The paper is Glatfelter Supple Opaque Recycled, an acid-free stock.

MANUFACTURED IN THE UNITED STATES OF AMERICA
06   05   04   03   5   4   3   2   1

*To the young women and men in my
classes at Elizabethtown College, with
the hope that they will take equal
opportunity to a new level by the sheer
force of their talent. If that isn't enough,
may they then learn from this story that
they can change the world.*

CONTENTS

ILLUSTRATIONS

TABLES

PREFACE

I grew up in a small Pennsylvania town, went to college, married, and started to teach English in a New Jersey seventh-grade classroom in 1963. Ten years later I was a card-carrying feminist and AT&T manager with the satisfaction that I had helped change how AT&T—the largest corporation in the world—treated women and minority employees. That change set a new standard and prompted other corporations to adopt affirmative action and equal employment opportunity policies.

From the fall of 1970 to the spring of 1973, I crossed paths with the major players in a civil war over women's rights. In this book I've told the story of that war from all sides, not just my own, and it is my hope that readers will see it as the adventure that it was. I also hope that readers will see how, with audacity, determination, and luck, individuals and small groups can change big institutions. Those interested in sources will find documentation in the footnotes, with references to academic, government, and corporate archives as well as to extensive interviews and original materials in my own files.

The story starts with women like me finding barriers to progress in our careers, with civil rights activists finding new ways to force companies to adopt new philosophies for the workplace, and with corporate executives who sincerely tried to adjust their organizations to a changing society. As a woman finding my way in a sometimes inhospitable or even hostile environment, I challenged rules and structures that didn't make sense to me. I questioned a company benefit program, while my friend Beth took on a company stag picnic, and another friend, Rosemary, challenged the way women were identified as married or single in the company phone book.

At first, I just wanted to change the barriers to my own progress. To me it seemed that if my benefits were lower, then the salary paid to me was worth less than it would have been if I were a man. I thought that if we were barred from social events with our peers, then we would be seen as "different" on the job as well. Additionally, carrying the tag of "Miss" or "Mrs." was making a primary identification based on whether or not I was attached to a man. All these distinctions got in the way of business and my career.

Unbeknown to me, others with more global concerns were taking stands on these and bigger issues. Ultimately we would join together in a battle to change the internal behavior of AT&T.

In 1970 the Equal Employment Opportunity Commission (EEOC), a fledgling federal government agency with virtually no power, leveraged the power of an established regulatory agency to challenge AT&T's treatment of women and minorities. AT&T was not only the largest company in America in terms of employees, assets, and shareholders; it was also the symbol of good operations management. AT&T's empire, known collectively as the Bell System, included AT&T General Departments and Long Lines, a research and development unit called Bell Telephone Laboratories, a manufacturing unit called the Western Electric Company, and local telephone companies across the country.

Shocked when the EEOC called it the "largest oppressor of women," AT&T struggled to define what was just and proper in a rapidly changing society and to defend its employment practices. The settlement reached in 1973 required AT&T to build the concepts and procedures for equal opportunity into the structure of its business. Government had challenged the best, not the worst, and raised expectations for all businesses.

The confrontation had political and personal dimensions. Its scope was all of American business, and the issues were matters of corporate social responsibility and social justice. *Women, Power, and AT&T* is a story about how change really happens, about courage and audacity, about power and leverage, and about how individuals altered the corporate environment.

On a personal level, I felt the problem before I knew its name, just as years earlier Betty Friedan in *The Feminine Mystique* had identified this same problem in the lives of housewives in the 1950s. I heard Caroline Bird, author of *Born Female*, decry the waste of talent that resulted from discrimination, and I knew exactly what she meant. At a rally, Bird talked about the invisible bars that locked women out, and I had seen them. I felt she understood my life, as few feminist writers did just then. She gave me support for my own views when she wrote, "Change is hard, but the way women are treated is just plain wrong." With her explanation of the "liberated woman of 1970" as "well-educated, privileged . . . idealistic, intense but soft-spoken, and . . . furious," she let me see that I fit in.[1]

With the perspective Bird provided, I could close the gap between my business persona and the feminist I wanted to be. I learned how to do something about the problems at work by associating with the National Organization for Women (NOW). Friends in NOW gave me tools for taking action and helped me connect my personal experience with the larger goals for which they fought. Founded in 1966 by Betty Friedan and friends, NOW had selected employment discrimination as one of its first targets. Later, when the time came to fight AT&T, NOW would be eager to learn more about the company and ready to do battle.

In the first phases of the battle, while the EEOC tracked discrimination complaints and NOW pressed for action, I was still just warming up to feminism. In 1970 I wanted to move one step ahead in my career. That's as far as I could plan. By 1974, when the case was over, I was confident enough to map out a career plan leading to CEO by 2000. In those four years, 1970–74, women went from nowhere to thinking we had changed the world and would have our chance to run it.

When I first got involved, like so many other early corporate feminists, I thought facts would dispel myths and change rules. I harbored no doubts about winning; I was sure that reason would change the system. Though not shy about my views inside the business, I was cautious in revealing my links with women's liberationists or government attorneys.

AT&T was "family," and there was tolerance for internal debate. In most cases, the company gave me room, literally and figuratively, to explore and air my concerns and to organize. I didn't have to be subversive. I had trouble explaining that freedom to outside activists, for they mostly imagined corporate executives as conniving capitalists bent on taking advantage of poor workers, especially women. Perhaps some businesses fit that stereotype, but the Bell System I knew did not. AT&T was committed to the communities it served and cared about its people.

This story is now thirty years old, and the telecommunications industry has changed significantly. No longer do telecommunications companies run "female" help wanted ads. Management training programs recruit women, and a few women do hold CEO positions. The companies that used to be the Bell System were separated by government antitrust action in 1984; divestitures and mergers since then have made it increasingly difficult to trace the effects or assess the long-term impact of what changed for women in 1973. The overall climate of business changed also, with less emphasis now on the long-term relationship between a company and its employees.

Corporate America looks very different today. I suspect that many women now working in telecommunications are unaware of the adventures of their predecessors. For some of those women, the promise of full and equal opportunity exists: they might not, however, understand the roles that feminists and the government played in securing that opportunity. For others the promise is still unfulfilled; the drama continues, and battles for equal opportunity remain quite personal and real. Two recent events highlight successes and failures. On January 7, 2002, Lucent Technologies (formerly Bell Laboratories) announced the appointment of Patricia F. Russo as president and chief executive officer.[2] Just two months earlier, AT&T was accused of sexual harassment and discrimination in complaints filed with the EEOC by 150 employees in nine different states.[3]

The people in this book are real people, dealing with the world as they find it and taking action to make it into the world they would like it to be. The essence of the story is, on a small scale, how one person works to clear her own path. On a larger scale, which I learned quickly by living it, we were working through the federal government to change the rules of the business game and to force corporations into opening the pathways for women and minorities.

The era of this story was an era of huge corporations—successful corporations like AT&T, IBM, GE, General Motors, and Sears. The fabric of society, however, was beginning to unravel in 1968. Martin Luther King Jr. and Robert F. Kennedy were assassinated. Riots erupted in the inner cities. Protestors marched for peace and for civil rights. The streets outside the Democratic National Convention in Chicago turned brutal. It was the era of Lyndon B. Johnson and Richard M. Nixon, an era bracketed by Vietnam and Watergate.

Against that background, the relatively civilized but nonetheless radical encounter between AT&T and the EEOC took place in the hearing rooms of the Federal Communication Commission. As in the other protests of the day, there were individual instigators, but the strength of the case rested on hundreds of individuals and a complex network of activists who operated without e-mail, cheap airfare, cell phones, or low-cost long-distance calling. Those activists rallied against a system that openly discriminated through formal practices and procedures for hiring, promotion, and compensation. Affirmative action, urged by civil rights activists, was designed to alter the structure, to clear the path for women and minorities to rise in the corporate environment.

The case had such visibility within the corporation that people could not avoid becoming aware of the inequities or the changes in the rules. Behavior was changed, and a halo effect existed in attitude. The affirmative action rules adopted by AT&T and other companies remained in place far longer than their authors expected, and the path to opportunity for some began to be seen as a barrier to others. Affirmative action itself would become a target. Women and minorities themselves were able to take their opportunities for granted — exactly the result the proponents of affirmative action wanted to achieve. To the extent that the opportunities exist, one could argue that affirmative action is no longer necessary. However, another part of affirmative action involved the good-faith effort to reach out and build a work force reflective of the available labor pool. In numbers, affirmative action has not yet succeeded, not even after more than thirty years. A new challenge faces corporate feminists and civil rights advocates now — ensuring that corporations meet the spirit of the law.

Herr Farm, July 2002

ACKNOWLEDGMENTS

M y first acknowledgment goes to the prime movers of this story, intense characters whose lives crossed in intricate patterns. Next, I owe a debt to the feminists and writers who gave those of us in the corporate world the words and the courage to fight from within. Their very presence in the streets enabled us inside.

Over the past ten years, as this book became more than boxes of "stuff" and an idea, I have been counseled and supported by three special people: Mary Jean Collins, a feminist friend for thirty years; James C. Armstrong, an AT&T colleague, coach, and critic; and my mother, Kathryn Nisley Herr, who always encourages and inspires me.

More than fifty individuals shared their memories and records of the case. They brought to life all sides of the story, and to them I am especially grateful. Finding them proved a challenge, and I was helped immensely by the development of the Internet and by Jacqui Ceballos, the prime mover behind the Veteran Feminists Association.

Professionals in academe and the archives helped me along the way, especially AT&T's corporate historian Sheldon Hochheiser, Fred Romanski at the National Archives, Joanne Donovan at the Schlesinger Library, and Patricia Bakunas at the University of Illinois at Chicago. Staff members at the Hagley Museum and Library, Columbia Rare Book and Manuscript Library, Tamiment Library at NYU, and the Library of Congress steered me to valuable resources. Together, they guided me through unfamiliar territory and, along with the anonymous readers who critiqued the manuscript, provided scholarly insight and suggestions that strengthened the book. Friends in the academic environment of Elizabethtown College encouraged my writing by their interest, examples, and advice. As the book was taking its final form I met Pamela

Walker Laird and had the opportunity to see my story in a wider historical and theoretical context.

In 1990 I retired from corporate life and New York to a farm in Lancaster County, Pennsylvania, but I did not find my writing space there. It was at Graves Mountain Lodge in Syria, Virginia, that I was able to create the first draft. A particularly relevant place, Graves Mountain Lodge was the site where the EEOC lawyers put together the most important document of this case against AT&T thirty years before. Major rewrites of my manuscript took place on Joan Risser Puchaty's cottage porch in historic Mt. Gretna, one of my favorite places in Pennsylvania. Places are important to me, and I revisited AT&T's old headquarters at 195 Broadway several times. Though new owners have remodeled the executive floors, the huge pillars and brass fixtures in the lobby still reflect the strength, power, and tradition that we associated with AT&T in the 1970s.

Elizabeth P. Swayze, Northeastern University Press's Women's Studies Editor, had faith in this book from the beginning and patiently and skillfully guided me through the publication process. Finding illustrations of specific events proved challenging, since at the time of the case we were more intent on changing the world than on taking pictures. With the research help of Mary-Ann Lupa in Chicago, and the wonderful cooperation of photographers Bettye Lane and Dorothea Jacobson-Wenzel, we found pictures from the time.

In the final stages, Doris J. McBeth tended the manuscript. Seeing every page so many times, she partnered with me in this, our first book. Somehow she continually approached my changes with good humor and good skills.

ABBREVIATIONS

195	195 Broadway, New York, New York—AT&T headquarters
AT&T	American Telephone & Telegraph
Bell Labs	Bell Telephone Laboratories
BFOQ	Bona Fide Occupational Qualification
C&P	Chesapeake and Potomac Telephone Company
CRBM	Columbia Rare Book and Manuscript Library
CRLA	California Rural Legal Assistance
CULA	Center for United Labor Action
CWA	Communications Workers of America
EEOC	Equal Employment Opportunity Commission
EPC	Executive Policy Committee
FCC	Federal Communication Commission
FEP	Fair Employment Practices
GEI	General Executive Instructions
GSA	General Services Administration
Hagley	Hagley Museum and Library
HEW	U.S. Department of Health, Education, and Welfare
IBEW	International Brotherhood of Electrical Workers
IBM	International Business Machines
ICC	Illinois Commerce Commission
IMDP	Initial Management Development Program
Justice	U.S. Department of Justice
Labor	U.S. Department of Labor
MALDEF	Mexican American Legal Defense and Education Fund
NAACP	National Association for the Advancement of Colored People
NACP	National Archives at College Park, Maryland

NAM	National Association of Manufacturers
NOW	National Organization for Women
OFCC	Office of Federal Contract Compliance in the Department of Labor
PT&T	Pacific Telephone and Telegraph Company
RG	Record Group
Schlesinger	Schlesinger Library, Radcliffe Institute, Harvard University
SMSA	Standard Metropolitan Statistical Area
UIC	University of Illinois at Chicago
WEAL	Women's Equity Action League
WIMDP	Women's Initial Management Development Program

1

TESTING THE RULES

No pants. Women were not allowed to wear pantsuits to work, not even on the coldest of Midwest winter days. To this day I don't know if it was a written rule for us at Bell Telephone Laboratories, but I do know it was a written policy for many telephone company employees in the late 1960s. Written or unwritten, "no pants" made no sense to me.

I was young and naïve, however, and I had a job, not a career. I saw a few nuisance rules, but I didn't see the walls.

The country's premier research and development employer, Bell Labs was a good place to work for a woman in the 1960s. Hired as a technical editor, I found not just work but a good life with lots of friends and after-hours fun. Company softball, golf, bowling, international film showings, picnics and parties—there was something for everyone.

Software was the new game in town then, with an electronic switching system installed for the first time in a telephone office in Succasunna, New Jersey, in 1966. When the Naperville, Illinois, "Indian Hill" location of Bell Labs opened later that year, seven hundred of us transferred there from New Jersey.

By organizational accident, technical editing at Indian Hill was part of a technical department, and I knew women who were taking on new technical roles beyond traditional secretarial, clerical, and administrative positions. Programming and computer work was new; to get its work force for the new computer technology, Bell Labs looked for math majors. Women held some of those math degrees, so the company hired them. Programming was a less valued job than engineering, however, and programmers could be hired in lower-ranked, lower-paid positions than the engineers who had come in as "members of technical staff."[1] There had been women members of technical staff before, but not many, and those who did get through became legends, like Hildegaard Vellenzer and Erna Hoover. All of those women ranked above me in the corporate framework; because they did, I began to think about upward career steps.

All was not easy for the female programmer, however. When my friend Frank Goetz, a technical supervisor, was out recruiting programmers, his guidelines told him to offer male math graduates one salary and females another. Though the company had a rationale, it bothered him, but we never talked about it then. When he moved to Illinois in 1966, Goetz connected with a liberal wing of the Catholic Church and hence to issues of civil rights. He was primed to understand, but there was no reason to challenge company practices. Goetz told women the truth. He explained that math degrees would get them programming positions and they *might* be able to pursue graduate studies. He told men that a job offer meant they would definitely be supported through graduate school. Different risks, different opportunities, different expectations, different pay. No one objected—that is just the way it was.[2] At the time, women did not know what particular courses and paths to take to become eligible for a position equal to their male peers. Women were hired as "senior technical aides"; in some cases they joined as part of a "courtship" program, which offered women the opportunity to be promoted after a year of graduate school and proving themselves on the job. Few men came into the company via that courtship program.[3]

The numbers went up; more and more women joined the ranks. On the administrative staff side, there was a fast track, or "jet" management program, but that was still for men only. In a few years, female programmers would band together and fight the caste system, but for the moment, they accepted it. I didn't know the details of Bell Labs' hiring, but I knew there were women in higher ranks. I pushed ahead.

Daily life had its trials, like wasting time explaining why "girls" wasn't an appropriate term or why it was not necessary to squirm in the elevator to let women out first. Petty little issues, the trappings of larger problems. We found ways around the unspoken rules when we had to. And while some men blocked our paths, others became mentors and friends.

When it came to clothing, those unwritten rules applied. Pantsuits had come into fashion, and I bought several. The first was a light blue tweed suit with wide-legged, cuffed pants and a long, sleeveless tunic that doubled as a miniskirt. Add a blouse, and I was really covered. The tunic was acceptable by itself, of course, but with the pants it was unacceptable. That did not make sense to me.

The other outfit—pink—featured a long belted jacket; a jewel-collared, short-sleeved top; and long, tailored pants. The Pink Panther could not have been less threatening. On days when I felt less brave, I could wear a matching miniskirt instead of the pants.

After testing the pantsuits on social occasions, I finally got the nerve to wear the pink suit to work. Nobody said anything. The day passed. Circuits functioned, programs ran, meetings and phone calls went on. Bell Labs–Indian Hill had experienced a nonevent—its first woman in a pantsuit.

Almost thirty years later I would learn that my boss, Charlie Kuhl, mentioned the appearance of the pants to his department head, Caesar Marchetto, who ran into his boss's office in a sweat. With what must have been uncharacteristic anxiety in his voice, Marchetto warned our director, Werner Ulrich, that I was wearing pants. Ulrich calmed Marchetto and put the situation into perspective.[4] In his ability to separate work-related issues from stereotypical reactions, Ulrich was ahead of his time.

In other parts of our building, similar confrontations took place. Fran Chessler, tagged by her friends to be the leader, approached her boss, Jack Scanlon, to test how he would react to women in the technical department wearing pants, that is, nicely coordinated suits with pants. Puffing on his cigar, Scanlon mused that he did not give a damn if they came to work buck naked as long as they wore closed-toed shoes, because that was in the GEI (the General Executive Instructions—the rule book).[5] Western Electric manager Beth Chilton encountered a different objection when the head of the secretarial pool complained about her pants to managers and suggested they send her home, which they did not.[6] No one in that very rational place could build a case against pants. The unwritten rule simply disappeared, and we went on to other issues. I was beginning to see that the rules were different for men and women. I also saw that we could change the rules.

Discriminatory treatment was everywhere. Some clues were not so subtle. Women noticed and started to talk with each other. It was personal and it was political.

"Charlie," I told my boss, "I'd like a job like yours. I know you think engineering standards is a necessary background, so how about transferring me across the hall into engineering standards?" Kuhl put me off by saying that the guys in that group came from the drafting department and I had not been in drafting. All draftsmen were men. As an awakening activist, I perceived an illogical barrier, though at the time I thought it was a matter of my experience. Whether or not that standards job was the only or even a good option for me, being denied the opportunity to consider it was a challenge. If there were other avenues, such as technical writing, I did not see them as real. I saw a brick wall.

Otherwise, I found opportunities and freedom that were well above what many of my friends in other companies encountered. Bell Labs was truly a collegial environment. My editing job had expanded to accommodate my new interests. I investigated computer text processing with IBM long before it was a solid commercial offering anywhere; I set up classes and taught technical writing to the engineers; I took software programming classes to understand the electronic switching programs we were documenting. It seemed as if I could do whatever I wanted that would help the company and me. Not being considered for a job I felt was quite within my capabilities seemed unusual and irrational.

Ready for a fight, I claimed I could learn. My boss promised to talk it over with his boss, Marchetto. On up the ladder the question went. Even from Ulrich the answer was no. This decision did not make sense to me, particularly from someone who was an early supporter of women in the technical departments. Why was this such a big deal to them? If I could do the job, why not?

In frustration, I decided to look outside the company. I called on Roland Women, an employment agency in Chicago, but they had no jobs for women that paid anywhere near my salary. Roland Women suggested I go to Roland Men, where on Wednesday, April 8, 1970, I dutifully filled out their forms, feeling very awkward as the only woman on the applicant side of the desk. I was ignored.

Kuhl had an alternative opportunity for me—transfer from the technical department to supervise a typing pool. He meant well, but he did not have my growing feminist perspective or my sensitivity to "pink collar" jobs. The typing pool job offer confirmed the patterns of female employment that I had been hearing about. None of my male managers understood that I was unhappy to be blocked and would be even unhappier walled into a female ghetto. I could not explain my problem because I did not yet have the words. It seemed that if only we could explain ourselves, men would understand and all would be well. On some days it seemed hopeless; on others I felt like taking on the world.

In my late twenties, I was semiconscious of the larger world, celebrating Earth Day and worrying about the Vietnam War, but not deeply involved. The company provided friends and social life as well as job satisfaction. With its generous treatment of employees, Bell Labs made me feel like part of the family. We might have squabbles, but they were family fights.

Until the spring of 1970 I had been on a traditional path—college to marriage to apartment to town house to four-bedroom ranch with a Ford Fairlane in the driveway. I made draperies, baked apple pies, and planted strawberries. Not satisfied with domestic successes, I found challenges at work and began to want more responsibilities. I decided to prove I was serious about a career. I did not know what a feminist was, but I felt I could compete with the men I knew.

By summer, I would be living in a condo and working on an MBA at the University of Chicago. I was more than ready for the National Organization for Women (NOW) to come into my life. After only a few meetings, I joined the Chicago chapter for their retreat weekend at Lake Geneva, Wisconsin. Bette Vidina, a natural fit for the membership job she held in Chicago NOW, talked to me when I arrived, and I felt welcome. Mostly I listened. In some ways, I felt as though I were on another planet—they talked in shorthand about laws and groups and people I did not know. They hugged. I was a conservative kid from a small town in Pennsylvania, but that was okay with them. They let me talk, and though my corporate experience was foreign to many of them, they listened. I was not yet at home with this crowd, but I was drawn to them.

Later I would understand that, like me, women all over the Bell System were recognizing sex discrimination. In those days AT&T included the General Departments and Long Lines, Bell Labs for research and development, the Western Electric Company for manufacturing, and twenty-two operating telephone companies. One of every fifty-six working women worked for Ma Bell.

NOW helped us a great deal and sensitized us to little clues that were everywhere—including the way organization charts listed men by their initials or names, but women by Mrs. or Miss, clearly noting whether or not they were married. (It would be another year till *Ms.* magazine hit the newsstands and Ms. would become common terminology.)[7] One brave soul, my patent attorney friend Rosemary Ryan, questioned the different patterns in a note to the company newsletter. They responded by discussing Ms., Mrs., and Miss without reference to Mr.:

> *There has been a noticeable trend towards use of the title "Ms." as a substitute for "Miss" and Mrs." The development has occurred partly because of the frequent need for an expedient alternative when the marital status of the person addressed is not known, and partly as the result of a heightened*

awareness in our society of possible discriminatory practices based on sex and marital status.

While the use of "Ms." is growing, at this juncture it is by no means generally established as the preferable title to use. For this reason Bell Laboratories will continue for the time being to use the more widely accepted titles "Miss" and "Mrs." This decision in no way detracts from the Company's expressed commitment to a non-discriminatory policy in all aspects of employment.[8]

Ryan and I continued to challenge Bell Labs with letters to the editor. We started to pick up on stories in the newspapers about women's rights and then talk about them at work. In the *Chicago Tribune*, Carol Kleiman wrote a "working woman" column, which I read religiously. Once she wrote about state laws, starting off with these two sentences:

Here's a real shocker: There are no Illinois laws that work for the working woman.

That means there is not one single state law that prohibits employers from discriminating against women in hiring, firing, fringe benefits, wages, promotion, job categories, classified ads or training programs.[9]

She went on to commend "Bell Telephone," meaning Illinois Bell Telephone Company, for challenging the current labor laws that "protect" nonadministrative women workers by restricting their work to eight hours a day. She sent me running for the rulebook—the General Executive Instructions. What did *my* company have on its books with respect to these matters?

Benefits was not a "sexy" issue, but it opened my eyes. I discovered that our company benefit plan did treat men and women differently. I read the fine print. If my husband died at work—for instance, while flying to New Jersey on company business—then I, as his wife, would receive a death benefit in addition to all other payments. If I died in a similar business situation, he got not a penny from the benefit provision because he was not "totally dependent" on me for support. Bottom line, my salary was discounted because the benefits were lower.

That was not fair, and in the tenor of the time, I naïvely thought that if I pointed out the inequity, the company would see the logic and change it. Surely my company would not design a system that blatantly treated working women so differently. Wrong.

Not long after that revelation, I posted a notice about "Women's Rights" on the company bulletin boards, calling attention to the inequities in education and employment and benefits in particular. "Let's get together and discuss this issue," I suggested. In the notice I also announced NOW's plans for a national strike on August 26, 1970, and gave a telephone number people could call. The strike would celebrate the fiftieth anniversary of women's right to vote.

I sent a letter to Morgan Sparks, chairman of the Bell Laboratories Employees' Benefit Committee; I purposely dated the letter August 26, 1970, though I would be "striking" on that actual day. The letter was blunt: "I am aware of instances of specific discrimination, based on sex, in our benefit plan." I went on to cite chapter and verse from the GEI, listing the sickness death benefit, the accident death benefit, the pension survivor options, and the retirement age. I reminded him that the company had recently bragged about the value of benefits to employees. Hanging out with activists, I had learned to be direct: "In effect, this differentiation appears to be a violation of: 1) the GEI which, in 5.1–6, defines the obligation to treat employees without regard to sex, saying 'such actions shall include, but not be limited to, the following . . . rates of pay or other forms of compensation . . .'; and, 2) the Civil Rights Act of 1964."[10] Little did I know at the time that Ruth Bader Ginsburg (the future Supreme Court justice) was arguing cases dealing with sex discrimination, and with benefits in particular, before the Supreme Court, cases that ultimately would change those corporate benefit plans.[11]

On Tuesday, August 25, Wheaton mayor Marget Hamilton and I were interviewed by an Aurora radio station—the tape to be broadcast the next day. Meanwhile, on the actual day of August 26, 1970, I skipped work—a "strike for equality." The slogan that year came from Dr. Ann London Scott, an academic and relatively new NOW member herself who would later be very much involved in Bell System issues. She coined the phrase "Don't iron while the strike is hot." My friend the Chicago activist Mary-Ann Lupa did the artwork. On the day of the strike, I took the train into Chicago, handed out leaflets on State Street, attended the noon rally, and watched the pickets at the Civic Center. At noon, as arranged by NOW the day before, NBC interviewed me for a few minutes for the noon news. I thought it was important to show that professional women were supporting the movement, but I was nervous. At the microphone in the Civic Center that day, Mary Lynn Myers represented Federally Employed Women and reminded everyone that "women who work full-time and year-round earn 58 percent of what men earn on the average and this wage gap has been increasing for over a decade." Clara Day, from the International Brotherhood of Teamsters, spoke of women's working conditions. Polly Connelly from the Abortion Coalition pointed out, "Nationally, approximately 1,500,000 illegal abortions were performed in 1969, resulting in more than 5,000 deaths due to complications." And the Women's Liberation Union representatives argued, "There is something wrong when an attractive woman can make more money as a Playboy Bunny or cover girl than anything else." Northwestern University's student body president, Eva Jefferson, added that "one of the qualifications for being president of a university is having a charming wife. That eliminates women right off." And so it went, as women listed the reasons for revolution.[12] In the evening, my husband met me at the Conrad Hilton Hotel, then we walked over to the rally at Grant Park to hear civil rights speakers like Fannie Lou Hamer. August 26, 1970—we'd been to our first demonstration.

Back at the labs, my boss, Charlie Kuhl, had a problem with my "I'm joining the women's strike in honor of the right to vote; I don't expect to be paid for today" note. As a reportable event, it did not fit. There were no codes for this kind of situation. They could not figure out how not to pay me.

Knowing NOW people and the comfort of their company, I looked for that comfort with others at work. And I took the advice of a new NOW friend and organizer, Mary Jean Collins-Robson—"Do something."

I found a dozen coworkers from Bell Labs and Western Electric who had responded to my posted notice and wanted to talk about women's rights—five men and seven women, counting me. Under the umbrella of the "Open Forum" club structure of Bell Labs, we set ourselves up as a "Women's Rights Committee"; that gave us permission to use bulletin boards and meeting facilities at work. We met almost daily for a while, gathering around a table in the cafeteria or in a meeting room. We built a list of two dozen agenda topics, from advertising to religion, insurance to literature. Beth Chilton, who would soon become a department chief at Western Electric, brought information from the Chicago Women's Liberation Union; I brought material and announcements from NOW; we shared books such as Caroline Bird's *Born Female* and Betty Friedan's *Feminine Mystique*. Meeting often during the fall and winter of 1970–71, the Bell Labs Women's Rights Committee planned meetings on topics such as equal pay for equal work, child-care centers, sexsell ads, equal say in the political process, and manners.[13]

Like many other groups throughout the Bell System, our Women's Rights Committee put together a statement of purpose. Unlike some parts of the Bell System, Bell Labs had an academic bent and was a relatively easy environ-

Mary Jean Collins Robson and Jim Collins-Robson.

Reprinted with permission of the photographer Bettye Lane.

ment in which to talk about controversial topics. The Women's Rights Committee was more public, and the Statement of Purpose was more assertive, than many other internal women's rights groups could be; we freely incorporated NOW philosophies into our mission statement. Not only did the committee want to raise the level of awareness concerning the facts and problems pertaining to women, but we clearly intended to take action "to change discriminatory and demeaning attitudes and behavior."[14]

Members of the committee shared the work—Chilton was assigned to find out about Western Electric's affirmative action, and I promised to find out about the Bell Labs program. We compared notes on December 9, 1970, unaware that the very next day would be a momentous one. By January 28, 1971, when Illinois Bell's Harriet White came to talk with us, we knew that the Equal Employment Opportunity Commission (EEOC) had on December 10 declared war on AT&T.

White connected with us through NOW, being one of those who could communicate with both corporate types and activists. Before joining Illinois Bell as one of the few women at district level in February 1968, White worked for the National Conference of Christians and Jews and had dealt with issues of equality for thirteen years. Friends thought she "abandoned ship" when she went to work for a corporation. Illinois Bell hired her to do sensitivity training on minority issues, but she soon became embroiled in other equity issues as well. The U.S. Labor Department's Office of Federal Contract Compliance (OFCC) did one of its early reviews at Illinois Bell. From her personal contacts, White knew the OFCC officer and welcomed her to a chicken casserole dinner party at home.[15] White helped those of us at Bell Labs understand the networking we could do and how we fit into the larger context of the issues women faced in the Bell System. She also was an example of how a woman could advocate for women and still be a part of the management hierarchy.

White reviewed the genesis of affirmative action and the requirements of Revised Order no. 4, which extended the OFCC's contract compliance rules to cover women. She noted that the company recognized the problem and was attempting to deal with it. She added that the company was involved at many levels, with an AT&T headquarters vice president of personnel having been on President Richard Nixon's task force on women, and more recently, by establishing a Bell System task force on women.[16] All of this was new to us. We quickly learned about government agencies, laws, and the executive orders that would become so important in our fight. We even learned more about our own company—about the relationships of AT&T's corporate headquarters personnel group with various parts of the Bell System—Bell Laboratories, Western Electric, and the telephone companies like Illinois Bell.

In addition to having outside speakers, our women's rights committee staged consciousness-raising events by designating days to spread out at tables in the cafeteria and intentionally start conversations about women's rights. We hosted movies, such as "The X Factor: Women as People."

No one held us back formally, and outsiders encouraged us. It felt good to read supportive articles, such as Kleiman's column, which in January covered Mary Jean Collins-Robson, the president of NOW's Chicago chapter. My calendar is filled with references to calling Collins-Robson for support and guidance; she became a key person in my feminist life.

As a group and individually, we achieved minor victories. Chilton, for example, went to war over a stag picnic. Western Electric had plans for its annual picnic on June 18, 1971. Before they even got organized, Chilton went to the picnic chairman to request that the event be open to women. The committee vetoed the idea by a vote of eighteen to one. Chilton appealed their decision to her managers, only to be castigated in front of the entire engineering group.[17] Believing that they could just as easily make it a picnic for "whites only," Chilton explained to all of us that women are conditioned to being excluded and cannot always see the discrimination unless we substitute race in place of sex and hear it again.

Chilton did her homework and found that committee members used work time for meetings, each department donated the time and efforts of one male representative, ticket sales were solicited during working hours, the company provided supplies, and management was encouraged to participate. She brought possible solutions to the Women's Rights Committee: we could send documentation of the sexual discrimination to the Equal Employment Opportunity Commission (EEOC), picket the picnic with signs, call the local press, write letters, obtain tickets illegally and attend, or do nothing.

Under pressure from Chilton, Western Electric kept the picnic low profile and took "stag" out of the name. Bell Labs denied them permission to place posters on the bulletin boards, mail flyers through the mailroom, or have tickets printed in the reproduction department. In time, the picnic would include women. It sounds so easy. It was so hard.

Ever alert, Chilton noticed a new safety poster—a woman in bed saying, "Just wanted to remind you to wear your seat belt"—and on March 3, 1971, called the administrator in charge of safety. She was told it was important to promote safety, that the poster came from AT&T headquarters, and that the poster would stay in place. Win some, lose some.[18]

My patience sometimes grew thin, especially when I was asked, for what seemed the millionth time, "Tell me again why you don't like being called 'girl'?" I tried to explain that it is a demeaning term if women are girls in the work environment where the men are men, not boys. What could be easier to understand? Yet they countered with, "My wife likes to be called a girl," or "The secretaries call themselves girls." That's not the point, I tried to argue, but I lost.

Meanwhile, I did a research project for my MBA work at the University of Chicago, naturally, that project studied a related issue. I compared NOW member statistics with what suburban Chicago women expected NOW women to be. From that I concluded that here was an opportunity. With the help of Chicago NOW members, my husband and I hosted a meeting on April 18, 1971, to form a NOW chapter in DuPage County, one of the first NOW chapters in the suburbs. Everywhere I turned there was an opportunity for feminist action.

NOW became a major calendar entry for me; I edited the newsletter and attended chapter events and board meetings. At work, I was added officially to the company's Affirmative Action Committee (May 4, 1971). While the top issue was minorities, women's issues surfaced, and one of the early topics was maternity leave. One computer programmer, forced to take a leave of absence at seven and a half months into her pregnancy, was actually welcomed back with the same job and a raise that kept her even with her peers.[19] Bell Labs was ahead of AT&T on maternity leave, albeit sometimes through unofficial means.[20]

From company sources, the official Affirmative Action Committee heard that the EEOC in Washington was "bogged down with complaints," and while the Labor Department contract compliance efforts showed "promise," the definition of a bona fide occupational qualification (BFOQ) was still "fuzzy."[21] How easy was it to define a job as male or female because of some "BFOQ"?

In June I presented a paper on automated text processing to the national conference of the Society of Technical Writers and Publishers. While there I convened a caucus on women's rights in the editing and publishing field and interviewed for a job with AT&T's Management Sciences Department in New York City. I went from a Bell Labs Affirmative Action Committee meeting on June 8 to a NOW Board meeting on June 9 and a DuPage County NOW organizing meeting on June 13. Everything revolved around feminist issues.

Meanwhile, my husband and I planned a move to New York City, based primarily on his transfer to AT&T headquarters. While I might wish we were on equal terms, his job provided the majority of our income, and he had a career path. Besides, I was ready to get to corporate headquarters.

My "to do" list expanded as I tried to wrap up work on a variety of projects, including finding a job, videotaping a technical writing course, keeping up with my technical editing responsibilities, and as a member of the advocate corps of Chicago NOW, advising a woman who felt aggrieved by sex discrimination at a meat-packing company.

Fortunately, classes at the University of Chicago were over. The move to New York City was only three months away. In my notes were references to AT&T "EEO" folks like Don Liebers and the highest-ranking woman in the system—Amy Hanan, in environmental affairs. People to meet when I moved to AT&T.

Every activist I knew had a long list of projects and threaded women's rights through all of them. Not content to change our own lives, we moved out to influence others everywhere we could. On NOW speaking engagements over the summer, I talked with the American Friends Service Committee, Wheaton High School, and the Brandywine Mothers Club, among others.[22]

At the NOW National Executive Committee Meeting in Milwaukee on July 4, 1971, I met the leaders of NOW. Wilma Scott Heide, the new chair of NOW, and I got to know each other and talked about the possibility of creating an administrative director position for NOW. Heide was concerned about the organizational structure and responsibility assignment in NOW; everything was done on a volunteer basis. She also wanted to build a good communications network. Mary Jean Collins-Robson's husband, Jim, took over running the NOW national office and would subsequently process national NOW membership and publications. Heide wanted to understand the national office's capacity "without volunteer help" and to know just how much volunteer help would be needed. One of her concerns in building the organization was finding a way to get information on national policy and actions out to local chapters. I liked her management style and her approach to running NOW.

Talking with Heide at length, I learned more of her philosophy. Grandmotherly in appearance, she cut through to the real issues quickly and directly. She talked about the view that women don't get along with other women, seeing that not as natural but as an "indicator of oppression." She noted that it is "safer to imitate the oppressor." Heide often talked about the only uniquely female job—incubator—and the only uniquely male job—sperm donor.[23] Heide's style put you at ease, and her incisive words brought you to attention.

Attendees at that board meeting included Aileen C. Hernandez (president), Dr. Ann Scott, Sylvia Roberts (southern regional director), Lucy Komisar (public relations vice president), Mary Jean Collins-Robson (NOW Midwest regional director and coordinator of NOW task forces), Dr. JoAnn Evansgardner (founder of KNOW, Inc.), Shirley Bernard (western regional director), Faith Seidenberg (NOW legal vice president), Paula Bernstein, Dr. Mordeca Jane Pollock (academic from Brandeis University), Karen DeCrow (eastern regional director), Nan Wood (business owner), and Eliza Paschall (NOW board secretary).[24] Many of these women would play important roles in the future battle over discrimination in the Bell System. I was impressed.

At the board meeting, NOW's executive committee talked about plans for archives at the Schlesinger Library at Radcliffe College in Cambridge. They

Wilma Scott Heide

Reprinted with permission of the photographer Bettye Lane.

talked about the next August 26 event, which would be a fund-raiser to get $100,000 for the legislative office in Washington, and about a legal defense and education fund, bylaws, and the NOW national conference planned for September in Los Angeles.[25]

NOW had moved into my life. The men and women in NOW formed a circle of friends as well as a workforce. We came from different backgrounds but shared a common understanding. Collins-Robson, educated at Alverno College to teach, had opened a new feminist bookstore after failing to find books on suffragists and feminists in local bookstores. Scott, a poet and English professor, became incensed at the inequities in faculty ranks and translated the concepts of affirmative action into academia; she would quickly take on legislative matters and Washington lobbying for NOW.

Little things became big questions, from whether women could get management jobs to whether "girl" was appropriate terminology. Being with NOW friends was a haven for me—a place of psychological rest. However, it was not a place of stillness. We were always busy plotting, planning, or working. And the opportunities almost overwhelmed us. The number of action items grew each day.

Elsewhere, others were equally but officially drawn to righting the wrongs of discrimination. In Washington, the EEOC had been watching AT&T and other corporations for several years. Created by the Civil Rights Act of 1964, the EEOC worked to ensure equal opportunity, but it lacked enforcement powers and struggled to influence corporate behavior.

In December 1970 the EEOC discovered an opportunity of its own.

2

THE CHALLENGE

One small line jumped out at EEOC attorney David A. Copus when he leaned down to pick up the *Washington Post* after his morning run in Washington on a cold November day in 1970: "The Bell System is seeking a 6 percent increase in its long distance revenue."[1] Economic conditions had changed, the *Post* noted, and AT&T asked for Federal Communications Commission (FCC) approval for an increase in nationwide long distance rates.[2] Copus immediately jumped to the conclusion that the FCC could intervene in the case and perhaps hold up the rate increase in order to force AT&T, the largest employer in the country, to toe the line on equal opportunity. On his way to the EEOC office, Copus thought out a plan based on his earlier work for the Urban League in a Potomac Electric Power case. He would argue that discrimination is economically inefficient and, thus, that discriminatory practices cost ratepayers money.[3]

This was it. This was the avenue—the way by which a major corporation, the largest in the world, could be coerced into becoming a corporate power that would do the work of affirmative action throughout the U.S. business establishment.

Copus talked his idea over with a colleague, William C. Oldaker, knowing he would be interested. As special assistant to EEOC chairman William H. Brown III, Oldaker had made no secret of his intent to lay down a marker, to force a process through which employment discrimination would be rooted out internally by professionals within companies or those they would hire to do it. The Bell System, known casually as Ma Bell and corporately as AT&T, was the largest employer outside the government. The number of employees who had been with the company less than a year (136,000 in 1971), that is, the new employees themselves, made up a "company" larger than the total employed by many of the largest industrial corporations in the country. One year's new hires for AT&T equalled the number of all employees in the nation's next eight largest utilities.[4] Looking ahead, AT&T expected to increase its telephone operator workforce by 130,000 by 1980, growth equivalent to the total workforce of RCA, then a major corporation itself.[5] Founded in 1885, AT&T was arguably the strongest and most respected corporation in America, and the company with the most widely owned stock—3 million share owners held AT&T stock.[6] AT&T's assets of $47 billion in 1969 made it the wealthiest corporation in the world.[7]

The EEOC had been tracking the performance of several industries and tabulating the number of race, sex, and national origin discrimination complaints filed against each. Because of the number of cases, the company at the top of that list was AT&T.[8]

Employment discrimination was a hot issue in Washington. The focus of government civil rights efforts, Oldaker had observed, was drifting away from busing and education, which were politically controversial, to the more acceptable themes of job integration and opportunity.[9] At that time, major government agencies involved in equal opportunity matters included the EEOC, the Department of Labor with its Office of Contract Compliance and the Wage and Hour Division, the Department of Justice Civil Rights Division, and the General Service Administration (GSA) Contract Compliance Office.[10]

While President Richard M. Nixon soothed conservatives with rhetoric, he supported employment programs for minorities and the development of affirmative action. Leonard Garment, then a "special consultant to the president," carried the message about "goals and timetables" to audiences both inside and outside the government. Nixon supported affirmative action and its goals-and-timetables approach as "benign outreach programs to remedy cases of actual discrimination."[11]

When Copus approached Oldaker that morning with his intervention idea, Oldaker was sympathetic. Just a year earlier, when he worked in the Broadcast Bureau of the FCC, it had been his job to write employment guidelines for the broadcast industry. With Copus's plan, the EEOC, even without enforcement powers of its own, could leverage the power of the FCC. Officially, the FCC's primary regulatory role dealt with the rates charged by communications companies. Familiar with the need to get concerted government action,

Oldaker saw intervention in the rate case as a way to squeeze AT&T from both Labor's Office of Contract Compliance (OFCC) and the EEOC.

Oldaker called his friend George P. Sape, who worked at the FCC and had put together the employment guidelines for common carriers much as Oldaker had done for the broadcast industry. AT&T, through its regulatory vice president, Dan Emerson, had worked with the FCC's Sape and the head of the Common Carrier Bureau, Bernard Strassburg, on issues related to employment testing, educational requirements, evaluation standards, men-only job distinctions, and a policy that no mothers of illegitimate children could be hired. A letter from Strassburg to Emerson dated November 13, 1969, reported to AT&T that the EEOC had materials indicating that "discrimination may be present in certain of the companies and that the employment practices of certain of the Bell companies may contain built-in opportunities for discrimination."[12] The proposed rulemaking on nondiscrimination in employment practices was issued by the FCC on November 19, 1969. AT&T filed its comments on January 15, 1970.

Sape conferred with Strassburg and Asher Ende (head of the FCC's trial staff), both knowledgeable and respected in the telecommunications world and experienced in regulating AT&T. A career FCC employee, Strassburg was heavily involved in the issues of the day—the first private microwave services proposed by the fledgling Microwave Communication, Inc. (MCI), ongoing debates about industry structure, and whether non-AT&T equipment could be connected to the telephone lines without harming the network.[13] With positive feedback from Strassburg and Ende, Sape then went to discuss the Copus plan with Oldaker and Copus. Sape, in his business suit, found the other two in jeans, eating potato chips and Snickers bars. All agreed it would be a great idea to make a statement of some sort, and the intervention struck them as a real opportunity. Sape went back to the FCC and told Strassburg and Ende about the plan.[14]

FCC guidelines on employment for common carriers such as AT&T, written by Sape, required that "equal opportunity in employment shall be afforded by all common carrier licensees or permittees to all qualified persons, and no personnel shall be discriminated against in employment because of sex, race, color, religion or national origin." Furthermore, the guidelines required the FCC to work with the EEOC. Few federal regulatory agencies had such specific requirements.[15] The stage was set.

Oldaker and Copus went to see Brown, who had taken over the chairmanship of the EEOC in 1969. Brown asked a few questions but quickly saw how this action would be a perfect fit with his goal of changing systems rather than dealing with one case at a time. A memorandum was circulated to the commissioners, and though there was opposition from Dr. Luther Holcomb, they voted to go ahead.[16] Holcomb, the vice chairman of the commission, had been appointed by his friend President Lyndon Johnson and had in fact been working at the EEOC since its first days.[17]

Brown welcomed the opportunity to act. A target of friends and foes alike, the EEOC had been struggling in the late 1960s and into 1970 to establish itself. Charged by former commissioner and NOW president Aileen C. Hernandez with failing to exercise equal employment opportunity internally (i.e., not practicing what they preached) and with the inability to move on specific complaints, the EEOC was on the defensive.[18]

In the 1960s, Brown and other individuals came to Washington bent on changing the world. Lawyers came with a civil rights interest; for some it was the best place to make a difference or the most interesting environment. Oldaker and Copus were drawn to it. The twenty-six-year-old Oldaker moved from the FCC to the EEOC in November 1968, and Copus, after a Peace Corps tour, took a job there in December, the eleventh lawyer hired. Sape, hired by Strassburg at the FCC, had been involved with the Civil Rights Council in law school and was naturally interested when called upon to write guidelines for common carrier compliance with civil rights legislation. The judge who eventually would handle the AT&T case, A. Leon Higginbotham, then a member of the Federal Trade Commission, was close to President Lyndon Johnson and had recommended Brown for the EEOC in 1968.[19]

Brown assigned attorney Lawrence J. Gartner and Susan Deller Ross, a new hire just out of New York University law school, to work with Copus on writing the intervention by the deadline of December 10, 1970. Ross was an activist and a feminist by the time she enrolled in law school. Now she ensured that the issue of sex discrimination would be a key element of the EEOC filing. This was not her first exposure to such issues; during her last year in law school she had an American Civil Liberties Union fellowship to research state labor protection laws and their impact on women. During that work, she received guidance from Pauli Murray, a well-known feminist lawyer and author, and Eleanor Holmes Norton, then assistant legal director at the American Civil Liberties Union. When Ross finished her research, Catherine East from the Department of Labor Women's Bureau called to get permission to use her report in congressional hearings.[20]

The EEOC's early reputation as a defender of women's rights was sketchy at best. Representative Martha Griffiths of Michigan, NOW, and others criticized the EEOC for its failure to deal with women's issues.[21] Within the EEOC, racial discrimination was the dominant concern, but Ross made certain that sex was included in the tough language she wrote into the Petition for Intervention in the AT&T case: "pervasive, system-wide, and blatantly unlawful discrimination in employment against women, blacks, Spanish-surnamed Americans, and other minorities."[22] On December 10 Brown signed the petition to the FCC. The forty-eight-page memorandum was accompanied by a request for relief asking for investigation, relief including back pay, prosecution, and orders to AT&T to cease discriminatory employment practices. Even at this early stage, the EEOC put forth a substantial argument, charging that AT&T violated rules of the FCC, the Civil Rights Act of 1964, the Equal Pay Act of 1963, executive orders, the Constitution, laws of thirty states, and ordinances of numerous cities.[23]

In the filing the EEOC quoted AT&T's own statements of size. For example, Frederick R. Kappel, AT&T's chairman of the board in 1967, had said, "We have more people at work than any other organization except the government. So the matter of how we handle ourselves has more than ordinary significance."[24] At the time of the filing, about 700,000 people were employed by the AT&T companies directly charged in the case.[25]

In the petition, Copus included examples of the sex-segregated jobs in the company and statistics on the dearth of minorities in skilled and higher-level positions. As further evidence of the situation, the petition noted that "whereas AT&T's employees account for less than 1% of the nation's workforce, they filed nearly 7% of all EEOC complaints in fiscal 1970. In addition, over thirty Title VII lawsuits have been filed against Bell Companies." Such lawsuits were charges of discrimination. Using terms such as "appalling" and "flagrantly," the EEOC aggressively charged AT&T with discriminatory behavior, arguing that "the time to end this discrimination is *now.*"[26]

The EEOC's constitutional argument was perhaps the most creative, referring to "the Commission's constitutional obligation to insure that those subject to its action receive due process." The petition also claimed that there is a "correlative affirmative obligation" on the FCC and referred to the Supreme Court's declaration that "state or federal agencies must take affirmative steps to insure that those with whom they participate do not engage in practices which violate the constitution."[27] In a closing argument, the petition reiterated that the FCC's approval of a rate increase would "impliedly authorize the discrimination to continue and such implicit approval clearly contravenes the constitution."[28]

On Friday, December 11, 1970, the day after the intervention, other groups filed in support of the EEOC's petition; they included the National Associa tion for the Advancement of Colored People (NAACP), the National Organi zation for Women (NOW), the NOW Legal Defense and Education Fund (LDEF), the American Civil Liberties Union (ACLU), the California Rural Legal Assistance (CRLA), the Mexican-American Legal Defense and Educa tion Fund (MALDEF), and the American G.I. Forum. In effect those actions constituted a "protective strategy in the possible event the EEOC was prohib ited from intervening in the proceedings of another government agency."[29] The NOW LDEF petition added that the request for relief be "expanded to include the establishment of child care centers for the children of employees of AT&T."[30]

Going beyond the complaint itself, the EEOC petition requested relief in terms of an investigatory board, the prosecution of officials responsible, cease and-desist orders, and orders from the FCC that the company change six speci fied employment practices immediately, that currently employed women and minorities be given the opportunity to fill vacant positions before new appli cants are considered, and that the company proceed with affirmative action programs, training programs, and whatever other relief the FCC deems neces sary. This was not a casual brief but a detailed charge of discriminatory behav ior, a major step for the EEOC. It would not be without challenge in Wash ington. In due course, Brown would hear from the White House, but Leonard Garment ran interference for him. While Garment did not see himself as sympathetic to the women's movement, he was interested in racial justice.[31] His role in the Nixon White House, as Garment described in his book *Crazy Rhythm*, turned out to be "in the distant swamplands of Republican politics, such as civil rights, Jews, and cultural affairs, activities that no sane and rea sonably ambitious person in my position would have touched in 1969."[32]

While Copus ignited the case and Brown let it burn, the EEOC had plenty of fuel. Three years earlier, in April 1967, the EEOC's director of compliance had provided a "listing of actionable complaints against the Bell Telephone System." The list of complaints included four deferred cases, five pending more information, fifty-one under investigation, five with draft decisions, twenty-two before the commission, five conciliated, and ten unsuccessful and referred for possible legal action. Charges included race, sex, religion, nation al origin, and medical complaints, but most involved race and sex.[33]

In 1967 EEOC staffer Chris Roggerson, working for the director of Re search, Charles Markham, put together a full dossier on the Bell System along with an eight-point "itinerary for action."[34] Roggerson suggested that the EEOC dossier on the Bell System be completed by November 13, 1967, in preparation for possible commissioner charges or private litigation. Other branches of government were to be involved—Justice, Defense, Labor, and the General Services Administration. Once all pending cases involving AT&T were reviewed, the EEOC would "contact the heads of the Federal Communication Commission and other interested governmental agencies for the purpose of mounting a joint and concerted attack against AT&T and its subsidiaries." Beyond that Roggerson foresaw "round table conciliatory discussions with officials of AT&T Company and the Communications Workers of America." The goal for the EEOC would be "a written agreement from AT&T and its subsidiaries which spells out specific remedies and a productive affirmative action program, with appropriate time tables on reporting."[35]

By January 1968 the EEOC had proposed a coordinated government action against three specific Bell System companies—Southern, Southwestern, and Pacific—based on underutilization of minority employees.[36] The attorney general declined to participate "at this time" but suggested to Clifford L. Alexander, then chairman of the EEOC, that their staffs work together on investigations and meetings with AT&T. The assistant attorney general, Department of Justice Civil Rights Division, indicated he would work with the EEOC on possible litigation if appropriate.[37] Later that year, the EEOC staff prepared for a high-level meeting between Alexander and AT&T chairman H. I. Romnes. Alexander laid out the EEOC's concerns and let Romnes know that the Southern, Southwestern, and Pacific companies were not in compliance and that "major corrective action was necessary." By this time, the EEOC knew the Bell System's organization and its employment trends and patterns.[38] Romnes had his personnel vice president, William C. Mercer, write back to Alexander, restating the company's commitment to equal employment and affirmative action.[39]

As the EEOC staff analyzed Bell companies in 1968, they noted several particularly troubling situations. It was Southern Bell's policy to deny employment to mothers of illegitimate children. Moreover, testing and "disparate application of employment standards" often affected opportunities. EEOC conciliators who dealt with AT&T found the company people to be "very knowledgeable, tough, and very smooth."[40] The staff assembled a briefing background for Alexander and a paper for Romnes with background data and a list of questions.[41] They wanted to see results: "negotiation of master conciliation agreements covering the three companies cited, involvement of a high ranking person from AT&T, and perhaps someone from a company, such as New York Telephone . . . , which has had success in this area."[42] Once Brown took over as EEOC chairman, he continued to pressure AT&T, visiting the Bell companies with the significant cases—Southern Bell executives in Atlanta on April 7, 1969, and South Central Bell in Birmingham on April 9.[43] Without enforcement powers, however, the EEOC could not force change.

On November 19, 1969, the FCC issued its proposed rule requiring common carriers to show nondiscrimination in their employment practices (Docket 18742). Bernard Strassburg, head of the Common Carrier Bureau, wrote to AT&T requesting detailed information on Bell System employment practices.[44] AT&T vice president Dan Emerson responded in detail on December 9, affirming the company's policy and its effective implementation.[45]

In Washington, Brown kept the idea of a joint government effort alive, reaching Dean Burch, then chairman of the FCC. Burch wrote to AT&T chairman Romnes on March 19, 1970, indicating his interest in discussing "the steps that can and should be taken by the Bell System companies to rectify any of their employment practices which require correction."[46] Six days later Romnes wrote back, assuring Burch that the "Bell System recognizes the importance of full compliance with the policies and objectives of the Civil Rights Act." He was "disappointed that the EEOC feels it necessary to involve the FCC in this matter," adding that involving another agency in the EEOC's area "can only lead to confusion and duplication of effort." In spite of his "disappointment," Romnes offered to provide information, visits, and meetings—whatever was necessary to reassure the FCC.[47]

AT&T and the EEOC had been talking about employment practices for years, but complaints about the company still came in. It was against this background that the EEOC's Brown evaluated the prospect of a major AT&T case. The case proposed by Copus would force the issue, but it carried risk as well as huge potential. AT&T was capable of a formidable defense. The intervention approach was unorthodox, and even the EEOC had doubts about how the FCC would rule.

Copus thought AT&T would certainly object. And as expected, AT&T responded to the intervention with shock and indignation. Their opposition, filed December 18, 1970, replied in equally passionate language, charging the EEOC with "intemperate and irresponsible charges." AT&T argued that the charges focused on the past and did not take into account that "the Bell System has led the employers of this Nation in affirmative programs to foster equal employment practices." AT&T accused the EEOC of wanting to "punish the Bell System" and argued that if the relief requested were granted it would require that rates be higher, not lower. Signed by John F. Preston Jr. and Howard J. Trienens, attorneys for AT&T, the opposition objected to the attachment of employment issues to a rate case.[48]

With AT&T's opposition was an exhibit, the affidavit of William C. Mercer, vice president of personnel. Mercer argued that the performance of the Bell System in complying with Title VII of the Civil Rights Act of 1964 would be an appropriate place to begin. He quoted Clifford L. Alexander Jr., chairman of the EEOC in 1968, who praised New York Telephone, noting that it had a "most impressive record" and had "led the way in finding minority group members to work and hopefully continue to advance as rapidly as possible." In concluding, Mercer "vigorously" denied the EEOC charges.[49] Just as the EEOC players had a cause they believed in, so did the company officers; they believed that AT&T led the country in management skills and took its social responsibility seriously.

Publicly, AT&T's chairman, H. I. Romnes, reacted strongly, arguing that the EEOC's charge was "outrageous" and would harm the cause of equal opportunity. He found it unacceptable that a company with a good record of progress was "singled out for public attack by a presumably responsible government agency."[50] Much of Romnes's attention as chairman had gone toward dealing with minority and urban problems.[51] Early in his chairmanship of AT&T, Romnes referred to the crisis in the nation's cities; he said, "To the simple question, 'What business is that of ours?' there is a simple answer: 'What happens in the cities happens to us.' "[52] He felt the company had been unjustly singled out by the EEOC. At the 1970 annual meeting, Romnes noted that nonwhite employment had risen from 29,000 to 100,000 over the previous ten years. Of the 311,000 people hired in 1964, 22 percent were black. "These numbers are," he said, "I think sufficient evidence of our practical commitment to equal opportunity in our business." He went on to enumerate activities under way to build skills and "overcome the effects of generations of discrimination and hopelessness."[53]

Generations of Bell System officers had spoken about the role of business in solving social problems. On June 22, 1962, AT&T president Eugene J. McNeely joined Lyndon B. Johnson, then U.S. vice president, in a joint statement "reaffirming the Company's established policy of employment based on merit," otherwise known as a "Plan for Progress."[54] Between the enactment and the effective date of the 1964 Civil Rights Act, the next AT&T chairman, Frederick R. Kappel, sent a letter to all officers reaffirming the importance of complying:

> We have already accomplished much progress that is consonant with the spirit and intent of this legislation. I am certain however that at this time of major social adjustment, our continuing diligent effort is required. By our demonstrated responsibility and in association with other business leaders in each community we serve, we can help importantly to bring about a peaceful and lawful transition. President Johnson has discussed this with me on several occasions, and I have assured him that we in the Bell System will take every appropriate means to advance compliance with both the letter and the spirit of the law.[55]

Kappel and Joseph A. Beirne, president of the Communications Workers of America (CWA), received Equal Opportunity awards in 1966 from the National Urban League. Kappel stressed the need to search out people, to open doors, to teach, and to motivate, and to "stay with them to see that they really get the full opportunity they are entitled to."[56] In 1968 AT&T president Ben S. Gilmer focused on results, which to him meant more than good intentions. The company's health and the health of its surrounding community were "inseparable," he noted. What business could do was to provide jobs. The corporation set goals for hiring and focused on blacks and worked with urban educators and leaders.[57]

The Bell System in word and deed had made progress in minority employment; the strength of that effort helps explain why AT&T officers felt so hurt by the EEOC's charges in 1970. They did not then see the sex discrimination that would become the main issue of the case.

What good deeds AT&T had done in the past were not the topic as the new year—1971—began. On January 21 the FCC partially acquiesced to the EEOC's request and issued its Memorandum and Order establishing a separate case to review AT&T employment practices and the EEOC charges. The new case (Docket 19143) was the FCC's first formal inquiry into AT&T's employment practices. Brown suspected that AT&T had negotiated a deal with its regulator: separate the issues and we won't object to the employment case.[58]

Pressure began to reach both the EEOC and AT&T from the business community, especially from other common carriers and the National Cham-

ber of Commerce. The chamber was flat-out resistant to government intervention and zealous in making its views known in Washington. The National
Association of Manufacturers (NAM) had a less aggressive stance on the case,
and Oldaker's strategy was for NAM to be neutral.[59] These two powerful lobbying organizations represented corporate America in Washington and had
considerable clout and access to the politically powerful. They viewed EEOC
activism as a threat.

Brown helped Copus and Gartner by adding Randall L. Speck, from the
Office of Compliance, and William O. Wallace, from the Office of Research,
to the AT&T task force.[60] All kept their regular EEOC jobs for a while, in addition to being on the AT&T team. Gradually they acquired dedicated space
in the offices at 1800 G Street and later, finally, added women to the team—
Katherine Mazzaferri and Marjanette Feagan. Mazzaferri was a law student,
Feagan a career employee. Wallace, a "counterculture guy" and friend of Copus's, knew statistics and had worked with Copus before, on hearings in Houston in the summer of 1970. Gartner joined the EEOC from Harvard. Speck,
not yet a lawyer, joined the team as a researcher and investigator. When he
came to the EEOC as a management intern, Speck thought he would be
there six months and then go to a regional office.[61] No one on the team had
ever been to court or even seen a trial, but they collectively were David going
after Goliath. They were true believers on a mission.[62]

The FCC appointed Frederick W. Denniston as hearing examiner for
Docket 19143.[63] Denniston was regarded as "flexible," and he was amenable to
hammering out employment issues within the rules of administrative proceedings. Sape would probably have been assigned to the case but had in the
meantime responded to a call from Oldaker and Brown to come to the EEOC
and help them get enforcement powers from Congress.[64]

The EEOC and AT&T were expected to file pretrial briefs, and each was
expected to put the other through a "discovery" process to gain information
and prepare for the actual hearings, with witnesses, exhibits, and findings of
fact. AT&T assigned the case to two company lawyers, George E. Ashley and
Harold S. Levy. Eventually, they would employ outside counsel, N. Thompson Powers from the firm of Steptoe and Johnson. Powers was one of the few
attorneys those days with considerable equal employment experience. From
his first post at Labor, Powers moved on to serve as special counsel to the 1962
President's Committee on Equal Employment Opportunity, and from there to
EEOC as the EEOC's first executive director in 1965. For the case, Ashley and
Levy would handle the Bell witnesses and Powers the outside experts and gov-

ernment witnesses. From the beginning, their legal strategy was to show that the EEOC overstated and misrepresented facts.[65]

Troops assembled and preparations began for a war fought in public with memoranda, stories, and letters from the past. From the start of the case, AT&T maintained that it should be judged by its current intent and not by the past. AT&T would claim it helped lead change for minorities and women, that it was aware of changes in society, and that it was changing its practices to deal with that new world. By 1970 the Bell System had considerable experience dealing with issues of race but was still finding its way with respect to issues of sex discrimination.

The women's movement had infiltrated government—Ross and others at the EEOC; Catherine East at the Women's Bureau of the Department of Labor; Dr. Bernice Sandler at Health, Education, and Welfare (HEW); and others in the executive and legislative branches of government. The lawyers in particular formed a close network. Organizations such as NOW and the Women's Equity Action League were beginning to lobby effectively and to build informal ties. NOW in particular would have important connections to government agencies involved in the AT&T case. Both the EEOC and NOW had worked to build connections to women in the Bell System and its unions.

3

GOOD INTENTIONS

In the late 1960s civil rights, women's liberation, and the war in Vietnam fueled conversations and debates, especially in New York and Washington and in the media emanating from New York. Those of us in corporations were not immune to those causes. For example, M. Elizabeth (Liz) Brydon, one of the few female district managers in New York Telephone, went to the Plaza Hotel and marched down Fifth Avenue to Bryant Park in the National Organization for Women Strike for Equality March on August 26, 1970.[1] Brydon then was one of only 120 district level (midlevel management) women in the entire Bell System, a system that had 9,363 men at that level; only 16 of the 4,490 managers above that level were women.[2]

At the time of the EEOC filing, AT&T had seven management levels, including the senior executive levels. The lowest two levels—first and second—involved the supervision of nonmanagement employees. At the third or "district" level, managers had significant organizational responsibilities. The pyramid narrowed as it went up through fourth or "division" level, fifth or "director" level, and sixth, assistant vice president. Above that were the senior executives. For many EEOC reporting purposes, however, levels "three and above" were grouped together. In 1968 the numbers for total management in the AT&T headquarters, the operating telephone companies, and the Long Lines Department combined included 98,332 men and 49,084 women. The aggregate number hides the differences by level, which are shown in table 1.

By 1970 official publications of AT&T were carrying stories about the women's movement. *AT&T News*, a weekly in-house report for employees, staged a mock protest in the lobby with volunteers carrying feminist signs to get a cover photo for the June 5 edition. Inside, the major story covered pro and con stories about "the weaker sex." Robert D. Lilley, then AT&T's execu-

TABLE 1: BELL SYSTEM MEN AND WOMEN IN HIGHER MANAGEMENT IN 1968

Third-level male	9,363
Third-level female	120
Fourth-level male	3,023
Fourth-level female	13
Fifth-level male	1,099
Fifth-level female	3
Above-fifth male	368
Above-fifth female	0

Note: Includes AT&T headquarters, Long Lines, and the Operating Companies, but excludes professionals (medical and legal) and all of Bell Laboratories and Western Electric.

Source: *AT&T Answerback* no. 798 (June 5, 1973).

tive vice president of human affairs, forecast that "women one day may fill the positions of president or executive vice president of AT&T," and he restated AT&T's commitment to equal opportunity. Lilley developed a greater awareness of societal changes than many of his peers because of his experiences as New Jersey Bell president during the Newark riots, as a Columbia University trustee during massive 1968 student protests, and as a key executive on the New Jersey Governor's Select Commission to Study Civil Disorder. A task force to study the status of women in management had recently been appointed, and Lilley noted that it would be a source of recommendations, whose implementation would be tested in selected telephone companies.[3]

In August 1970 the task force released its findings in a report entitled "The Utilization of Women in the Management of the Bell System." The report laid out problems, described opportunities, and made recommendations; it would ultimately become both the blueprint for company action and the primary data for the EEOC's charges of discrimination against women in management.[4]

The task force came about in an unusual way. In 1969 President Nixon appointed William C. Mercer, AT&T's vice president for personnel relations, as one of the two men on the President's Task Force on Women's Rights and Responsibilities. As the only man in most meetings, Mercer had his understanding and his assumptions challenged regularly by a group of aware and articulate women. It was an unparalleled experience for Mercer. When he returned to AT&T, he put AT&T's task force in motion.

Led by Joel L. Moses, personnel supervisor for research, the AT&T task force worked through the summer of 1970, analyzing employment data, holding fact-finding meetings with the operating departments at headquarters and at telephone companies across the country, and putting together "Guidelines for Implementing Progress in Management for Women." The task force report provided some stark numbers: of a total population of managers at third level and above of 14,566, women represented only 1.1 percent. Of those in high levels, few women were found in line (as opposed to staff) management jobs. Women represented 7.6 percent of second-level managers and 46.3 percent of all first-level managers. The picture seemed so bleak that the task force turned to investigating "why women were not utilized more fully."[5]

Traditionally, most women in the company worked in "traffic," as the department was commonly known. Primarily "operators," they assisted customers in making calls, provided directory information, and recorded data for billing. Another large population of women worked in what was called the Commercial Department, handling service, sales, and billing matters. In both of these departments women predominated at the nonmanagement and first management level. Their numbers dropped off sharply at second level and almost disappeared at third level. Male college hires slipped in to fill third-level positions as part of their training for further management development.

The task force report dealt with attitudes toward women in management using four categories: women at work, male-female competition, characteristics attributed to women by men, and society's role expectations. It left few stones unturned. Then the task force turned to organizational factors inhibiting the advancement of women managers. It cited four factors as the most important: manpower planning, selection criteria, training and development programs, and utilization factors (jobs not open to women or dead-end jobs). The report candidly described the problems to be overcome and outlined how the company should get the job done.

As a member of that team, Edward Mahler brought real line experience; most of the others represented professional research disciplines. Mahler came with a background in the respected operations part of the business—providing dial tone. Others on the team included a psychologist, Sidney Gael, the "work itself" specialist Malcolm Gillette, and a personnel specialist, Virginia Becker from Michigan. In many of their discussions with men in the field, the team met traditional resistance to women's breaking into jobs that had been held by men historically. There would be other, similar arguments about reintroducing men to jobs usually thought of as women's jobs, such as telephone operator.

Mahler had learned about recruitment hurdles and line opposition during the time he spent recruiting at black and women's colleges. Personally, he had been upset that women from the top of their college class could not be considered for the initial management development program (IMDP) at his home company, Bell of Pennsylvania. There, in the 1960s he had been able to get women into a management training program eventually known as the women's IMDP (WIMDP).[6]

Change would not be easy in a corporation with a million employees. AT&T owned twenty-two operating companies and had minority ownership of two others (18 percent of Southern New England Telephone and 27 percent of Cincinnati Bell).[7] The Bell System operated with each telephone company as a subsidiary, with its own president and board of directors. In overly simplistic terms, AT&T established policies and practices, and the companies managed implementation and operation.

Pacific Telephone, Bell of Pennsylvania, and Southwestern Bell had reputations for being staunchly independent—none wanted to be told what to do by AT&T headquarters in New York City. Southern Bell, though it had its problems with EEOC complaints, was not as confrontational with headquarters and had in John Hopkins an assistant vice president of personnel who was receptive to the task force issues. According to Mahler, the task force found allies in Ohio Bell, Indiana Bell, Pacific Northwest Bell, and Illinois Bell as well.

In the late 1960s company actions to hire women often began because of a few motivated managers in field positions. In Ohio Bell, for example, Harold W. (Hal) Burlingame hired six college women in 1967 to be trained as managers. An IMDPer himself, Burlingame envisioned a career track for those women that would be like IMDP. Why did he get involved? As he and some of his cohorts progressed through IMDP, especially in the Commercial Department, they saw that women at first and second level were the ones training the new men. It seemed to them unreasonable that none of the women got into middle or upper management. Thus was created one of the early Bell women's management development programs. The women in the program received a higher level of pay than women in lower positions, but still they were not officially in IMDP and did not make as much as the men.[8]

AT&T's team studying women reported officially to John W. Kingsbury, assistant vice president for personnel relations. By the time the team walked over to Kingsbury's corner office on the Broadway & Dye Street side of the twenty-first floor to present the task force report, they were a "group of advocates" presenting their case to someone who was "encouraging and sympathetic."[9] Not a traditional manager, the Phi Beta Kappa Kingsbury staffed his department with college faculty types.[10] Still, he had an operations background, having come to AT&T after twenty-eight years with Indiana Bell, mostly in the Traffic Department.

Officers at the top of AT&T at that time all had experience running operating units. Headquarters was staffed with a mix of managers rotating in from the various operating units for a few years and a corps of professional managers permanently a part of the headquarters company. Just before Mahler returned to his home company — Bell of Pennsylvania — Mercer brought in Michigan Bell's Don Liebers to manage the college employment function in Mahler's organization. (Liebers would later play a major role in the EEOC case.)[11]

The position of women and minorities differed widely among the various units of the Bell System; New York Telephone, for example, led the system in its hiring of minorities. In terms of higher-level management women, the 1968 numbers in table 2 showed a disproportionate share of the women at headquarters, not in the operating units. [12]

Issues of sex discrimination were discussed in the halls and in company publications. For the September/October 1970 issue of the *Bell Telephone Magazine*, editor Tim Henney engaged Susan Brownmiller to write a feature article entitled "Liberty for Women." Brownmiller's byline identified her as "a professional journalist with experience in TV and the print media. She frequently writes on politics and social problems. She is a member of the New York Radical Feminists." For AT&T readers, Brownmiller wrote about the lack of women who like and have experience in the business world. Then she bluntly stated "that it has been in men's interest . . . to keep us believing that success, ambition, a good job, high pay, etc., were strictly within the masculine province and therefore unfeminine."[13]

Writing several months before the EEOC challenge, Brownmiller related how the EEOC, "aided and abetted by alert women who are aware of their

TABLE 2: 1968 PLACEMENT OF MANAGEMENT MEN AND WOMEN

Level	AT&T Headquarters	Long Lines	Operating Companies
Third-level male	715	408	8,240
Third-level female	43	4	73
Fourth-level male	274	187	2,562
Fourth-level female	3	0	10
Fifth-level male	139	64	896
Fifth-level female	1	0	2
Above-fifth male	63	24	281
Above-fifth female	0	0	0

Source: *AT&T Answerback* no. 798 (June 5, 1973).

rights," was taking on issues of sex discrimination. Telling personal stories, she related her experiences trying to get ahead as a researcher at *Newsweek*, as a news writer for ABC, and as a writer for the *New York Times Magazine*. Not being considered for promotion, being viewed as an intruder in the newsroom, or being held in the "woman's waiting room" of clubs like the Harvard or Yale Clubs had all begun to wear on her. Men, it seemed, were comfortable with women at work so long as the "balance of power" was "clearly delineated." She wondered if big business would be "able to adjust to the demands of the women's liberation movement." In a foretaste of AT&T's future, she talked about how men do not willingly give up power. She stated, "It's not that we expect to replace men with our own female supremacist hierarchy, but we do expect that men will have to move over or step aside to give us room." She recognized that the burden of this change would fall most heavily on the "mediocre man in middle management." Women, she warned, meant to move forward. "If we step on your toes, don't expect us to say 'pardon.' The anger is boiling over in us. We've been watching our step for too long. We're putting our own interests up front at long last."[14]

My friends in New York connected with Brownmiller and "clicked" with the stories she told. Those of us who were beginning to challenge the system internally gained confidence and added to our arsenal of arguments and terminology.

In Chicago that summer, the National Organization for Women directly challenged Illinois Bell. J. B. (Jack) Gable, Illinois Bell's vice president of personnel, responded that neither Illinois Bell, nor society as a whole, had always provided opportunities for women to move up. "We recognize the changing situation and we are doing something about it," Gable claimed. Furthermore, he said that though NOW did not represent all women, "the organization has articulated legitimate concerns similar to the objectives of our Affirmative Action program. And we'll work with such groups."15 NOW gained legitimacy with each negotiated encounter.

Certainly the feminist movement, both inside and outside the Bell System, gave ample warning of its intent.

In the midst of the turmoil was Mercer, who happened to be in a key personnel position at the time. His career had led him from his first job as an auditor with Western Electric through a variety of management roles there and in New England Telephone and Telegraph. He had important line and staff jobs on his way up the ladder and served as a general manager by 1959. In the pattern of company executives, he went to another operating company—Indiana Bell—as vice president for operations (where he knew Kingsbury), then to AT&T headquarters. At headquarters he held alternating marketing and personnel positions. Mercer would go on to be president and CEO of New England Telephone and Telegraph.

On Tuesday, November 24, 1970, Mercer met with EEOC chairman William H. Brown III and his staff to go over test validation issues. The Bell System subjected potential new hires to a battery of tests, which the EEOC claimed were discriminatory in effect. In a letter to the operating company presidents and AT&T vice presidents, Mercer noted that the EEOC finally agreed that the company had good validation studies. However, Brown had challenged AT&T on how well the companies administered the tests. Mercer feared that the Bell System's use of any pre-employment tests might be in jeopardy if tests were misused.16

At nearly the same time, Mercer would be talking about equal employment for women in a quite different context: Mary Baldwin College, a women's college in the Shenandoah Valley of Virginia. The National Association of Manufacturers, the Women's Bureau of the Department of Labor, American Can Company, AT&T, General Electric, International Paper Company, and Mary Baldwin College put together a session on "Women in Indus-

*William C. Mercer,
AT&T Vice President for
Personnel Relations (1967–71),
New England Telephone and
Telegraph Company President
and CEO (1971–82).*

Photograph property of AT&T Archives.
Reprinted with permission of AT&T.

try." There in early December 1970, Mercer found himself standing next to Dr. Luther Holcomb, vice chairman of the EEOC. After a brief introduction to the Bell System's history on equal opportunity, Mercer referred to "dramatic changes" in society as a whole. Directly referring to feminist street protests on the fiftieth anniversary of the right to vote, August 26, he acknowledged the social turmoil that was part of the scenery of 1970. AT&T addressed these changes through the Task Force on Women; the reasons for the task force, he continued, were fourfold: "our moral obligation to utilize each employee to her or his fullest capacity . . . the desire and necessity to have the very best talent running our business . . . the desire to comply with the law . . . the desire to respond to the changes in society."[17]

As he described the issue, he used phrases such as "the Women's Liberation Movement" and referred to Lucy Komisar, a prominent NOW activist. Komisar, he noted, was a board member of the New York City chapter of NOW and a guest speaker at Bell System college recruiters' conferences. Mercer closed with a quote from John F. Kennedy:

When at some future date the high court of history sits in judgment on each one of us—recording whether in our brief span of service we fulfilled our responsibilities—our success or failure, in whatever office we may hold, will be measured by the answers to four questions:
  —Were we truly men of courage?
  —Were we truly men of judgment?
  —Were we truly men of integrity?
  —Were we truly men of dedication?[18]

Mercer joked that his speech might be "foolhardy" in the presence of not only the vice chairman of the EEOC but also Elizabeth D. Koontz, director of the Women's Bureau, and Leonard Biermann, director of program review, Office of Federal Contract Compliance (OFCC) in the Department of Labor. Mercer jested that when he finished, "a race will begin to see who can be first to serve me with a complaint for sex discrimination." He took that risk because he thought the problem was "ubiquitous" in business and because AT&T had already made a commitment to deal with it.[19]

Only days later, the EEOC would shock AT&T with its intervention filing and charges of discrimination.

Throughout many documents and in frequent discussion, the topic was indeed being talked about across the Bell System. Women's liberation movement advocates set foot in conferences and gave talks at AT&T's invitation. Aileen C. Hernandez, the EEOC commissioner from 1965 to 1966 and a future NOW president, advised Pacific Telephone on its affirmative action plan.[20]

Much earlier, just after passage of the Civil Rights Act of 1964, personnel managers throughout the Bell System had compared notes on the implications of the "sex" provision and what it would mean to their operation. In 1965, when he was an assistant vice president, Mercer himself sent a letter to the companies discussing the need for further rules on bona fide occupational qualification (BFOQ) decisions. At the same time, he pointed to the need to end sex-segregated job advertising, which by its position in a particular column, by its statements, or by its pictures indicated that a job was for men or for women. He called for the review of all employment literature to avoid conflict with Title VII and suggested that companies begin to use references to jobs that did not limit the jobs to one sex or another. More important, he asked the companies to review the duties and compensation of men and women with the same title or those doing substantially the same work "to make sure no differences based on sex could be claimed to exist."[21]

Still, AT&T in 1966 sent the operating companies a position paper entitled "Application of Title VII of Civil Rights Act to Traffic Operating Jobs in the Telephone Industry." In that document, sex was determined to be a BFOQ for the operator's job, and the companies could defend designating the operator's job as a female job. The defense rested on six arguments: quality of service, "the voice with a smile," the physical closeness of the work positions, the physical design of the positions, the need for separate lounge and rest facilities, and the lack of a mixed force precedent in the industry.[22]

A few of the companies took other positions. Michigan Bell prepared a backgrounder for "questions that might arise in the minds of MBT employees." In response to the question "Are there any jobs at all in our Company that should be filled exclusively by men or women?" the company response was: "None that we were able to discover."[23]

At a Bell System public affairs conference on September 25, 1968, Mercer talked about dealing with the "racial problems of the cities" and the "growth of black power." He emphasized that pressures would increase and the company's "only defense will be our performance in providing work opportunities and the assistance we render in the communities in which we operate and yet this may not be enough. Certainly we just can't mouth high-sounding policies and statements of the problems and what we'd like to do. At the very least our words must be supported by our actions." Before this group, which handled the company's relationship with the government, he added that the EEOC was pushing for enforcement power and might very well get it. In thinking about that possibility, he noted that the company was "fearful" of the future in that case, because there would be more complaints. He saw the future in saying, "We would anticipate broad and rather extreme decisions not only on racial questions but perhaps even more disturbing decisions relating to sex discrimination." And he concluded, "We will be judged in the future on what we do tomorrow, not what we did yesterday."[24]

When Mercer pressed for change internally, he met some opposition. A letter from San Francisco in 1969, commenting on females entering plant positions, forecasted dire results: accidents, absences, disabling injuries, costs of constructing toilet facilities, assaults on female employees in urban areas, and high turnover. Yet the writer had a sense of humor, noting, "Undoubtedly there is some male bias here but we are probably reflecting the general feeling amongst Plant managers." He added, "If we *must* [emphasis his] do it, then let's open all jobs."[25]

By 1970 the topic turned to dress codes. Could women wear pants at work? If so, on what days and what hours? Did they have to have matching tops? A division manager in Illinois Bell confused the spelling of "chic" and ended up with a letter that said, "We feel the 'chick' pant suits and dress slacks are acceptable attire."[26] Another memo admitted "pantsuits and matching ensembles" for women but required that the "top must cover the hips at all times."[27] In San Jose a woman could wear pants with a coat or jacket of the same material in matching or harmonizing colors, but she could not wear "slacks with a contrasting mini-dress worn as an overblouse."[28]

In the midst of this, on December 10, 1970, came the EEOC intervention in AT&T's rate case. Brown knew enough about AT&T's practices and procedures to take a chance with Copus and use the FCC for leverage.

AT&T's Washington office, alerted by the FCC, called the executives at 195 Broadway in New York with the news that the EEOC filed a petition to intervene in the long-distance rate filing. AT&T had announced on November 17 that it would ask the FCC for an increase in revenues of 6 percent — or $385 million — and a boost in the allowable rate of return to 9.5 percent.[29] AT&T's filing, known as Docket 19129, was unprecedented in terms of its size, and AT&T knew it would be months, perhaps years, before a decision was arrived at. Intense regulatory scrutiny was not new to AT&T, but they had never expected anything on employment issues. The EEOC had not been high on the list of important agencies for AT&T's Washington office; they had no contacts and thus no advance information about the filing.[30] Total shock blended with absolute indignation.

The EEOC had not been silent with AT&T on the matter of race and sex discrimination; what upset the officers was that the EEOC was now meddling with something really important to the business — its finances — and at best delaying what the executives saw as a crucial move for the company's future. In a way, the EEOC had stepped on holy ground — it was meddling with the regulatory process.

AT&T and the FCC were also in the midst of major industry issues at the time. For example, FCC decisions had allowed competition in both equipment and high-capacity circuits for the first time. In the Carterphone case, the FCC opened the door to manufacturers of phone equipment other than AT&T's Western Electric. And in the MCI case, the FCC allowed a non-Bell

company to provide point-to-point transmission at low cost.[31] To AT&T, competition represented a serious threat. Employee issues did not seem to represent a major problem. Personnel officers knew about the EEOC and NOW,
but generally the executives at AT&T knew little about the organizations and
their leaders. In the months and years ahead, they would get to know William H. Brown III, David A. Copus, Wilma Scott Heide, and Ann London
Scott.

AT&T was taken by surprise on December 10, 1970, but acted fast. By
9:30 A.M. that day, Bob Lilley had convened a meeting to address the EEOC
issue. In the next few weeks he and John Kingsbury would delve into the
charges and meet frequently. Brown's phone number would be prominent in
the first pages of Lilley's pocket calendar.[32]

Don Liebers, having just been promoted to a fifth-level job as director of
employment, was on vacation, enjoying time with his youngest child, who was
still a kindergartner, when he got a call from Don VanGilder: "Have you seen
the front page of the *New York Times*? Call the office." Liebers called Kingsbury, only to hear that "all hell is breaking loose" and that he needed to go
back to the office immediately. Liebers would be working on the case and its
follow-up till that kindergartner was in high school.[33]

A Bell System–wide personnel conference was in progress when the call
came there. In the midst of routine presentations on personnel practices, an
announcement was made of the EEOC action, and the printed agenda went
out the window. First the group of personnel vice presidents sat in stunned
silence; then dozens of heated conversations broke out, no one, of course,
knowing the full meaning of the event. From the podium came a call for order, "Gentlemen, gentlemen . . ."—for in fact all were male.

At least this audience knew what the EEOC was about, making their responses that much more emotional. These were the officers who oversaw the
business of equal opportunity. They knew how much or how little their companies had done. They knew the EEOC for what it then was—a small agency
with no enforcement power and with a few young, liberal lawyers. They knew
that the companies had, in general, gone beyond the call of duty to bring the
cities of the nation back to stability after the riots of the 1960s. They felt, and
in many cases justifiably so, that the companies they represented had been
leaders in the hiring of minority workers. They felt they had always treated
women well, that the Bell System had been regarded as a good place for
women to find jobs that paid well. They knew the statistics on race and sex.

That was part of their jobs. And some were proud of what they had accomplished recently. To them, the Bell System was a leader and did not practice "blatantly unlawful discrimination."

The rest of the personnel conference agenda was replaced with discussions of this new development. The New Jersey Bell representative, Eugene Kofke, watched as the group solidified in defense of the system they had helped build and almost sworn to support. By the last day, nearly all were prepared to defend the business, not to ask questions of it. In a few minds, however, the "click" of recognition made them see that the data they had could be viewed from a different angle. The very data the group used to defend its behavior could be used against it.[34]

Equally stunned, AT&T's public relations forces called an emergency session and argued over the best position. Some felt outraged and argued that the company should strongly plead not guilty. Others countered that the company was guilty and that to say otherwise would be to lose credibility. Transferred recently from Long Lines to headquarters, Kim Manna had the assignment to handle day-to-day public relations for the case. Like many AT&T women, Manna worked on the case for AT&T but found that the case also worked on her consciousness. She stood her ground: "At least half the population knows you're guilty. You may not be sympathetic but our public posture can't go counter to the facts," she argued. It was a fine line, balancing reality with legality, accepting that the good intentions of the past would not match the expectations of the present. All of corporate America could be guilty in that sense.[35]

Officially, AT&T's response came from Chairman H. I. Romnes at a press conference on Friday, December 11. Emotionally charged, the response reflected the wounded pride of a proud company. AT&T argued most strenuously on the basis of its efforts to deal with race. On the matter of sex, the statement simply referred to percentages, as if that would be argument enough: "Women account for 55.5 percent of Bell System employment; they account for 33.5 percent of management and professional employment."[36]

In offices across the country, some of those women managers noticed the case. To many of its employees, the Bell System represented an extended family, with loyalty and support a part of the unwritten bargain on both sides. Relatively speaking, women managers in the Bell System had good jobs. Change was uneven across the system, however, and those who broke barriers could find themselves in hostile work environments. Most of us were absorbed in our own battles and did not then know about government or NOW national actions or how we would be drawn into the larger war.

4

NOW TAKES ON AT&T

In its first years, NOW aggressively tackled employment issues for women. Sometimes that meant working with the EEOC, sometimes pressuring it to pay attention to sex discrimination.[1] With Betty Friedan as president and Kathryn Clarenbach as chairman of the board, NOW had charged onto the scene in 1966. The first twenty members of NOW's national board "came from all walks of life—business leaders, housewives, union officials, academics, scientists, lawyers, television commentators, advertising executives, community organizers."[2] Elected as NOW's first executive vice president, Aileen Hernandez had resigned as EEOC commissioner, frustrated at the EEOC's lack of action and its "little or no commitment to eliminating sex discrimination."[3]

In March 1970 Hernandez became president of NOW and Wilma Scott Heide became chair of the board. A black woman with a background in civil rights, union activism, and both state and federal government, Hernandez came to NOW with considerable knowledge and connections. Heide, with interpersonal skills and a tradition of nurturance from her health care profession, felt the need to see the problems of women in a social context. Together Hernandez and Heide pushed for more formal organization and a budget that would provide financial stability for NOW.[4] Local chapters existed all over the country, and membership had grown to about five thousand, or so we said (the address file was just a box of index cards on the table in NOW's office on the south side of Chicago). Heide recognized that NOW members did important work but were scattered across the country and depended on informal ties to keep each other up to date. Board meetings had been the primary structure. Under Heide, the organization became more formal, with four regional directors and vice presidents for finance and fund-raising, legislation, public relations, and legal matters. Task forces and committees began to coordinate the work of NOW. Ann Scott took an active role in addressing employment discrimination, providing for the chapters an affirmative action how-to kit.

Given her experience with the EEOC, Hernandez worried about the relationship between the government agencies and NOW. Pondering how NOW should concentrate its efforts, she was confident that Labor's Office of Federal Contract Compliance (OFCC) was prepared to respond to charges of discrimination against government contractors. She felt that NOW needed more assurance that the EEOC would take action. Later, when there was a move to merge the OFCC into the EEOC, Scott and Hernandez would lead NOW to oppose the consolidation. Heide supported Hernandez, feeling strongly that it was "important to stand up for what was just, to go after justice in the public realm." Like Hernandez, Heide had the "willingness to challenge giants, the authorities, and the powerful."[5]

Already, individuals and NOW chapters had taken on the Bell System, with actions loosely coordinated through ad hoc committees and national board decisions. For example, the Chicago chapter tackled Illinois Bell, the Detroit chapter Michigan Bell, the Pittsburgh chapter Bell of Pennsylvania.

The "Scott plan," a NOW version of affirmative action, was circulating by March 1970. Ann Scott's friend Dr. Bernice (Bunny) Sandler acted on the knowledge that universities and colleges had federal contracts and thus would fall under the Executive Order banning discrimination.[6] Sandler intended to submit the "Scott Plan" to Robert H. Finch, who was Nixon's secretary of Health, Education, and Welfare (HEW) and George P. Shultz, secretary of Labor, as "a model for the kind of affirmative action plan that their contract compliance officers should be asking for." The report also had a second value, she felt, in that it would educate anyone who read it. Sandler, who shared Scott's academic interests, offered to give her the materials she had developed for the Women's Equity Action League (WEAL). She also offered to join NOW, citing what she called "Political Ploy #38: double the number of organizations for the *same* members and you have twice as much political muscle."[7]

The very day the EEOC intervened in the AT&T rate case, Scott heard from a New Yorker who agreed to be NOW's compliance coordinator for the New York chapter. That volunteer was Joan Hull, who worked for the textile firm Celanese. Hull thanked Scott for sending what was a "very good explanation of what a class action is" and went on to describe current individuals working grievances against Salomon Brothers. She explained that New York NOW was going to "strengthen our employment activities," noting they were "delighted" by the EEOC action against the telephone company. Hull also reported that NOW had recruited six people to take the test to qualify for jobs with the EEOC or other agencies working on equal employment. She added a postscript suggesting that NOW testify at telephone rate hearings. She was incensed that the company bragged about how many women were in management. Knowing women managers were at low levels, Hull claimed they were just monitors of company rules and regulations and were nowhere near the decision-making process.[8]

Meanwhile, Lucy Komisar, working with Scott, developed "The NOW Phone Company Anti-Discrimination Affirmative Action Kit." This kit explained the appropriate laws and described how a local chapter or individual should get and analyze a telephone company's December 1970 affirmative action program.[9] Included in the kit were copies of a call for a nationwide demonstration against AT&T on March 29, 1971, and copies of letters. JoAnn Evansgardner, coordinator of an AT&T Ad Hoc Committee, sent the notice out from her offices of KNOW, Inc., in Pittsburgh on behalf of NOW.[10]

The NOW national board, at its meeting in Houston on January 15–16, wanted to follow up on its support for the EEOC intervention and to express support for Lorena Weeks, a Southern Bell employee in her battle with Southern Bell. Instead of being required to commute to another town, Weeks wanted to work in a local office where a job vacancy had been posted for a "switchman" job, a position in connection with the maintenance of the telephone central office switch. She knew the job and knew she could do it. In addition, the job paid well. It had never entered her mind that the job was off-limits to women. Refused the opportunity, Weeks turned to the EEOC. When charged by the EEOC with the complaint in 1966, Southern Bell claimed a sex BFOQ based on weight lifting and "odd-hour" call-out work that required driving alone at night and working at lonely and isolated locations.[11]

Hernandez wrote to Frank M. Malone, the president of Southern Bell, stating NOW's support for Weeks and criticizing the company's tactics. Hernandez alerted Malone that NOW planned "a national action against Southern Bell and its parent company, American Telephone and Telegraph." She warned him the protest would include "letters and multi-city demonstrations" and noted that "new tactics will be determined as the need arises," promising that NOW "will continue opposition until we can be assured that the Bell System is indeed the 'equal opportunity employer' its ads proclaim." NOW included the AT&T case as one of its major efforts, along with such projects as women in poverty, the equal rights amendment, child care, and the stockholders' action project.[12]

Ever watchful, NOW members across the country reported instances of offensive behavior on the part of EEOC officials. Hernandez heard about an EEOC executive director who participated in a Wisconsin panel on equal employment opportunity at a statewide Chamber of Commerce meeting. His cavalier treatment of the sex provision of the EEOC's responsibility as a joke sent the wrong message to the employers attending the meeting, according to Hernandez, and she let William H. (Bill) Brown know about it. In a January letter to Brown, Hernandez also took the opportunity to express NOW's concern that this one director's insensitivity to sex discrimination might be permeating the staff:

> We see no evidence that staff is selected on the basis of a full commitment to eliminating sex discrimination as well as racial and ethnic discrimination. Experience with many of your regional offices, in fact, indicates callous disregard of the whole subject of sex discrimination and, frequently, annoyance that such cases have been filed to add to the caseload.
>
> NOW is appalled at the small number of women at the higher grade levels in EEOC and in supervisory positions either in the field offices or at headquarters. In view of this situation, we request a breakdown of EEOC staff—in field offices and in headquarters—by race, sex and position, and an account of EEOC's internal affirmative action program to ensure equal employment opportunity.[13]

Another NOW leader, concerned that "the EEOC had not done much to help the cause of sex discrimination," urged caution in NOW's relationship with the EEOC, advising, "I don't think we should get too cozy with EEOC, even if we are on the same side at the moment." She cautioned against an alliance with the EEOC, given the "brush off" individuals had received and the sad state of the EEOC's own policies and staffing. Even the bills in Congress extending the powers of the EEOC made her cautious, and she questioned what NOW's position on that legislation should be. "It might be risky to put this much power in one agency which has not demonstrated much interest in sex discrimination."[14] Clearly, within NOW there were policy decisions to be made; employment issues covered government structure and legislation as well as employer behavior.

Hernandez met with Brown at the EEOC to talk about three topics that were paramount to her. In response to the first, hiring and promotion within government, Brown showed her a list of women in high levels of government services but did not give her the list. Next, Hernandez wanted hearings on sex discrimination in Washington; Brown agreed that hearings in Washington should be held, though he had budgetary and security concerns. Last, Hernandez pressed Brown on the Weeks case. For five years, Weeks had waited for the switchman job; during that time she found work "almost unbearable at times" because of the constant harassment. With NOW and attorney Sylvia Roberts's support, Weeks appealed to the Fifth Circuit Court, which ruled in her favor in March 1969. "Appropriate relief" was to be determined at the district level, and Judge Griffin Bell told Southern Bell to put her on the job as switchman in Wadley immediately with the same base salary as the man who had gotten the job before. The company delayed, Roberts got another hearing with Judge Bell, who issued another order, and on March 3 Weeks went to work as a switchman at Wadley. The final meeting with Judge Bell resulted in a back pay and expense award to Weeks of thirty-one thousand dollars.[15] Still, Weeks found a hostile work environment. Brown agreed to look into the matter further.

After the meeting, Hernandez wrote to Brown, reminding him of their discussion and presenting eight other suggestions. She offered to meet again in late March, indicating she would like that meeting to be with the commission and top staff. A previous commissioner herself, Hernandez knew the ropes.[16]

Hernandez was not the only NOW leader pressuring for action. Scott, now federal compliance coordinator for NOW, lobbied New York Representative Bella Abzug to have the House Government Operations Committee hold hearings "to evaluate Federal enforcement against sex discrimination in both its internal and external programs." She attached a detailed agenda for action.[17]

NOW chapters across the country were gearing up for protests and demonstrations against the Bell System. Action committees included experienced members but mostly were composed of volunteers getting their first exposure to "movement" protest activity. On March 29, 1971, the picket lines went up at Illinois Bell's headquarters, 222 W. Randolph Street, with local NOW members and some who stayed over after the NOW Midwest regional conference the day before. Posters advocated support for Lorena Weeks and charged AT&T with unfair treatment of women.[18]

The conference passed a resolution officially joining in the protest action against AT&T and "strongly" urging the Bell System to put affirmative action in place for minorities and women "immediately." In line with the demands other NOW groups would push, the Midwest region pressured Illinois Bell to

Chicago NOW's Bette Vidina and Kathy Rand protest against Illinois Bell. "Members of the National Organization for Women," photograph by Perry C. Riddle.

Photograph property of the University of Illinois at Chicago, the University Library Department of Special Collections—National Organization for Women, Chicago Chapter Records. Reprinted with special permission from the Chicago Sun-Times, Inc. © 2001.

"communicate its equal employment opportunity programs to the public, potential employees and human relations groups such as NOW." In closing, the resolution reiterated support for Weeks and demanded justice.[19] On March 29, Mary Jean Collins-Robson, as Midwest regional director, and Gene Boyer, a NOW national officer from Beaver Dam, Wisconsin, jointly made a statement to the press. After covering the Weeks case and the brief filed by the EEOC before the FCC, the statement challenged the local Bell company. NOW argued the "affirmative action programs are not worth the paper on which they are written unless they have goals, timetables, procedures, and accountability for results." NOW questioned whether Illinois Bell met the FCC requirement that it "communicate its equal employment opportunity policy, program and employment needs to sources of qualified applicants and solicit their recruitment assistance on a continuing basis."[20]

NOW had done its homework and was ready to talk business. Members had arranged a meeting that same day with Jack Gable, vice president of personnel, and John Bauman, assistant vice president of personnel. Harriet White, of course, was there in her Illinois Bell role. If the executives did not know it before, Gable and Bauman could see by her hello that she knew the NOW women. After the meeting, Gable turned to White and asked her if it bothered her to be a representative of the company in a meeting with NOW. She told him no but admitted she used data internally to get changes made and externally to show progress.[21]

Later in the week, NOW prepared three thousand leaflets to hand out to Illinois Bell employees as they left work. Summarizing the meeting with Gable, the leaflet claimed that Gable agreed with NOW's charges of "discrimination within the Bell System" and would be willing to have NOW work with management to set up timetables. Other changes were said to have been negotiated at the meeting: new nonsexist job titles, encouragement for women to seek management and plant jobs, opening all jobs to both sexes, and a "new way of looking at female employees that makes their special needs the norm and not the exception," meaning that "maternity leaves and benefits should be an accepted part of the employment package." NOW urged Bell women to apply for plant and management jobs.[22]

On April 7, 1971, in its internal *Bulletin*, Illinois Bell described the meeting with NOW as "a good exchange of views . . . probably leading to a continuing dialogue." Gable, however, claimed that the NOW leaflet "went well beyond the context of our discussions" and cited the job title changes as an example.[23] Illinois Bell chairman Charles L. Brown was on vacation, but *Chicago Daily News* reporter Betty Washington got to a spokesman, who claimed, "Our skirts are clean," regarding NOW's charges. The spokesman reminded the reporter that "Illinois Bell led the fight to get rid of the Illinois law that prevented women from working overtime." He stressed that "more than 4,000 women— 37½% of our employment" were in management and that "hundreds of our women earn $15,000 or more with some getting as high as $30,000 a year." "Does this sound like discrimination?" he asked. The reporter noted that Collins-Robson "isn't impressed."[24]

The Maryland NOW chapter opted to meet with the general personnel manager of the Chesapeake and Potomac Telephone and Telegraph Company rather than staging a "premature demonstration which would have alienated the working woman (our main concern), the unions who are negotiating a contract with the company now, the company itself and the press." For Maryland, NOW reported to Scott: "We're delighted with the AT&T project and are planning long-term involvement. Lack of womanpower, time and knowledge about employment laws prevented us from organizing an effective action."[25]

In Pittsburgh, twenty NOW members picketed Bell of Pennsylvania offices, to the surprise of company spokesman Noah Halper, who said to the press, "I don't understand why these people are here today."[26] Demonstrations also took place in Boston; New York; Bethlehem, Pennsylvania; Miami; Huntsville, Alabama; Milwaukee; Youngstown, Ohio; St. Louis; New Orleans; Albuquerque; Houston; Los Angeles; Seattle; and other cities.[27]

The action was not a one-day event, however; local chapters had begun and would continue to keep the pressure on. This was but one of the many projects in motion. Action was the name of the game, and "failure is impossible" was its motto. In Chicago, for example, NOW activist Susan Dean reported on Chicago NOW committee's activities. "Pa Bell has the wrong number, and we will prove it," she wrote. The committee asked for more contacts within Illinois Bell and more members to help with actions. They planned to testify against Bell in an Illinois Commerce Commission (ICC) hearing on proposed rate increases, to put out a "PR campaign to reach women inside and outside Bell," to review Bell ads for "sexist overtones," and to work on child care as a possibility for Bell employees. The committee met every other Tuesday.[28] It seemed as though NOW moved on all fronts simultaneously. In addition to action events, the chapter received requests for speakers and established a speakers bureau to respond.

Still unaware of the work going on in Washington, I was involved within Bell Labs and in local NOW activities; I dealt with day-to-day concerns. One of my memorable speaking engagements for NOW was at the Cypress restaurant in Hinsdale, Illinois, with the LaGrange Area Chamber of Commerce. Lorraine Hardt, in the local paper, *The Citizen*, reported in bold type at the start of the article that I was "obviously sincere . . . extremely likable . . . and attractive. In her sleeveless white sheath, low-heeled pumps, and mild manner, she neither irritates nor offends." Then she went on to cover the topics I discussed, admitting that there is "strangely, actually little to argue, basically." She quoted me accurately, then concluded that NOW is "simply a civil rights group of women—and men—some more vociferous than others, to be sure, but all dedicated to the 'action plus information' cause of women's development toward their 'full human potential,' with both its privileges and its responsibilities."[29] The *Chicago Tribune* covered the same event, with the head-

line "Glen Ellyn Feminist Says Woman's Place Is in House—Senate, Too."
Patricia Stemper had a more aggressive article, giving more time to the content of my talk and none at all to what I wore.[30]

Purpose accomplished. One more step to reaching out in different ways to different groups. Each venture into an arena like that built up my ability to articulate the NOW position and to deal with questions.

Others in NOW would do the same. An AT&T Long Lines new supervisors training class heard Jacqui M. Ceballos talk about issues important to women. A NOW founder and president of the New York chapter, Ceballos presented statistics on working women and argued for full equality in jobs. "The Sunset Room at the Hotel Gramatan in Bronxville, New York, that afternoon was buzzing with questions long after the speech had ended." As reported in a company publication, Ceballos was asked questions like, "Why does a woman want more responsibility than she has in the home?" and "Are you willing to accept the consequences of true equality for women?"[31]

Meanwhile, other news in the papers covered the economist John Kenneth Galbraith's defense of the Women's Liberation Movement. According to the *Chicago Sun-Times*, Galbraith saw it was "very hard for women to do well in business, not because they are unfitted for it but because there is a secret and invisible barrier—the male world of luncheon clubs, golf, locker rooms and peculiar jokes, in which they do not participate and where so much business wheeling and dealing is done." The headline, however, came from his comment that he had "done his best to dissuade 'bright girls' from marrying less intelligent men by telling them: 'Better have an affair. It isn't so permanent and you keep your job.' "[32]

The same issue of the *Sun-Times* covered NOW's announcement that it had appealed to the Department of Labor to end "discrimination against women employed by the public schools." About 85 percent of elementary teachers were women, but only 22 percent of principals; half of high school teachers were women, but only 4 percent of principals, Collins-Robson noted. Collins-Robson and Charlotte Adelman, an attorney for NOW, explained that the appeal had to go to the Labor Department rather than the EEOC because the Civil Rights Act of 1964 excluded teachers from protection from sex discrimination.[33]

On the national level, NOW considered a variety of actions for the coming year—AT&T, the ERA, the United Crusade/Fund/Way, Sears credit cards, HEW. The discussion led to the conclusion that NOW needed guidelines for national actions that could be used by the task force and committee leaders.

Toni Carabillo, vice president for public relations, and Ann Scott, vice president for legislation, put together a proposal, the thrust of which was that the action should be an *"event* to dramatize an issue of *national concern to NOW* in which many or all NOW chapters can participate." The event needed to have *"press* value." NOW needed successful events that would "confront the power structure" and help build NOW. Coordination for national events would be partially funded by the board to cover printing, telephone bills, mailings, and so forth.[34] It may seem obvious now, but that was a key point; most NOW efforts ran on donated resources.

Many NOW members struggled on a daily basis not just with finding funds for events but with establishing their own careers in sexist environments. We worked hard keeping personal relationships in difficult days, not only with time pressures but also with the conflicts of sex roles endemic to the time and place. Nowhere could we escape the issues.

Almost every day I read about the feminist movement or sex discrimination fights. As a group, those of us in Chicago NOW knew we needed some time for renewal, and Lake Geneva again beckoned, with Bette Vidina organizing the trip. We went to the George Williams College Camp in Williams Bay, Wisconsin, on July 24 and 25. Among the topics for discussion? "How People Treat You as a Feminist," "How You as a Feminist Treat People," and "New Feminist Sexuality." For fun and funds, we had a "new feminist auction," with proceeds set aside for the August 26 Washington Lobby Fund.[35]

In the midst of planning for a big August 26 event, NOW members from around the country were making plans for another get-together: going to Los Angeles for the NOW national conference over Labor Day weekend. The Chicago chapter charted a United Airlines plane and made reservations at the Airport Marina in Los Angeles. All the other projects moved along as well, individuals and committees working feverishly on one event or another, printing flyers on mimeograph machines, making posters, writing position papers, speaking to anyone who would listen.

Except for a brief visit to Montana, Scott was busy in Washington, D.C. Hernandez's next meeting with Bill Brown and the EEOC had been postponed to August 23. Scott got information from women inside the EEOC on matters that needed attention. One particularly sensitive issue revolved around the potential of women's rights' getting in the way of minority rights or vice versa, in effect fighting for the same jobs in an environment where there might not be enough jobs to go around.[36]

NOW fund-raising event in Chicago. Left to right: Ann Scott, Betty Friedan, Judith Lonn-quist, Mary-Ann Lupa, Susan Dean, Kathy Rand.

Reprinted with permission of the photographer Dorothea Jacobson-Wenzel.

August 26 came closer. NOW planned events nationwide: in the Twin Cities of Minnesota, with twenty-one hours of free radio time; in Hartford, Connecticut, meeting with the heads of major insurance companies; in Cedar Rapids; Sacramento; Milwaukee; Pittsburgh; Des Moines; Cincinnati; Portland, Oregon; Richmond; Baton Rouge; St. Louis; Winston-Salem; Muncie, Indiana; Kansas City; and the biggest of all, in New York City.

In Chicago, the day would be full: City Hall in the morning, with political demands made to Mayor Richard J. Daley; the Civic Center at noon for talks, singing, and voter registration; Sage's East for a social hour; and Orchestra Hall for the evening fund-raiser, "From Promise to Power." Speakers for the program included Aileen Hernandez, president of NOW, and Caroline Bird, author of *Born Female: The High Cost of Keeping Women Down*. Special music would be performed by Bonnie Koloc, and Dorothy Donegan and her trio would introduce "Liberation NOW," a song written for the movement. No one knew the chapter's finances better than my husband, who was treasurer at the time; he and I put up the front money to rent Orchestra Hall. To me, that was a big deal, an act of faith in our fund-raising ability, not just to raise money for "the women's lobby in D.C." but also to pay our bills.

Early in August, the Chicago Police caught three "skulkers" putting up posters at 12:03 A.M. near LaSalle and Randolph. Nine cops caucused to determine the charge and ultimately gave them a traffic citation with a court appearance scheduled. Needless to say, the NOW skulkers planned more sophisticated lookout and placement tactics for future nights.[37]

Mary-Ann Lupa once again came through with great graphics, the buttons were ready, posters were up on the streets of Chicago, volunteers mimeographed hundreds of leaflets, and we were set for the day. I did not leave a secret note for my boss. By this time my role in NOW was no secret.

When they had a going-away party for me at Bell Labs, my present was a plaque inscribed to the "technical editor and resident feminist." The flyer announcing the party spotlighted me within a feminist symbol. Not a quiet leave-taking. The party was on September 2. The next day we left for Los Angeles, and on September 15 I was due on a new job with AT&T in New York. Action was the key word, everything was in motion.

In a rousing speech at the L.A. conference, Hernandez honored the work of NOW over its first five years, from 1966 to 1971, celebrating the victories, recognizing those who stood up and fought. Part of the speech was lofty, calling the organization to move the nation into humanity, to urge caring about people, to be determined to change the world for the better. She reminded the audience of unfinished business but tempered that with the observation that "women are now beginning to move as a political force. . . . We will not be co-opted! Neither will we be limited!"[38]

The sisterhood, the tears, the laughter, stirred us all. What went on after the conference was just plain work. Judith Meuli, Scott, and Hernandez served on a "conference implementation committee" to organize the resolutions coming out of the national conference and route them to the appropriate committee or to the board, if board action was needed. They felt it was important that the organization follow up on every item and that annual reports provide feedback to members. Issues of employment found their way to Mary Lynn Myers, newly elected to NOW's national board and chair of the Compliance and Enforcement Task Force.[39] Myers stepped up to national leadership easily, having served as the Chicago chapter's compliance coordinator for four years.[40] In the fall, Scott provided Myers with volumes of information. They were considering advertising and selling Scott's model affirmative action program, perhaps at a low cost for educational purposes.[41]

On December 1, 1971, the EEOC would file thousands of pages in its case against AT&T. By December 20 Myers had an "AT&T Happy New Year Action" ready to roll. Again, NOW sent its chapters lots of help in getting the action going. Basically, on January 3, 1972, or "as soon after that date as you can get yourselves together," each local chapter was to present its local phone company president with holiday greetings along with a lump of coal. Myers would be sending a message to the four corporate headquarters (AT&T, Western Electric, Bell Labs, and Teletype). The suggested verbiage was:

> *Seasons Greeting to a vital partner in the Sexist Corporation of the Year . . . from (the name of the local chapter). Santa, in the guise of the EEOC, has already presented you with the proverbial lump of coal for your past and present behavior.*
>
> *We would like to add that thousands of NOW members across the country support the EEOC action and will be following the case carefully.*
>
> *We wish you a Happy New Year full of changes to bring women into full partnership with the men in your company.[42]*

Attached to the report were "notes and quotes from the EEOC report," along with the names and addresses of the top officers of each Bell operating company and, where useful, the heads of state operations. Toni Carabillo sent along suggestions for press contacts and a sample press release.[43]

In 1971 NOW built its knowledge of AT&T and learned how to challenge the company. The EEOC had used all of 1971 to build its case, much of which rested on documents AT&T had so conveniently provided. As 1971 ended, AT&T faced the flurry of pages from the EEOC and protests from NOW.

My move to New York brought me closer to the center of AT&T policy but took me away from close contact with NOW local actions. My feminist energies turned almost completely to what I termed corporate feminism, trying to change the system from within, while still keeping the ties to NOW's AT&T task force and thus indirectly to the EEOC's AT&T task force.

5

WHAT REALLY WAS TRUE

Once the FCC's hearing examiner, Frederick W. Denniston, started the case, AT&T and the EEOC levied requests on each other for data. AT&T would ultimately ask for everything the EEOC had on the case, specifically the backup material for every allegation and for all materials the EEOC had provided to the FCC regarding employment practices since 1966.

David Copus negotiated with AT&T's attorney Hal Levy in preparation for making document and data requests. AT&T and the EEOC agreed that the locus for data would be the thirty largest metropolitan areas, known to statisticians as the standard metropolitan statistical areas (SMSAs). In those thirty SMSAs were more than half of the Bell System's operating company employees.[1] AT&T agreed to provide data on magnetic tape; thus the case became one of the first to rely heavily on computer records and analysis. AT&T agreed to provide discrete data on 125,000 employees and over a million documents. Computerized information would enable the EEOC to undertake its first national analysis of an employer; AT&T may have been unique in its ability to provide data for so many people in every major area of the country.

In Washington, D.C., at 2000 L Street, AT&T set up the eighth floor just for the EEOC files. Lighting and air conditioning were installed, together with row upon row of steel bookshelves. AT&T labeled the documents, provided work areas and tables, and at the end of each day made copies for the EEOC of what Copus and his colleagues requested. AT&T did a perfect job of gathering the documents, Copus later observed. He felt at the time that he and his team were "gnats surviving by their mere indulgence."[2]

Copus and Levy communicated by phone and letter, negotiating requests. For example, in April Copus sent Levy seven items, including such things as "Employment Patterns in the Utilities Industry, 1966–67," the "Table of Contents for Confidential Employment of Minorities and Women in Commercial Banking," and "copies of charges against AT&T and Bell subsidiaries." Detail, detail, detail. The kinds of documents being discussed included, for example, New Jersey Bell's "personnel and/or supervisor's manuals," a management compensation binder, an employment guide, and the "flip chart and leader's guide for orientation of traffic women."[3]

On June 17 Copus asked for missing documents from *his* April seven-page request. He talked with Levy about the list again on July 27, and Levy admitted that some items had not yet been located. By September 10 Levy claimed that some documents were nonexistent, "orientation materials" would not be provided, and "certainly most everything else" would be sent. They talked about the list again on September 15.[4]

Copus originally perceived the case to be aimed at the race issue in spite of prodding from NOW, Susan Deller Ross, and other women's rights advocates. As the data and documents from AT&T were analyzed, however, it became clear that this was a sex case.

A routine developed at the EEOC. Larry Gartner and Copus walked to work from Foggy Bottom; Randy Speck rode his bike. They met at 7 A.M. to review and share notes. At 9 A.M., they reviewed documents at AT&T's 2000 L Street location. The young EEOC group stood out among the more traditionally attired and coifed AT&T lawyers. Speck took pride in the image and

David A. Copus, EEOC attorney

Photograph from personal files of David A. Copus and reprinted with his permission.

Harold S. Levy, AT&T attorney.

Photograph property of AT&T Archives.
Reprinted with permission of AT&T.

guessed that the image had something to do with AT&T's underestimating what the EEOC could do.[5] The *Village Voice* referred to the EEOC team as the "nest of freaks."[6]

By 5 P.M. each day, the "freaks" were back at the EEOC, organizing documents and writing notes on three-by-five cards until late at night. At times, Copus, suffering from migraines, slept under his desk. Rarely at home to watch television, he brought his TV set to the office.[7] Copus dominated the landscape with his wit, energy, and intellect. While others saw him as arrogant, his colleague Bill Wallace observed that "only Copus had the combination of audacity, insight, and unremitting drive" to deal with the magnitude of the case.[8] Copus worked at the case day and night, following leads and lines of thought with a hound's persistence. He knew the case in incredible detail, and the case consumed him. Others moved with him as the case developed, but no one knew more about it or could keep pace throughout.

Starting to think about witnesses, Copus worked with an advisory group pulled together by Dr. Phyllis Wallace and went out to interview prospective witnesses. Speck traveled to Wadley, Georgia, to talk with Lorena Weeks. The team's strategy precluded a collection of individual stories, but the Weeks case was too significant to ignore, having been through the courts and having nationwide visibility, thanks to NOW. At her kitchen table Speck heard firsthand about her long fight to get a transfer within Southern Bell to a job close to home, a job she knew she could do but, she found, was not open to women. She would be an excellent witness, and he made plans to bring her to Washington. Other potential witness meetings took him to places such as New Orleans and Albany.[9] Like Copus, Speck persevered through long hours and almost total absorption in the case compared to Gartner, Wallace, and Kathy Mazzaferri, who liked to think they still had a meaningful life outside the case.[10]

As they developed their case, the EEOC put together an impressive set of expert witnesses. Phyllis Wallace aided in finding and preparing social scientists, lawyers, and experts on employment discrimination.[11] Altogether the EEOC filed testimony of seventeen witnesses including psychologists Sandra and Daryl Bem, Wharton assistant professor Bernard Anderson, and from the CWA, Charles J. McDonald.[12] The FCC's Common Carrier Bureau prepared two witnesses, Robert Nathan and Barbara R. Bergmann.

Knowing that summaries were recommended for big cases, the EEOC's AT&T team began organizing its note cards by topic and writing drafts. Two secretaries were kept busy typing, and a copy machine was commandeered specifically for the task. Whatever experts were needed were hired. Marjanette Feagan, perhaps better grounded in reality than the lawyers, managed the clerical process. Her hard work, excellent skills, and good sense kept day-to-day operations from falling into chaos. Eventually, everyone on the team took a turn at photocopying each with a daily assignment of an hour and a half.[13]

Bill Brown felt that the union perspective should be included, but his pleas went unanswered by the union itself. On January 29, early in the process, Brown met over lunch with Communications Workers of America (CWA) president Joseph A. Beirne and invited the CWA to join as a plaintiff. Repeatedly, Copus and Brown entreated the union to join the process. While the union tried to represent minorities and women, it defended its seniority system and other trappings of the status quo. Eventually Copus got Charles McDonald, administrative assistant to the CWA president, to survey CWA members for the EEOC.[14]

On February 24, 1971, as had been assumed from the beginning, the FCC officially named the twenty-two operating companies of the Bell System as parties to the hearing. AT&T needed, and received, a thirty-day extension on the data request to July 1. The EEOC filed its prehearing memorandum on April 15, and FCC Order 71M-602 invited comments, which AT&T filed on April 19. Hearing examiner Denniston set the prehearing conference date for May 11, but AT&T again asked for an extension, this time for its prehearing brief. Denniston set June 2, 1971, as the new date and set September 1 for AT&T to file its written testimony. He also indicated that California hearings would follow the EEOC presentations in Washington.[15]

That spring, AT&T faced the threat of a nationwide strike. Sixteen union contract agreements were expiring on April 30 and seven on May 1; day-to-day "no strike" extensions were granted as talks continued. AT&T's regulatory department maintained a full-force effort with its interstate rate request, working with the FCC trial staff's head, Asher Ende. Meanwhile, the business continued—Bell Laboratories scientists and Western Electric engineers had just worked out a new breed of transistor, encased in plastic, providing a way to use transistors widely for the first time. Domestic satellites for communications purposes had been proposed and were awaiting FCC action.[16] What worried AT&T executives the most, however, was the continuing problem of service quality.

In the summer of 1971 Bob Lilley authored a "Concern for People" column in the *Bell Labs News*:

> *Traditionally a "people business," we in the Bell System are discovering that a significant number of employees and a substantial body of customers feel that we are not meeting our basic obligations to them as individuals, that we have become so occupied with the technical aspects of the business that we have lost sight of the human needs of human beings.*
>
> *A long-term policy is underway at AT&T to restore public and employee confidence in our company. But we recognize that confidence won't be restored until our service is brought back to the level that the public has every right to expect, until absolute dependability of communications becomes not only a goal but a reality. That has to be the first order of business.*
>
> *But important as it is—as essential as it is—good service will not be enough if it is provided in a cold and impersonal way, or if we neglect other areas of corporate responsibility and accountability. Our good reputation will not be regained until we achieve top performance with respect to treatment of employees, equal opportunity, the rights of women, concern for the environment, and concern and more concern for the needs, the dig-*

nity and the aspirations of every human being affected by our operations.
And that is virtually every man, woman and child in America."[17]

Even with the service crisis demanding his attention, Lilley never set aside
his concern for employees. Equally committed, Copus worked day and night
to understand the Bell System's policies, structure, and results. Copus became
the head of an official EEOC AT&T task force. Brown knew the dean of the
University of Puerto Rico's law school and from that school recruited students
to help over the summer; enthusiastic and hardworking, they dug energetical-
ly through the documents provided by AT&T.[18]

Brown felt strongly that the EEOC had to behave as the independent
agency it was. He fought to keep the agency apart from other government departments, and he fought for the EEOC budget. When Congress attempted to
cut the EEOC budget, Leonard Garment intervened for Brown and con-
vinced Nixon to push senators to restore it. Brown was not averse to arguing
with Nixon himself, having already had a role in convincing the president that
employment would be a good avenue for civil rights attention. Nixon knew
Brown as "that thin fellow that heads equal opportunities," acknowledging in
a conversation with Patrick Moynihan that, contrary to many blacks, in his
opinion, "He's got it."[19]

Accustomed to pressure, Brown kept those who objected to the EEOC's
challenge of AT&T away from the team. At hearings in Houston in the summer of 1970, he had demonstrated that he and the EEOC would be aggressive. Even calls from Vice President Spiro Agnew did not deter him. Prompted by a call from Houston's mayor, the vice president told Brown that his
hearings there would be too disruptive. Houston had been selected, Brown explained, precisely because of the significant number of charges filed there and
because so many major corporations had a presence. It was "the place to go."
Agnew relented, Brown called the mayor, and plans went ahead.[20]

Brown had invited major corporations to the Houston hearings, some refused to appear in public. The EEOC caught senior managers in words without results and provided an opportunity for the victims of discrimination to be
heard. Twenty-year-old Gregory Salazar proved eloquent in challenging the
commission to get enforcement power and act. Sociologist Dr. Sally Hacker
appeared for NOW, and many individuals told their stories.[21]

Taking on AT&T was just another step. Brown ignored those who said,
"You can't do it," and those who argued that the best results would be
achieved by winning individual cases. The more Copus and his team heard

that they should not be challenging AT&T—or heard that Justice, not the EEOC, was where the action was—the more they were motivated to build a good case. Brown allowed the team to gear up and gave them the necessary budget and resources when staff was lean and budgets sparse.[22] Tackling systemic discrimination was where Brown saw the most significant opportunity for change.

From July on, the adhoc advisory panel of university social scientists chaired by Phyllis Wallace and informal representatives from NOW provided input to the EEOC team as it built its testimony.[23] At the same time, Ann Scott established a NOW lobbying office in Washington. As NOW's legislative vice president, she made her views heard and would become an important witness. Renting offices across the hall from George Sape, Scott became a familiar face at upper levels of the EEOC.[24]

Copus and his team knew there were rumblings among the women at AT&T, and they knew about the NOW actions, but those actions were on the periphery as the team waded through statistics and documents in 1971. By summer's end, the team was surrounded by piles of note cards, many pointing to issues of sex discrimination. The statistics were stark, the sex segregation blatant. Even the statistics about race—most of the black employees of AT&T were female—had sex discrimination as an important factor. AT&T was so proud of its record as a good employer of women and as a leader in dealing with urban employment issues that it filled its documents with explicit statements and willingly provided tons of statistics. Neither AT&T nor EEOC had previously seen what was obvious when they put it together.[25]

Prompted by Denniston, AT&T and EEOC exploratory talks began in the fall of 1971 with the charge to find a settlement. Copus, Charles Wilson (chief of the office of conciliations), and John (Jack) deJ. Pemberton Jr. (deputy general counsel) represented the EEOC. Levy, Lee Satterfield (a Chesapeake & Potomac Telephone Company attorney detailed to AT&T), and John Kingsbury (assistant vice president for personnel) represented AT&T. Satterfield was no stranger to the subject of civil rights, though he started out as a tax law specialist. In 1967 and 1968 he investigated violent civil unrest as part of his work with the National Advisory Committee on Civil Disorders (the Kerner Commission). He knew about AT&T's involvement with urban crises, especially in New Jersey, where Lilley had been chairman of the Governor's Select Commission to Study Civil Disorder. Then, while in the general counsel's office at the EEOC, Satterfield learned of the number of cases filed against the Bell System. He had a memorable exchange with Southern Bell on a particular case in which he requested an organization chart and the company refused to provide it. When given the opportunity to work with the C&P Telephone Company, Satterfield thought he might be able to learn just enough to step back and nail the company. Once hired, however, he liked the company and learned to know "good" people within the business. He resolved to change the company from within.[26]

For the negotiations, Satterfield booked a suite at the Hay-Adams Hotel on Lafayette Square in Washington and invited the EEOC team. They met on September 2 and November 1 and 5, 1971, in what were somewhat stiff, formal meetings without much interaction; Levy and Copus did most of the talking. Talks continued frequently up to early January 1972, when they ended abruptly over the issue of back pay dollars.[27] Copus wanted to pursue the case—settling carried a high price. AT&T was not really ready to negotiate dollars or to compromise on principles; the company had a cultural resistance to making changes as demanded by the EEOC, especially the idea of goals for men in operator jobs.[28]

The head of AT&T's Washington office, John Fox, had other issues to deal with and did not follow the discussions closely; AT&T's lead attorney Ashley, on the other hand, wanted reports from Levy at the end of every day. Within AT&T's Washington office, the most prestigious job was managing the company's relationship with the FCC. Others within the office were assigned to the legislative branch, and the newest or least favored managers drew the other executive branch departments and agencies. In 1971, small, powerless agencies such as the EEOC had the lowest priority of all.[29]

Satterfield did not know Copus before the discussions began but soon learned to respect him. Satterfield noted that Copus sometimes was not taken seriously within the EEOC because he had no real legal experience. Satterfield observed, over time, that Copus was motivated to change the employment processes of corporate America and that he was determined to get women into craft jobs at AT&T.[30]

Negotiations did not appear to be particularly productive, so the EEOC team focused on the case. With Brown's blessing, a Frisbee, and a football, Copus, Speck, Bill Wallace, and Gartner boxed up their notes and headed to Graves Mountain Lodge in Syria, Virginia, a place Copus had visited before with Peace Corps friends. The team needed to get away. At this point they were overworked, burned out, and just plain tired, but they needed to write, to put their case into words, to prepare the formal filing.

There in the Shenandoah Valley, holed up in a small cabin, they wrote for hours on end. Occasionally they left to shoot baskets on the court across the stream or toss the football on the lawn. Family-style meals in the main lodge provided all they could possibly want to eat. Only one phone was available, a pay phone at the lodge, so they wrote undisturbed by the rest of the world.

In the main room of the cabin, papers fell everywhere, with the fire in the fireplace kept going with rejected pages. When it got to be too much, Speck went out on the porch and listened to the stream below. Copus did not often take a break, and the work went on for twelve to fourteen hours a day. Copus, Speck, Wallace, and Gartner each had a section to write; they compared notes and read each other's work. For seven days, they wrote and rewrote. Wallace and Speck worked particularly on summaries of each allegation.[31]

The pace never slowed. By the end of the retreat Copus concluded, "We have them," and knew that AT&T did not suspect the magnitude of the EEOC's charge. With so much data, Copus felt that prosecuting the case would be like "shooting fish in a barrel," though in truth no one had ever tried a case like this before. No previous briefs, no transcripts, no findings of fact, no summaries, no judgments, no opinions could provide guidance.[32]

Writing the summary of their intense investigation required not just that they outline their findings but that they put them into an easily understood context. To do that, they first had to describe how the complex Bell System was organized and how it functioned from a personnel standpoint. Over the past months, the necessary help had come from previous EEOC research, from FCC staff personnel, from friends inside AT&T, and from responses to direct questions asked of Levy and his team. At this point, Copus and his task force probably knew the Bell System's employment practices as well as anyone outside ever could. It was all in their heads; now it had to get onto paper. The first section of their filed case provided a layman's guide to the large and powerful AT&T of 1970, an explanation of its corporate structure and processes.

Copus considered the race case strong, based on statistics, but the claims on sex discrimination were backed up not only with statistics but also with example after example from AT&T's own documents. Sex discrimination was a matter of fact. AT&T had documented the company's pride in what women had done during World War II and what they did in specific cases, such as doing wiring work on frames in Michigan telephone offices. Looking at the data, Copus saw that in every other Bell company, wiring work was men's work. Almost all nonmanagement jobs were known as men's or women's jobs but not both. Management ranks had clear delineations as well, though exceptions occurred now and then.[33]

Copus, Gartner, Speck, and Wallace worked and ate. Huge meals served by Jim and Rachel Graves at the main lodge were also social times, however, and the team, sometimes reinforced by Bill Oldaker, did not particularly try to be secret about its mission. Explaining what they were working on to strangers helped refine their style.

A 1968 quotation from AT&T vice president Walter Straley provided the lead for their document: "We think our experience as an employer, hiring some 200,000 persons each year, provides us with a unique competence to play a leading role in the improvement of employment opportunity."[34] Once they found that quote, the title of their document became obvious—*A Unique Competence: A Study of Equal Employment Opportunity in the Bell System.*

With the manuscript boxed, they returned to Washington, where the rest of the team polished it. No one editorialized or censored their work. Brown trusted his team.

The actual filing on Wednesday, December 1, 1971, included *A Unique Competence* complete with detailed footnotes, charts, and tables (515 pages), findings of fact (1,719 pages), a list of documents (450 pages), testimony of seventeen witnesses (690 pages), documents "of more than routine interest" (505 pages), the statistics database (462 pages) and over twenty-five thousand pages of backup documents. About 95 percent of the backup documents were reproductions of materials furnished by AT&T during the discovery phase of the case.[35] *A Unique Competence*, based not on theory but on documents and data from AT&T itself, hit all the hot buttons of women's employment. "Real world" information had provided evidence of discrimination in recruitment, hiring, promotion, wages, maternity leave, segregated jobs, and segregated routes to management. What might be seen by Bell System management as a reflection of society could be seen clearly from another perspective as the result of discrimination.

For analytical purposes, the EEOC studied in detail AT&T's work force in thirty agreed-upon SMSAs, ranging from New York, with a Bell System employment of 82,380, to El Paso, with 1,058 Bell employees. In each of the SMSAs, data were presented by department—accounting, commercial, marketing, plant, traffic, and other. Statistics indicated salaries, sex, race, and so on, and the descriptive material covered working conditions, turnover, job requirements, and recruiting. *A Unique Competence* addressed management statistics as well because 23 percent of all Bell employees in the SMSAs were in management positions.

From its study of the Bell System's employment structure and statistics, the EEOC noted that Bell had five major departments, the largest of which were "plant" and "traffic." Major nonmanagement jobs were craft workers in the plant department, clerical workers in the plant and accounting departments, operators in the traffic department, and service representatives in the commercial department. Operator and clerical jobs had the least desirable working conditions and the lowest pay. Craft wages were the highest, exceeding the pay of many first-level management jobs. "Virtually all of the 200,000 persons hired each year possess little or no skills and are completely trained within the System." High turnover aggravated costs. Bell promoted craft employees from within or hired college graduates.[36]

In subsequent chapters, A Unique Competence described how each of these factors related to equal opportunities for women and minorities. The first and most in-depth discussion was of sex segregation: "Although women continue to be employed in very large numbers, they are confined to the most stifling and repetitive jobs. Their compensation is so meager as to make them doubt their own self worth. Their prospects for promotion are in the distant future, if at all. It is little wonder, therefore, that many women flee from telephone jobs almost as quickly as they are attracted to them." Internally and externally, the Bell System identified jobs as either male or female, and the EEOC had a wealth of documentation to prove it. What amazed the researchers was the "absolute uniformity" of sex segregation in every company, with only minor variations. "In the 30 SMSAs, 92.4% of all employees in major job classifications are in sex-segregated jobs," and "in the 30 SMSAs, 54% of all employees in major job classifications are in 100% sex-segregated jobs." In dealing with pay, the picture painted in A Unique Competence was equally bleak: "In 1971, almost every major low-paying job in the Bell System is a 'female' job."[37]

In spite of the Bell System's official pronouncements and responses to Title VII, "only three companies (New England Tel, Ohio Bell, and Michigan Bell) employed any females in craft jobs" in 1966. "Craft jobs" were nonmanagement operations jobs in the plant department, usually paying far more than the traditionally female positions. By 1971 every company had at least one woman in a craft job, but "in only five companies did the proportion of female craft workers exceed one percent." In stark contrast to other companies in the Bell System, Michigan Bell employed only women in the craft job of "framework" and had done so for twenty years. But the job differed from similar jobs in other companies by its clerical entry requirements, lower pay scale, and the fact that "the promotional opportunities were into lateral clerical jobs rather than to higher rated crafts or management."[38]

A *Unique Competence* explored management opportunities and career paths, finding that, for a variety of reasons, "the Bell System's failure to promote females must be classified as one of the most monumental inequities in private industries." Studies of wages confirmed the discrimination for the EEOC:

> By any standard, the exclusion of females from craft jobs and middle and upper management positions is tragic. The psychological toll is incalculable. The toll in turnover is fantastic. The loss in wages is astronomical. The conclusion is inescapable that, in terms of providing equality of opportunity for females, the Bell System has been uniquely incompetent.[39]

Having gone through thousands of pages of internal and external AT&T documents, the EEOC could trace the company's reaction to Title VII, to the bona fide occupational qualification (BFOQ) arguments, and to state protective legislation. The Bell companies never claimed a BFOQ for clerk and service representative, but those jobs in 1971 were still "female" jobs. In some cases, the companies tried to claim a BFOQ for operator, outside sales, and craft jobs. Those efforts were inconsistent and short-lived, though the jobs themselves remained segregated by sex. A few of the operating companies challenged state protective legislation, requesting exemptions from the law that would allow them to use women in craft positions. Other companies maintained that women should not "lift heavy weights or work in hazardous areas." The EEOC concluded, "Whatever the rationalizations might be . . . there were no real differences among the companies in the sex composition of the jobs in the Bell System. All were just about as segregated in 1971 as they were in 1965." Having explained the sexist structure and corporate attempts to deal with requirements of Title VII, the EEOC went on to claim, "It is preposterous to think that these distinctions between males and females could have occurred by chance. The disparities are so egregious and the corporate explanations are so feeble and contradictory that the segregation of males and females must be ascribed to a deliberately sexist policy."[40]

And on it went to an analysis of recruitment methods, hiring, promotion, maternity leave. The 1971 maternity leave policies in eight companies required pregnant females to resign or take a leave of absence at the end of the sixth or seventh month of their pregnancy. Four of the companies limited maternity leave to married females. Health benefits were suspended during maternity leave, and only two companies (Mountain Bell and South Central Bell) "guaranteed reemployment." The EEOC quoted a New York Telephone regulation that ensured returning traffic employees would lose all promotions they had earned prior to their leave. Such "unreasonable and discriminatory maternity leave provisions" kept women from being able to take advantage of opportunities in the company. Additionally, the EEOC concluded that the recruitment, hiring, and promotion procedures, all of which they detailed, unfairly restricted women. "The 'pure meritocracy' claimed by Bell exists only for males. For females, competition and its rewards are limited to the feminine sphere. While telephone employment can be a rewarding vocation for men, it can be no more than a way station for women, a mockery of their career aspirations."[41]

Going further, the EEOC challenged the Bell System on its treatment of women in management, arguing that "women are in the lowest paying, least desirable, 'terminal' management positions." While AT&T proudly claimed that one-third of all its managers were women, the EEOC pointed out that 94 percent of those women were in the lowest level of management.[42] The EEOC's argument leaned heavily on the task force study Mercer had prompted within AT&T. Titled "The 1970 AT&T Task Force on Women," it had candidly identified problems for the company to solve for itself. The EEOC acknowledged the internal study but challenged the company's ability to implement its own recommendations.

With respect to sex segregation overall, the EEOC summarized by saying:

> The Bell monolith is, without doubt, the largest oppressor of women workers in the United States. This harsh conclusion is inescapable . . . Bell's women are forced either to adjust their ambitions downward to conform to the company's restrictive expectations or to seek more rewarding work with another employer.
>
> Bell's policies toward women are morally and ethically indefensible and since July 2, 1965, they have been against the law.[43]

To quantify the economic impact of discrimination against women, the EEOC's expert Dr. Ronald Oaxaca claimed that Bell System's women, "given their age, education, and experience are paid an aggregate of $500 million per year less than males with comparable personal characteristics." If the company employed women in all job categories, the EEOC argued, the savings would have been "an annual reduction of 2% to 4% in overall telephone rates." As a bottom line to the issue of sex discrimination and as a spur to affirmative action, the EEOC claimed, "Bell's history is replete with examples of conscious, calculated action to discourage interest in 'opposite sex' jobs. Their affirmative obligation to eliminate these pervasive inequities is now overwhelming."[44]

In chapters on racial discrimination, the EEOC documented hiring practices and a pattern of exclusion that kept blacks in particular jobs, usually the lowest-paying, least desirable jobs. The EEOC traced the employment of black workers in the Bell System from a position of "almost complete" exclusion in 1930 to a significant effort on the part of some Bell companies in the 1960s. By 1967, in four of the SMSAs studied, the Bell System hiring "exceeded or came close to the all industry average for black employment." Whether this was due to socially driven policy or economic reality was open to question. Dr. Bernard E. Anderson, whom the EEOC identified as "the chief chronicler of black employment at the Bell System," concluded that "labor market conditions in the North and East were a major, if not primary, force contributing to the increased employment of blacks as Operators during the 1950's." Commenting on the influx of blacks into the operator ranks, the EEOC described the conversion of the traffic department from a "nunnery" to a "ghetto nunnery."[45]

Overall, the EEOC summarized its finding on the Bell System's employment of blacks by noting that "Bell companies in most of the 30 SMSAs still employed blacks at a rate less than that of the population or lower even than the average of all major employers." While noting exceptions, the EEOC singled out the companies in the South for falling behind "even the minimal efforts of the rest of the System." The report claimed that the Bell System channeled black workers into the "lowest-paying, least desirable jobs in the companies." Black women "suffer from a dual handicap of both race and sex." The EEOC alleged, "The concentration of blacks into the operator job is no accident." In economic terms, discrimination cost black employees $225 million each year.[46]

Spanish-surnamed Americans suffered "persistent neglect" and were the "invisible minority" in the Bell System. A *Unique Competence* ends with a poem:

I am Joaquin,
Lost in a world of confusion
Caught up in the whirl of an Anglo society,
Confused by the rules,
Scorned by attitudes,
Suppressed by manipulations,
And destroyed by modern society.
My fathers have lost the economic battle,
And won the fight for cultural survival.

In a country that has wiped out all my history,
stifled all my pride.
In a country that has placed a different indignity
upon my ancient burdens.
Inferiority
is the new load.[47]

The EEOC saw "only one pattern in Bell's employment of Spanish-surnamed Americans: exclusion," and concluded the economic cost was over $137 million annually.[48]

The FCC itself filed over two hundred pages, including testimony of two witnesses—Robert Nathan on the economics of discrimination and Barbara R. Bergmann on statistics, goals, and methods. The FCC's Jim Juntilla told Speck that with respect to his career, this filing might well be the "most significant thing you'll have done." As the work progressed, Juntilla provided helpful insights and support to the EEOC in understanding necessary procedures; he and Speck often talked about the impact this case could have on business and government culture.[49]

After the yearlong cooperation and exchange of data, AT&T was surprised by the extent of the EEOC charges. What good AT&T did was not good enough. What bad it did was unforgivable. For a company that prided itself on being a good citizen, it was indeed a heavy blow. AT&T's Don Liebers was astonished—he had never expected the EEOC to respond so strongly, so fast.[50]

The filing actually got little press reaction—five or six major front page stories—and only perfunctory coverage, less than a minute, on the major TV news networks. AT&T issued a press release pointing out that in 1971, one out of every four new hires was either black, American Indian, Oriental, or

Spanish-surnamed. The company stressed that about 13 percent of total employment was minority, a percentage "fractionally higher than the proportion of minorities in the U.S. population." Furthermore, the release claimed, total Bell System employment from 1963 to 1971 grew 38 percent but the number of minority employees grew 265 percent.

The thrust of AT&T's statement dealt with race, but it provided some indication that the company had begun to understand the sex issues. For example, in the release, Bob Lilley cited the fact that eight thousand women earned promotions into and within management in the telephone companies in the prior year. He added, "We need more in higher levels and plan to have them." Beyond that, he argued that much of the EEOC's case dealt with "ancient history, long since mooted by changes we've already made." He went on to cite the changes in pension options and the opportunity for women to transfer into crafts that had been male jobs. The statement was tempered—Lilley admitted not having achieved all that should be done. "We don't claim to be perfect."[51]

In an internal publication, with material provided by AT&T headquarters, Southwestern Bell told its employees, "In its 2,000 pages of summary testimony, the EEOC zeroed in heaviest on alleged discrimination against women."[52]

Meanwhile, on Saturday night in Washington, the EEOC AT&T task force celebrated in Apartment 4, 3012 Q Street.[53]

Lilley, Ashley, and Kingsbury appeared on an AT&T internal closed-circuit television program moderated by Paul Lund. Seated behind a table piled high with the EEOC's testimony, they cried foul. Lilley emphasized, however, "We need to do better." He felt the company's goodwill had been challenged but reminded employees to "emphasize the positives." He reminded people that the Bell System has "tackled the problem head-on for a long time." The executives charged the EEOC with a "simplistic approach." They claimed that only recently had there been women interested in craft positions, and noted, "Time will tell about those interests." What they saw as the question was the distinction between the willingness of an individual woman to get a craft job and a corporate policy that says a certain percentage must be women. Lilley felt "our jobs are downgraded in the EEOC report; operator jobs, for example, are extremely important jobs in our society." Kingsbury called the charges "as serious a problem as we've ever had." Asked about copies, the audience was told that AT&T got two complete copies and would be providing a summary of about nine pages on the EEOC filing and three on the FCC part. Asked how many AT&T resources were dedicated to this case, they responded with twenty people and $2 million. The dollar value of the charges was bandied about, with one estimate being $959 million as the deficit in women's salaries. Laughter greeted a question, "What if cease-and-desist power is granted?" Whether or not the EEOC should have any enforcement power was still a question in Washington. Beyond that, people differed over whether the EEOC should have the right to take employers to court or to get cease-and-desist orders imposed on employers. At this point, the EEOC had neither.[54]

Internally, executives recognized it would be a long and difficult struggle to protect AT&T's reputation. And those who understood that change was inevitable knew that they would have a tough task managing that change in a responsible way.[55]

The closed-circuit television program was an indication of the company's openness and willingness to share information with employees. However, the program raised temperatures; awareness grew within AT&T, especially among its women. When A Unique Competence appeared, women in corporate headquarters were primed to respond, and we were close to the action. The more vociferously the executives disclaimed any discriminatory treatment, the more it became obvious to us that "they didn't quite get it." Having been well cared for in some ways within the company and being afraid of what being "a problem" might do to my career, I still approached the problem as a problem of communication—"If we explain, they will understand."

Intrigued by the EEOC charges and angered by AT&T's official response, four of us discussed the EEOC case over lunch, then recruited others for an evening meeting the next Monday, December 13, 1971, at the Manhattan apartment of Kim Manna, who worked for AT&T headquarters public relations. Twenty-two women would show up to talk about the status of women in AT&T at an all-day working meeting on February 7 on company time and company premises, Room 350 at 195 Broadway. Following that meeting, Dorothy Francis, Nancy Rathfelder, and Barbara Colbert would work on an attitude study; Jayne Sherman, Liz Brydon, and Suzanne Albert on our statement of purpose; and Amy Hanan on providing statistics for AT&T headquarters personnel. The AT&T Alliance for Women came alive and would be officially recognized by upper management, with Hanan as the company's liaison to the group.

In the halls of AT&T, individuals sometimes expressed support for our alliance but would not, or could not, lend their names to any action. Being identified with the cause meant always having to explain the issues, and it sometimes meant notoriety. In the long term that visibility would help, not hurt, careers; early leaders of the group went on to be firsts in many jobs on their way up the corporate ladder. One of the alliance's visible leaders and its first president, Liz Brydon, became fourth level during the case and ultimately would become an officer of the business. The group had far more power than we ever used or even knew we had, but at the time the risks seemed significant.

The alliance and other groups within the Bell System tried to resolve day-to-day problems while the EEOC complaint wound its way through the tedious process of fact finding. We challenged procedures, such as the hidden nature of management job openings. Dorothy Francis and I put together a slide show on the sexist nature of advertising to heighten awareness. Not waiting for the government to act, committees of the alliance struggled to change practices within the business, leveraging the existence of the case to accomplish what we could. The EEOC complaint had lumped together all management women at the third level and above; the alliance gathered data about women in specific upper management levels. Thanks to AT&T's willingness to respond to employee questions, we knew that as of 1971, the highest women in the Bell System were the six at fifth level: Lucile Dugan (assistant comptroller, Pacific Telephone), Clarene Pearce (assistant secretary, South Central Bell), Julia H. Gaza (assistant secretary, Southern Bell), Irene S. Ayres (assistant secretary, Bell of Pennsylvania/Diamond), Amy R. Hanan (director, AT&T General Departments), and Pauline J. Nelson (attorney, Mountain Bell). Moreover, there were at least two female secretaries of the Employee Benefit Committees. On Bell companies' boards of directors, there were two women: one on Wisconsin Telephone's board (Catherine B. Cleary) and one on Cincinnati Bell's (Frances Jones Poetker).[56] AT&T's board had no women.

At Illinois Bell, Harriet White convened the Women's Advisory Committee with a dozen management women. On November 16, 1971, after several work sessions, the group presented a letter to John Bauman, assistant vice president of personnel. The committee intended to identify what policies, practices, and attitudes hamper upward mobility for women, suggest means of reducing barriers, and define "reasonable" numerical objectives and timetables for the affirmative action program. White's committee identified and formed task forces to study barriers. In particular, they tackled hiring and career pathing, pay equity, attitudes, job criteria, and "mistrust and misunderstanding of the Affirmative Action Program." Ultimately, the committee suggested a program to "de-stereotype women." It suggested consciousness raising for women and sensitizing sessions for all supervisors.[57]

Issues arose even at Sandia, a New Mexico subsidiary of Western Electric that worked on government projects such as nuclear simulation testing. A women's committee there met resistance as it tried to address Sandia's refusal to hire spouses, the implications of New Mexico's community property laws, and equal pay for female draftsmen. The group disappeared soon after it appeared.

Other corporations, most notably IBM, had high-visibility programs. IBM appointed Barbara Boyle as head of their equal opportunity office in August 1970. Why? IBM cited several reasons: government, ethics, the number of women in their work force, and economics driven by a desire to utilize resources. They saw problems in classification, level achievement, job restrictions, salary, and development. Their action program included establishing Boyle's position, gathering data, involving top management, setting "targets and objectives," and running "awareness programs."

Polaroid acknowledged internal problems when three special-interest groups of women raised their voices. Polaroid's director of corporate systems, James Grinnell, set up task forces and charged them to look at current policies and their implementation, the current status of women in the company, possible awareness sessions for management, and government requirements.

General Electric appointed a corporate coordinator for EEO-Women, Jackie Pinckney. In the fall of 1970 GE's planning organization added women's issues to those of minority relations and appointed several task forces. In June 1971 GE appointed a fourteen-person women's advisory panel representing women from all kinds of jobs. The panel met twice in New York, with the task force trying out ideas on the panel and vice versa. The General Electric Foundation underwrote a play about equal employment opportunity and women in management, aiming it at an upper management level.[58]

A *Harvard Business Review* article in the July–August 1971 issue summarized corporate actions. One option was for the chief executive to issue a policy statement accompanied by equal opportunity officer appointments and committees or task forces to develop action plans. A second option was to use a more subtle approach, gradually moving women into visible management roles. A third option blended the first two but kept a low profile because of potential reactions.[59]

Corporations with an interest in social responsibility took on the issue, but most battles were fought by individual women in hand-to-hand combat, with words for weapons. Sexual harassment remained one of the unspoken challenges—it had no name. We privately shared stories and knew whom to avoid when traveling but rarely complained. To challenge a man openly, particularly a senior-level manager, could have led to a personal career disaster. Those battles continued to be private hells, taking their toll on our confidence and opportunity and waiting for another decade.

As 1971 ended, executive changes at AT&T moved William Mercer to the presidency of New England Telephone and Telegraph and brought David K. Easlick at fifty from the presidency of Indiana Bell to the position of vice president for personnel relations at AT&T. Easlick knew that AT&T's top executives expected him to settle the EEOC case. The next year would be an election year, and AT&T management most certainly did not want the case to drag on into a new administration in Washington. Easlick took command of the negotiating team and charged them with settling the case.[60]

Everyone now had access to the EEOC's argument, so carefully documented in A Unique Competence. However, neither the EEOC nor NOW nor women like me knew Easlick's marching orders. What we saw was the opening round of a lively FCC hearing that would go on through all of 1972 in parallel with settlement negotiations. NOW continued to pressure AT&T, the local telephone companies, and the EEOC. The AT&T Alliance for Women gently challenged AT&T's headquarters and officers, and other groups throughout the system kept issues very much alive on a local basis.

6

NO PLACE TO HIDE

For AT&T, the leap year of 1972 began with a holiday greeting and a lump of coal from NOW. AT&T's spokesperson, John Kingsbury, responded to NOW's task force leader, Mary Lynn Myers. Myers relayed the news to the NOW Compliance and Enforcement Task Force: "His feathers were obviously ruffled, but he managed to put down some of the usual rhetoric about 'trying to break free from traditional American stereotypes,' etc. etc." She continued with the news that the sociologist Dr. Sally Hacker, a task force member at large from Iowa, would take over coordination of the AT&T action. A two-year plan of attack was already in draft. The same newsletter contained a "questionnaire for use in evaluating company affirmative action plans," written by Betty Kersh of Seattle, and a list of "helpful resource materials" based on compliance work done for NOW's Eastern Regional Conference.[1]

NOW's Compliance and Enforcement Task Force, under Myers, planned a separate action directed toward the EEOC; she and Wilma Scott Heide were working on points to discuss with Chairman William H. Brown. NOW members elsewhere in the country were alerted to prepare to follow up with district and regional directors of the EEOC. NOW was willing to work with the EEOC on the AT&T case but would keep after the EEOC to practice what it preached.

AT&T was not ready for the EEOC hearings and was counting on negotiation with the EEOC to move closer to a settlement. The EEOC team was not ready either, but AT&T did not know that. On January 5, 1972, AT&T filed for a continuance, arguing that it needed time to "take exception" to documents and material submitted by the EEOC and asking Frederick Denniston to delay the start of hearings from January 31 to May 1.

On January 18 Denniston denied AT&T's request. Money issues derailed negotiations. The EEOC estimated back pay requirements at $175 million. Other issues at the time included sex stereotyping in AT&T's recruitment advertising, the level and timing of the hiring and promotion of minorities and women in each occupation (including males in operator positions), and the terms and conditions under which minorities and women would be allowed to transfer, without jeopardizing their seniority rights, to jobs with better career opportunities.[2]

With data about AT&T's employment practices, local chapters of NOW planned actions against the individual telephone companies. The Detroit chapter was no exception; President Joan Israel led a discussion of "various suggestions to generate mass public action and publicity against Bell." By January 21, the *Detroit News* reported, the local leaders of NOW had demanded that Michigan Bell "divide among its female employees the $91 million they [the women] have allegedly lost because of sex bias since 1965." Michigan Bell's personnel vice president, W. Ricks Littell, and the assistant vice president in charge of their "upward mobility program," Edward N. Hodges, met with local NOW leaders. Bell spokesmen attempted to explain, once again, how women held approximately a third of all management jobs. Littell reported that "94 of the company's 2,125 female managers could be classified as 'middle management or higher,'" and Bell had ordered all departments to set "goals and timetables for the utilization of women and minorities at all levels and in all job classifications." At a subsequent meeting with Michigan Bell, NOW put specific demands on the agenda: advertising practices, education programs, employment and testing procedures, operator working conditions, maternity leave and child care, and equal pay issues.[3]

Detroit chapter president Israel called a press conference to discuss NOW's charges and Michigan Bell's response. The company was under pressure from its union not to talk with NOW. The *Detroit Free Press* reported that the Communications Workers of America (CWA) was considering "filing unfair labor charges against Bell if they discussed contractual matters with NOW." Still, a CWA representative, Gloria McKay, Local 4000 president, told reporter Helen Fogel that her local was pleased by the interest of NOW concerning the "condition of women workers in the Bell System." The press tried in vain to persuade Israel to reveal the sources of NOW's information about Bell. A NOW member was quoted saying, "Don't forget that every document is typed by a secretary, and in that organization, every secretary is a woman."[4]

Aware of the issues being debated, Bob Lilley expressed AT&T's understanding that the government now seemed most interested in results when it reviewed corporate progress toward equal opportunity. "Intent," he perceived, "has become a secondary consideration."[5]

Negotiations resumed on January 19, this time with the FCC staff present. AT&T's negotiating team reported directly to Dave Easlick, though they kept Lilley, Don Liebers, and Gene Kofke informed. Kingsbury also established an EEO committee of vice presidents from the operating companies and Western Electric. The group met frequently with Liebers and Kingsbury as the case wore on.[6]

Hearings started on January 31, in accordance with Denniston's original schedule. NOW had petitioned the FCC to appear as a public witness, and, Jim Juntilla, from the FCC's Common Carrier Bureau, recognized NOW as a party in the case. Ann Scott, articulate, knowledgeable, and well connected, would be NOW's primary witness.

The EEOC relied on Phyllis Wallace to recruit expert witnesses, but Bill Wallace, Randy Speck, and Kathy Mazzaferri briefed them for the hearings. Bill Wallace and Mazzaferri went to work with Sandra and Daryl Bem, while Speck traveled to meet with Lorena Weeks and other Bell System employees who might testify for the EEOC. Speck and Bill Wallace also prepared their own testimony to defend the findings of fact and the summaries.

As the hearings approached, the EEOC team realized it had little real experience in presenting and cross-examining witnesses. Luckily still in the office next door to Copus at the EEOC was Susan Deller Ross. Ross connected the EEOC team with Judy Potter, one of the few female lawyers in Washington with litigation experience in federal court. A 1960 Cornell graduate, Potter's experiences living and working in Eastern Europe after graduation motivated her to study justice and become a lawyer. When she graduated from Michigan's Law School, she was one of only ten women in a class of 330. She had difficulty getting a job in Washington but eventually settled in with a small but politically powerful firm. One day, without any particular motivation other than a feeling of being irrelevant, Potter looked up NOW's telephone number and called. Through NOW she met Ross and other activist women; they worked for Congresswoman Shirley Chisholm in her precedent-setting run for U.S. president in 1972 and on other projects, providing a supportive environment for each other.[7]

Ross and Potter, who became good friends, were part of the group of women lawyers who founded the Women's Legal Defense Fund. In December 1970, at Ross's home, that group organized the fund, later known as the National Partnership for Work and Family. In the beginning were Ross; Potter;

Potter's twin sister, Anne; Nancy Stanley; Gladys Kessler; Hope Eastman; Barbara Underwood; Cindy Gitt; Kathy Mazzaferri; and Lucy Komisar.[8]

Recently back from a vacation in Venice, Italy, Potter arrived on the EEOC scene knowing little about the AT&T case, scheduled to begin in a matter of days. Arriving for her first day at the office, she found Copus and the team surrounded by piles of paper. AT&T had produced more than the EEOC ever needed, perhaps even wanted, to know. Fortunately the material could be computerized, but that would prove costly. Afterward, in retrospect, Potter would conclude that no private law firm could have had the resources to do what the EEOC did against AT&T.

What pushed the case also was not just the "cause" but also competition between the Civil Rights Division of the Justice Department and staff at the EEOC. Having been cast in a support role, the EEOC needed a win. Most EEOC staff tracked cases, going through procedural hoops to achieve action. Only the cases that went to Justice ever went to court in those days. Potter's husband had spent many days trying civil rights cases for Justice. Thus she knew something about the situation.[9]

Daily life for Potter became a routine of taking her baby, Molly, to day care, biking from the town house at Thirty-sixth and P Streets to work by 7:30 or 8 A.M., and getting home at 6 or 7 P.M. Approaching the case, Potter understood there were no precedents; nobody knew the bottom line. No predictability.

AT&T also did not have a clue. No company had ever been involved in a major government investigation of its employment behavior. In the FCC's hearing room, the contrasts were stark—The AT&T uniform? White shirts and dark suits. The EEOC uniform? Anything goes: Copus in a blue crushed velvet suit or his leather jacket, Wallace with jeans and shoulder-length hair. It was briefcase versus knapsack, wingtip versus sandal.[10] Only Potter's presence prevented the legal representation of AT&T and the EEOC from being all male.

Early in the process, AT&T realized that the company needed to beef up its staff for the case. Lilley picked Kofke, then assistant vice president for personnel in New Jersey Bell, to be staff coordinator of the case. Liebers had initially suggested Kofke to Kingsbury, who passed the suggestion along to Lilley. Lilley reacted favorably; he had worked with Kofke earlier at New Jersey Bell, and Kofke had served as his executive assistant on an operating company reorganization project. Acting for Lilley, Liebers called Kofke, suggesting lunch but saying only that he wanted to talk about the EEOC case. When they met, Liebers told Kofke that negotiations with the EEOC had broken down. AT&T

was clearly not ready for hearings. Somehow they had to get ready. They needed Kofke to pull the case together.

The possibility caused Kofke to pause—such an assignment would dominate his life indefinitely. He took a day to think about it. He discussed it with his wife, Sally, and warned her that if he accepted, he would disappear and be eaten up by the case. Kofke said yes partly based on belief, partly for the opportunity, and partly for the adventure. Kofke set down two conditions: he would not lie, and he needed a free hand and would not report to Kingsbury or anyone else on a traditional report-after-report fashion. He also insisted on administrative help, no budget nonsense, and no layering for approvals. Lilley agreed.[11]

Kofke's first meeting with the AT&T legal team took place in George Ashley's office at 2000 L Street in Washington. Kofke walked into the room, noting a circle of chairs with one in the middle for him. Having been a witness in many rate cases and often interviewed by the press, Kofke did not panic. In the ensuing discussion, Kofke learned that the legal team put a lot of emphasis on witnesses and hoped through their testimony to prove AT&T was not guilty of conspiracy and crime. The FCC and EEOC witnesses would appear first, however. Kofke set up his Washington headquarters in the Grammercy Inn, studying the testimony there and developing strategy for cross-examining EEOC witnesses.[12]

The first witness was the EEOC's own twenty-two-year-old researcher, Speck, who took the stand to present the "summaries" and "findings of fact." Copus had no experience introducing witnesses. Potter was horrified that they had put a team member on as a witness, and Speck, as the day went on, felt worse and worse. No one had thought to do mock cross-examination in preparation, and Speck struggled to establish his credibility. Thompson Powers, the experienced attorney from Steptoe and Johnson whom AT&T retained to help with the case, cornered Speck more than once. The hearing examiner, Frederick Denniston, intervened repeatedly, determined to hear the EEOC's arguments and not to let the case be derailed by a skilled lawyer or inexperienced witness.[13]

Powers queried Speck on how he chose material for the summaries. Speck explained that the summaries, typed from his stack of hundreds of index cards, covered what was "relevant." Denniston asked him, "Do I assume that your mission was to look for what you construed to be violations of non-discrimination regulations and laws rather than an overall evaluation of the employment practices?" Speck replied, "That is correct." Powers kept on,

working to show that Speck had been looking just for "unfavorable material."
AT&T's attorney Ashley believed the EEOC's summaries were full of errors
and distortions. If the hearing examiner admitted the summaries, he felt, then
the AT&T team was entitled to point out those errors.[14] Powers argued that not
only were the summaries not accurate but the AT&T documents used were
being taken out of context as well. He challenged every one.

Denniston did not object to the AT&T inquiries, but he pointed out to
Powers, "You are overdoing it, so to speak." Shortly thereafter, Denniston asked
for a break, easing the tension. When they reconvened, AT&T urged Denniston to invalidate the "whole study" on the basis of flawed summaries. To do so,
Denniston realized, would put him in an unenviable position of dismissing a
proceeding and having no facts to present to the FCC commissioners. "On
the other hand," he noted, if AT&T proceeded to deal with each and every
fact and document, he would be "left in a hopeless position of not making any
resolution of the problem short of digging into the pile myself." That, he
stressed, was not "feasible."

Powers feared that accepting the summaries would jeopardize AT&T's future options. Copus and the EEOC team felt tricked because AT&T had not
provided a list of their objections ahead of time. Potter offered a compromise
where they would deal with the objections and work toward an agreed summary of facts or at least alternatives. Juntilla, from the FCC staff, agreed that a
cooperative effort could produce results. If it didn't, Denniston observed, "we
will have a voluminous record with no facts." He was "chagrined" to find out
that the conferences that took place in December and January apparently had
not dealt with this problem. Those conferences, Juntilla said, had focused
more on "possibilities of settlement."

Copus objected to summary-by-summary bargaining, though he said his
two years in the Peace Corps in India had taught him to be a skilled bargainer.
"He saw no purpose in haggling" and feared "we will be here forever" if each
and every AT&T document is reviewed in context. Denniston concluded that
the important thing was to get the exhibits into the record. Until the opportunity for cross-examination occured, however, they would not be "evidence."

Getting the hearings started involved posturing on a variety of items. Powers objected to the EEOC's filing of documents that came from earlier EEOC
investigations. He asked Denniston to have Copus state why the EEOC is not
precluded from entering that data. Denniston, getting tired of the banter, re-
torted, "Obviously, he thinks it proper or he would not have submitted it in
the first place." And the day ended on that note.[15]

Wallace had a somewhat easier time as an EEOC witness. He was cross-examined by Levy, who was less aggressive than Powers. Yet establishing the challenges, one by one, was a daunting task. AT&T aggressively challenged every detail.

Lighter moments occurred. As Wallace defended his experience in the field, Levy asked, "What is a target, Mr. Wallace?" Copus chimed in, "Strange the Bell System should ask," and Denniston joined, "I would say guess who." Levy quickly defended his question, saying he asked "What not who."[16]

As Levy led Wallace through his qualifications in personnel matters and how one measured qualifications, he asked about how Wallace would measure his own abilities and then suggested, "intangible qualities, deep insight, considerable tact," at which point Potter objected and Denniston headed off the objection by objecting himself. "Going into the mysticisms of personnel classification is something which I think is quite unfair to put to this witness."[17]

The EEOC escaped that day, and Potter became more involved in planning case strategy. The animated and knowledgeable Copus and strategist Potter worked the case in partnership to the EEOC's advantage. Speck, Wallace, and Gartner, assured that they had the information they needed, suggested lines of attack, carried out the necessary analyses, and helped prepare witnesses. AT&T fell on the defensive for the rest of the case, never quite building the momentum they had hoped for.

A few days into the hearings, Professors Sandra and Daryl Bem appeared on the stand and testified together. Surprisingly, AT&T did not object to that arrangement. As part of their testimony, the Bems took existing AT&T job ads and illustrated how they could be done in a nonsexist fashion. They theorized that sexist ads discourage male and female applications for nontraditional jobs. While one spoke the other had time to think. The Bems artfully responded to questions, each filling in when the other had missed a point.

Levy pursued a line of questioning related to terminology, distinguishing between generic references that use "-man" in the word and those which have been defined as female, such as "waitress." The questioning evolved to a discussion of what impact socialization has on job preference and what impact a company could have. Sandra Bem commented, "Eighteen years of socialization does not mean nothing, but in fact advertising seems to have an enormous impact on how a person views a job and whether or not he or she sees himself or herself as appropriate for a job. So it seems to me in fact even in adulthood, if we can treat 18 year-olds like adults, even then the impact is great for altering the kinds of stereotypes that people have of jobs and that people have of themselves as fitting into particular jobs, so I think the impact would be great." Daryl Bem followed with, "I would like to enlarge with respect to the telephone company in general. Many jobs are so pervasive throughout our country, such as secretary and nurse, that no institution by altering that fact could have an impact by itself, but the job of telephone operator is almost defined de novo by a single company. As with the case of Michigan Bell, with a single policy decision, they can alter in the public mind who fills a particular job."[18]

On Monday, February 7, 1972, the sociologist Judith Long Laws and Susan B. Leake, the assistant placement director of Simmons College, appeared. Laws claimed that sex-oriented ads affect recruiting; she argued that hiring methodology must be validated to job performance.[19] Leake testified about the sexist recruitment brochures that AT&T used on the college campus. Appearing first on Tuesday, AT&T employee Helen Roig discussed the harassment and intimidation she experienced when she sought the traditionally male test deskman job at South Central Bell, a job she ultimately won in court. On Wednesday Roig reappeared; then Lorena Weeks began the story of her long struggle. Months earlier, Speck had traveled to Georgia to meet her, and it was he who met Weeks and her sister Elizabeth when they came to Washington to testify. The sisters stayed at the Francis Scott Key Hotel at Twentieth and F Streets, near the EEOC. Weeks appeared at the hearings for two days, explaining that she had confronted Southern Bell in the spring of 1966 simply because she thought the company was wrong to deny her a particular job. AT&T asked few questions of this witness. She had, after all, already won her court case against Southern Bell and was NOW's "poster child" for protest rallies around the country.[20]

Juntilla, representing the FCC's Common Carrier Bureau, questioned Weeks on her experience after she bid for the switchman job. Weeks described how her work, which had been characterized as excellent for a year, suddenly, six days after she applied for the job, was characterized by her supervisor on the record as "less than satisfactory." Juntilla queried Weeks about her appeal to the CWA; Weeks said the local union president told her she did not get the switchman job "because the man is the breadwinner in the family and women just don't need this type of job." Juntilla pushed on, asking Weeks about her statement that two days after she lost her case in District Court she was suspended for refusing to lift a typewriter that weighed thirty-four pounds. The men in her office seemed to be amused by her loss, she noted, so she reacted.

"I told him the typewriter on my desk weighed thirty-four pounds and I had to move it, and since I had just lost a job—and working at home meant so much to me—I didn't see why I should have to lift this 34-pound typewriter . . . it looked to me like the telephone company was using this both ways and either way I was just wrong."[21]

After Weeks responded to Juntilla's questions about how women were treated in the company, Levy asked four questions of Weeks to establish that he did not believe "this witness has the established competence or qualification to testify" about the experience of women in general. He moved to strike portions of her testimony, but Denniston denied the motion on the basis that what was said was an expression of Week's own personal view, "anecdotal," and "within the framework of her experience."[22]

The breaks were going the EEOC's way and, as Potter understood, luck can make a case. The EEOC was incredibly lucky as the case, which initially could have gone either way, just got better and better for the EEOC. AT&T focused on settlement while the EEOC team focused on winning the case. AT&T's proposed terms of settlement did not approach the EEOC's idea of justice; the EEOC would not consider them seriously as an alternative to proceeding with the hearings. It was, after all, a cause in the heyday of causes.[23] At various points others might have settled, but Copus would not quit without getting significant change.[24]

NOW followed the case closely and followed other, more long-term EEOC initiatives as well. On February 2 NOW's Whitney Adams had written to Joan Hull, the New York leader of NOW's Compliance and Enforcement Task Force, sending information about a "targeting procedure" that NOW had submitted to the FCC. "It was developed," she wrote, "with the help from our friends at the EEOC and gives an indication of the type of targeting procedure the EEOC will be using to identify those large companies to go after." She referred Hull to Bill Wallace, who worked on targeting, and whom Adams identified with Copus as "the leading experts at the EEOC—and perhaps anywhere—on the use of statistics in proving sex discrimination." She closed with the promise to help the compliance task force by keeping in touch with the EEOC and the Department of Labor, and by doing "a little consciousness raising with the Department of Justice."[25]

At AT&T headquarters the case was followed closely by those of us with a vested interest in the result. I managed to keep equal employment on the list of issues we analyzed in corporate planning, and I could justify attending relevant conferences. On February 16 and 17 I heard both NOW president Aileen

Hernandez and EEOC chairman Brown speak at the Urban Research Corporation's "Equal Opportunity for Women: Corporate Affirmative Action Programs" conference in Chicago. Brown discussed the AT&T case. He also reported fighting hard for court enforcement power, which would allow the EEOC to take cases to a three-judge court; appeals would go directly from there to the Supreme Court. Conference attendees worried about the magnitude of the job ahead, some feeling it might be impossible to attack both race and sex discrimination with the same staff. Black EEO managers strongly reminded advocates for women that, first, black women should be included, and second, a "let's not rock the boat" approach could lead to a time frame for resolution of one hundred years or more, as it had for blacks.

Covering this conference, the *New York Times* reported, "600 Government officials, corporate executives and feminists traded insults, intelligence, and speculation about the new regulation [Revised Order 4]."[26] The *Times's* implication of three armed camps—government officials, executives, and feminists—overlooked the overlap, however. Some key officials and executives at the conference were also activists on women's issues. Catherine East of the Women's Bureau of the Department of Labor and Barbara Boyle of IBM were two examples. The "insults" the *Times* reported were of little consequence compared with the amount of information exchanged and the experiences companies traded.

We listened to presentations on relevant laws and legislation, company experiences, and feminist perspectives. AT&T's current difficulties with the EEOC were often discussed. The magnitude of the AT&T case illustrated the seriousness of the subject and provided a clear example of just what type of government investigation other companies could expect. Quite possibly the national attention and seriousness of this case had something to do with the large attendance of Bell System people at the conference (at least 6 percent of the audience). The telephone companies, Bell Laboratories, Sandia Laboratories, Western Electric, and AT&T headquarters were all represented.[27]

While personnel experts met in professional conferences and the EEOC hearings continued to discuss AT&T's employment practices, the company took a major step. On February 18, 1972, AT&T announced two new Board of Directors nominees—William J. McGill, president of Columbia University, and Catherine B. Cleary, president and director of First Wisconsin Trust Company. Cleary's nomination was a first for the AT&T board, though two women had been nominated from the floor at the annual meeting in 1971—Sandra O'Connor, director of the First National Bank of Arizona, and Jessica

Hobby Cato, a director of the *Houston Post* and chair of the state's bicentennial. Both were defeated, but O'Connor received 41,399 votes and Cato 42,922.[28] Some of the Bell System operating companies included women on their boards. Frances Jones Poetker served on Cincinnati Bell's board, and Pacific Telephone's board included Leslie L. Luttgens.[29] Wisconsin Telephone had elected Cleary to its board in 1971.[30] A graduate of the University of Chicago in 1937, she was a contemporary of Katherine Graham of the *Washington Post.* Both Cleary and Graham would ultimately be listed in *Fortune*'s "Ten Highest-Ranking Women in Big Business."[31]

Well prepared for a board position, Cleary had earned her law degree from the University of Wisconsin in 1943 with highest honors and practiced law with firms in Wisconsin and Chicago before her long career with First Wisconsin Trust. Cleary had connections. She had been on the board of Northwestern Mutual Life Insurance (NMLI) since 1955, serving there with Joseph Morrison, then head of C&P Telephone. In fact, she served on the NMLI Executive Committee with Morrison.

When John deButts, the newly announced head of AT&T, came out to talk with Cleary about joining the AT&T board, she was serving on the board of Wisconsin Telephone, an AT&T subsidiary. She knew deButts; they both served on Kraft's board; later they would serve on the General Motors board. Unfortunately, the AT&T board met on the same day as the Northwestern Mutual executive committee. Cleary felt her loyalty lay with Northwestern Mutual and declined deButts's invitation. Back in his office, deButts called Morrison, the telephone company president who served on the Northwestern Mutual board. Soon, the Northwestern Mutual board changed its executive committee meeting dates, and Cleary joined AT&T's board.[32]

NOW, delighted in the news about a woman being appointed to the AT&T board, spread the word quickly. By the day after the announcement, the Chicago NOW board added the details to its "AT&T Action" agenda item for its meeting.[33]

The word around the AT&T Alliance for Women in New York was that Catherine Cleary was a lawyer, she was fifty-five, she was not a feminist but was "educable," she had received an award from Alverno College in Milwaukee, and she was bright and pleasant. The Alverno reference meant something to me particularly because Sister Joel Read and Sister Austin Doherty from Alverno were among the early founders of NOW and were mentors of many of my midwestern feminist friends such as Mary Jean Collins-Robson and Mary-Ann Lupa. Other leaders of the feminist movement came from Wisconsin—Kay Clarenbach and Catherine Conroy. It was a good sign. No one from the alliance tried to contact Cleary. We had an "official" liaison and chose not to go around the chain of command. We were cautious.[34]

A significant changing of the guard was about to take place at AT&T. When H. I. Romnes retired at the end of March, North Carolina native John Dulany deButts took his place as chairman. Led by the imposing Virginia Military Institute graduate deButts, the new team included Robert D. Lilley as president and William Lindholm as vice chairman. This Lindholm, some of us noted, was the same Lindholm who gave a talk to Bell Labs directors in 1971 on the topic "Learning to Live with the 70's"; at that time he referred to the complexity of the telephone network and asked, "Will we be able to hire enough young men to do our plant craft job?"[35] Interestingly, Lindholm's first Bell System job was as a service representative—the only male service representative in all of Texas at the time. All three men were tall, imposing, and accustomed to leadership.

Almost at the same time, Wilma Scott Heide added the more powerful position of president of NOW to her role, remaining chair of the board. Sally Hacker officially took over NOW's newly formed AT&T Task Force, and Mary Lynn Myers provided her with all the background and "under the table" stuff she had accumulated.[36] Hacker had testified for NOW in the Houston hearings the EEOC held in 1970, hearings that gave the first indication of an aggressive EEOC move on corporations.[37]

The *Saturday Review* voted the retiring Romnes "Man of the Year" based primarily on "Equal Employment Opportunities of AT&T." Never one to let anything go unobserved, Heide wrote to the editor, commenting that the honor "has got to be the 'Mistake of the Year' if not the decade." She accused the magazine of "either an absence of homework or lack of sensitivity to the seriousness of employment discrimination by AT&T against women of all races and minority men." She went on to cite and quote the EEOC's documentation in its case against AT&T.[38] According to stories in the *AT&T News*, Romnes had been chosen for the honor by a panel of 250 business leaders, educators, editors and other opinion molders:

> The honor was not conferred "entirely for proficient administering of a man's own business," according to the magazine. At least as important was what the publication called, "a service to public interest projects, educa-

Robert D. Lilley, president; John D. deButts, chairman of the Board; and William L. Lind-
holm, vice chairman of the Board, AT&T.

Photograph property of AT&T Archives. Reprinted with permission of AT&T.

tion, government and broadly based civic pursuits with special emphasis
on current social problems." Said the Review, *"In this regard, Mr. Romnes*
was a decade ahead of many businessmen."[39]

From inside the business, it did look as if Romnes paid more attention than
his predecessors or most business leaders did to social issues, whether problems of the cities or antiwar sentiments. DeButts's views were not as well
known. The company heard about EEOC charges from the chairman-elect at

his first presentation after the announcement—at the Human Affairs Conference in Chicago on March 8, when deButts took an aggressive position on competition and then talked about equal opportunity:

> When the EEOC charges were first announced, most of us felt they were a "bum rap." I still feel that way. I still feel that we have been a leader in this area and ought to be congratulated rather than castigated. But we cannot let our resentment of those charges or our efforts to rebut them distract us from the more fundamental task of affirming through action our commitment to nondiscrimination in every aspect of our personnel practices. I know that you have spent a good deal of time on this topic in the course of this conference. So I'll say only this: the time has long since passed when there was room for debate as to whether the Bell companies should commit themselves to affirmative action—including realistic, specified objectives—in assuring equal opportunity for minorities and for women in every occupation and at every level throughout our business.
>
> I am not so naïve that I am not aware that personal attitudes vary on this matter and I know, too, that there are honest differences of view as to how our policy ought to be implemented. But one thing should be clear: it is the policy of the Bell System—north, south, east and west—to assure that every employee has a fair and equal chance to realize his full potential and to progress to the limit of that potential along any career path he or she may choose. That's the way I read the law of the land. More fundamentally, that's the way I read our country's purpose, a purpose we have a responsibility to help fulfill. And, furthermore, that's what I personally believe is the right course for us. In short, affirmative action to achieve equal opportunity is a major factor in every Bell System manager's job—a factor on which he can expect to be measured on the basis of the results he achieves.[40]

Not everyone believed that AT&T meant what it said. In Illinois, the Chicago Women's Liberation Union published an issue of *Womankind* that went after the company. An article titled "Ma Bell: A Slick Operator?" portrayed with graphic detail the operators, clerks, and service representatives as slaves and small children mistreated by the company. Of all employees, it argued, the operators are "the most exploited." Automation took a hit as well, with the charge that the new machines allow an operator to handle "six times as many calls." "However meager operators' wages are, the company would rather not pay them at all," and the difference in pay between college-educated operators and non-college-educated operators was two cents an hour. In what became a much-copied segment of the article, an operator told about "fleas" that breed in the equipment and attack the operators. Someone drew up a cartoon about the fleas, and someone else sent it to a newspaper columnist. After the story appeared in a local column, the company sent in an exterminator. Suddenly the operators realized that public pressure made a difference. Next came a fight over pants. Operators were required to wear dresses on weekdays. Thinking it ridiculous, some women wore pants. At least one was sent home. When others wore pants to work, the company posted a notice that after January 21 anyone who wore pants to work would be "dealt with." The operators wrote a "People's Policy on Dress" to counter the company policy. The company backed down.[41]

And so it went across the land, and not just in the companies of the Bell System.

In the New York City headquarters of AT&T, those of us following the case reached out to feminists in other companies. I found informal and formal groups inside Polaroid, Raytheon, and Monsanto and made contact with women and sympathetic men, some in charge of EEO, at GE, IBM, Polaroid, Sears, and Atlantic Richfield. James Grinnell at Polaroid told us about their five task forces addressing women's issues. At that point Polaroid "management still misunderstands but is aware," he said.[42] GE's Jackie Pinckney told us about her work as "Corporate Coordinator for EEO-Women."[43]

We knew about women inside Michigan Bell, and we knew that Detroit had been an area of intense NOW activity.[44] A New York Telephone operator told us she would be interested in meeting with the alliance. She felt women were really stuck as operators; those who did get out of the ghetto were made miserable by the treatment they received from men in the other departments.[45]

I continued to attend conferences and meetings to learn about the corporate policy implications of EEO. One of those conferences, held by the New York Personnel Management Association, had IBM's Barbara Boyle as the speaker. Company personnel managers had a real need to learn how to deal with equal opportunity.

Within the Management Sciences Department at AT&T, five of us met with the department head to get his views on a new project, which we labeled Long Range Policy on Women in the Bell System. Our objective was to "inform and guide the Executive Policy Committee in establishing a policy for utilization of womanpower." We wanted to address a systemwide issue and felt the existing "human affairs" department (no longer "personnel") was just fighting the current fire and the threat to the rate case. Our department head heard us out and agreed that AT&T's Executive Policy Committee had an opportunity, but he concentrated his remarks on department strategy rather than on the broad issues. We kept talking but made no progress in generating systemwide policy from Management Sciences. It seemed to me the department, which provided support to the top executives of the Bell System, should be more aggressive on this issue.[46]

With NOW friends, I discussed establishing a NOW chapter at AT&T. The disadvantages we saw included: conflict of interest in terms of information, action, and local publicity; the initial shock of management and possible overreaction; the alienation of some women and men; the complication of dues; and the notion that such an organization probably went against some company rule somewhere. But establishing a chapter also held advantages: we could put together a good convenor kit and provide information easily; the initial shock to management could prod them to good actions or paralysis, either of which might be good; the action would be newsworthy; management would be almost obligated to recognize the group; our association with NOW would offer us protection; setting up a new pattern would destabilize the situation and aid change; and forming the chapter would stimulate participation with women in other NOW chapters and advance the cause generally and personally.[47] Despite the potential benefits, however, we chose collectively not to take this action.

The Chicago writer and feminist Susan Davis, meanwhile, used our story as she built a case and wrote an article, "Organizing from Within: Justice on the Job and How to Get It," which would appear in the August issue of Ms.[48] I kept the idea alive by working with Chicago NOW to set up a workshop on corporate feminism. The brochure for our program read, "Organize a Women's Rights Group in Your Company," and was sponsored by Chicago NOW's Employment Committee. Announced for May 6, the workshop covered the basics— laws, contacts, corporate politics. We stressed the need for both "patience" and "information." The workshop included experiential learning—small groups attacking the problem of organizing in "The Open Book Publishing Company, the Forever Insurance Company, The Last Traditional Bank, or the Dinga-ling Telephone Company."[49]

As a follow-up to the workshop, we drafted "Corporate Equal Opportunity for Women: A Bill of Rights." For my job in Corporate Planning at AT&T, I wrote "External Realities: Social Activists and the Corporation," which was revised for my own use as "Feminists and the Corporation." Later in the spring I appeared with Womanpower's Betsy Hogan on a panel, "Establishing Good Relations with Feminist Groups" at an Urban Research Corporation Conference.[50]

On the first day of that conference, Eleanor Holmes Norton said she saw a retreat under way—a reaction to social reform—that was becoming a conservative national trend, especially with respect to abortion rights and affirmative action. She felt "northerners" were out-of-touch with the law and too often defined discrimination as overt denial of jobs. Thus, she added, they were blind to what really happened on the job and objected to affirmative action. Norton's New York City Commission on Human Rights had seen a 1,000 percent increase in case load in sex discrimination cases. She saw the women's movement as a "wide spectrum of interest," a group that "may be able to become a real influence." She closed by saying she saw "reasons for hope but cause for mobilization."[51]

We searched for guidelines, for the business version of the "feminine mystique." It seemed we had to perform, to have the credentials, and be circumspect about our activism. I went to Fordham University at Lincoln Center every Monday and Wednesday for two years to get an MBA and gain some of that valuable credibility.[52]

Those of us willing to be tagged as in-house feminists were in demand as speakers and committee resources. Throughout the Bell System, the companies geared up with affirmative action programs, affirmative action departments, affirmative action committees, and various educational efforts. The Bell Laboratories Holmdel Affirmative Action Committee drafted a strongly worded memo challenging the way company publications portrayed women.[53] The IBM movie "51%" became a hot item. Dr. Olga Mitchell, a member of the Holmdel Affirmative Action Committee, invited me as a former Bell Labs–Indian Hill Affirmative Action Committee member to talk about programs for women that had been started at Polaroid and GE and show the film. The thirty-five-minute"51%" showed three vignettes of the lives of women in roles of secretary, systems analyst, and manager.

I reported the meeting to my boss in Management Sciences (soon to be known as Corporate Planning), adding that I had done a quick inventory of the committee members' attitudes toward women. (The statements were a subset of those used by the AT&T Task Force on Women in their 1970 study.) Included in the results were Mitchell and her friend (and fellow pilot) Dr.

Dot Kirby, who both had become strong advocates for women after establishing themselves in the predominately male research segment of Bell Laboratories. The results show that even those on affirmative action committees held stereotypes about women on the job. Faced with saying whether a series of statements were true or false, the Affirmative Action Committee members varied in their responses, as shown in table 3.

TABLE 3: ATTITUDE SURVEY RESULTS, BELL LABORATORIES AFFIRMATIVE ACTION COMMITTEE

Characteristic	True	False	Not sure
Women in management are specialists	5	5	0
The best women leave before a management job is available to them	4	5	1
Women are not as mobile as men	5	5	0
Women in management can't compete with men	1	9	0
Women in management are a threat to men	3	6	1
Women are not as competent as men	0	10	0
In order to manage, a woman must have "masculine characteristics"	0	10	0
Men cannot consider women as equals	1	9	0
Women just don't want to manage	2	6	2
Women cannot supervise men in the field	1	8	1
Women prefer staff jobs	1	5	4
Women are too emotional	2	7	1

Characteristic	True	False	Not sure
Men will not want a management job which women hold	2	6	2
Women should subscribe to a passive, domestic image	2	8	0
Men and women should not work together too closely	0	9	1

Often the women on company affirmative action committees were both formal and informal contacts of mine. I was sending out a newsletter, the *Private Line*, to all interested parties I could find in the Bell System—my purpose was to share information among internal activists. I received a call one day from a person in an operating company who wanted to be on the mailing list but wanted to be absolutely sure it wasn't a subversive publication. The *Private Line* went out from my office in New York as a newsletter full of reports on the status of the EEOC complaint, on what related activities were taking place in AT&T, and on women's rights in general. From February 1972 to February 1973 the *Private Line* circulated across the country. News about women's groups, updates on the EEOC-AT&T case, relevant news clippings, sources, and references filled the pages.[54]

On this as on other systemwide issues, I often operated independently. The alliance declined, formally, to be involved with the *Private Line*, consistently voting to concentrate on changing AT&T headquarters. Individual members of the alliance not only followed the EEOC actions but, in some cases, were also formally involved as part of their jobs. Several were in public relations and routinely provided all of AT&T with updates on the case.

When March 1972 arrived, the FCC and EEOC brought more witnesses in and again spent long days in the FCC hearing rooms. March 21 saw Bergmann and Nathan testify for the FCC. Nathan found the Bell System's affirmative action programs "as good as any in the country in research and marketing analysis" and added that once the system puts it into practice, the "cost of in-house compliance teams would be very modest." Goals and timetables should be used, he noted, to provide realistic goals and to motivate people in the company to achieve those goals.[55] By March 24 cross-examination of

Lois Herr Kerkeslager in her AT&T office.

Photo by Bill Schropp.

EEOC witnesses was completed, and we heard less company news from Washington. Behind the scenes, Levy and Copus met or talked daily. Levy and Ashley kept Liebers and the others at AT&T headquarters up to date. They met periodically over lunch at Miller's, the popular basement restaurant in the ornate Woolworth Building on Broadway, just a block north of AT&T's headquarters.

Though the EEOC had presented its case, Copus continued to review AT&T's data. On March 27 Copus went to New York to meet with Levy, Liebers, and AT&T federal regulatory representatives on data tables and EEO-1 data for 1970 and 1971. The EEOC had a "standing order" for all 1971 data as it became available. Three studies on the test battery for 1968, 1969, and a five-year look at the end of 1971 would be available in "a matter of weeks." Copus's notes over the next months covered endless exchanges about the time periods and formats (e.g., "machine readable" form). "Major—to exclude minor little piddly-ass memos" would be made available as soon as possible "unless it will impede the case." Copus demanded the company provide EEO plans for each location. In addition to providing what Copus requested, AT&T was working on its own case. Copus was promised a list of AT&T witnesses by June 1.[56]

As the case went on, Bob Lilley internally and privately lectured and coached the company presidents, together and separately, holding formal Affirmative Action Program reviews with each company president.57 Kofke updated the companies periodically on a closed-circuit television network. Kofke moved his New York team to 71 Broadway, the old U.S. Steel building, and borrowed his secretary from the New Jersey Bell payroll. Tons of data piled up. An early and critical task was to figure out what AT&T's lawyers really wanted those data to prove.

Kofke would play a major role in identifying and prepping witnesses, including external experts, but he got a lot of "free-floating advice" from company executives and attorneys. In particular he was urged to get Matina Horner, who had just published an article in *Psychology Today* explaining how women fear success. Kofke knew instinctively that her argument would not help AT&T's case. A number of prospective witnesses declined to appear because they did not agree with AT&T's position or did not want to be seen as apologists for the company.58

Kofke learned early that one of his primary responsibilities was to "keep us from doing dumb things." That was not always easy. Company witnesses were sometimes ultraconservative and combative. Those with power never give in willingly, he reminded himself, and norms and customs were tremendously powerful forces.

Running the task force, Kofke faced internal challenges beyond the question of how to prepare witnesses and plan the logistics. He had to motivate his team to work intensely even though everyone knew the case might be settled at any time and never reach the hearing stage. He also had to communicate with top executives to keep them comfortable with the pace of the case, keep the press relations group informed so they could deal with the outside world, and make sure employees had accurate and timely information. As the case progressed, Kofke and Levy would routinely spend hours at the Grammercy Inn in Washington, studying transcripts and planning strategy for cross-examination. Occasionally, the two would be diverted by nearby parties for Nixon; the offices of the Committee to Reelect the President, also known as CREEP, were nearby.59

As the fog cleared, AT&T built a file of memos documenting performance. The personnel types were philosophically and ethically attuned to what was going on, and public relations people were enlightened, but EEO rarely made the top corporate issue lists. The company had just gone through an intense period of concentration on minority problems—the priority of the 1960s—and was eager to be back to the basic business of providing telephone service. The effects of the 1960s and urban employment objectives were just merging into routines and practices.

Though AT&T had not been totally idle on the issues of sex discrimination within the company, many of the actions set up to deal with it were spontaneous and dependent on the motivation of local managers. Higher levels tolerated or sanctioned initiatives such as day care center experiments, but they did not initiate or decree such changes systemwide. Nor did they decree the opposite. Illinois Bell independently established a child care referral program in 1970. In 1971 Chesapeake and Potomac opened an experimental child care facility for its employees' children. Ohio Bell and Western Electric jointly opened a center in Columbus, Ohio.

Another example of local initiative surfaced in Ohio Bell. Hal Burlingame in downtown Cleveland had been instrumental in taking a Bell Labs science program into the inner city and bringing inner city youths in for training after hours when the business office was closed. Joseph D. Reed, head of Public Relations for Ohio Bell, recognized in Burlingame a young manager who would help him do a little attitude adjustment within the company and pulled him into public relations. One of the products of their 1971 collaboration was a film, "Is It Always Right to Be Right?," developed to change traditional attitudes about race, sex, and age discrimination. Sparing no expense, Burlingame had the film produced in Hollywood and narrated by Orson Welles. The short film got more attention than its initiators expected. One evening Reed called Burlingame at home, asking, "Are you watching the Academy Awards?" No, replied Burlingame, he wasn't. Reed observed that he should have been—their film had just won an Academy Award for best short subject.[60]

Efforts such as the child care centers or Burlingame's effort to change attitudes did not result in systemic change. Kofke himself had tried in New Jersey Bell to move women into nontraditional management jobs. Some of those early efforts to move women into traditional male jobs were naive, he knew, undertaken with inadequate support provided to those pioneers. Women in those circumstances had to fight to survive. Most fled or failed, not a surprising result given the inhospitable environment.[61]

Pulling together a coherent case meant sifting through voluminous data, attempting to deal honestly with the past, then taking a position. Throughout the case, AT&T stuck to its basic argument: the company had good intentions in keeping up with, if not being on the leading edge of, social change. To

Kofke, it was ironic: what aroused activists most was the idea of an evil conspiracy in AT&T perpetuating oppression of women. Kofke knew that such was not the case.

On occasion when the AT&T team members had worked very hard for very long, they gave up for a night and, in those late not-so-sober hours, amused themselves by creating facetious counterarguments. They were faced, it seemed, with unanswerable questions. Had AT&T discriminated because of a conspiracy or was it accidental? Were they powerless, sheeplike followers of societal patterns? Eventually it would boil down to, "How much is enough?"[62]

Quietly, AT&T negotiators had been working directly with the General Services Administration (GSA), the federal agency processing contract compliance. A holder of large government contracts, AT&T was already required to submit affirmative action plans to GSA. If the GSA would agree to a plan without back pay and without tough goals and timetables, AT&T perhaps could finesse the EEOC case. Satterfield and Liebers submitted a model plan to GSA in February. When Copus heard of the filing, he called Levy immediately. After many calls and a few harsh words, on Tuesday, March 28, Levy told Copus over the telephone, "What was given to GSA was a preliminary draft and is undergoing revisions, so it is not a '195' document yet," referring to AT&T's headquarters at 195 Broadway in New York. Copus responded, "We want the 'preliminary draft'—we don't care what it is." Levy didn't want to set a precedent, fearing it would inhibit development of additional material. Copus offered, "We'd emphasize the difference between in-house and out-house materials." Levy again refused, stating that the material had not yet been reviewed with unions or with the presidents of the operating companies. He wanted a commitment for short-term confidentiality.[63]

On Wednesday, Copus was told that Levy could not reach Lilley, whose "underlings were unwilling to make it available before getting input from the companies." Copus simply said, "Okay," and went on to talk about the data requests. He had already gotten a copy of the plan from friends in GSA. Liebers was helping to obtain information from the companies to respond to data requests of the EEOC, but sometimes he could not tell how burdensome that task would be. Both Copus and Levy knew that 1971 was the first full year of data gathering, and there would be errors the first time around. It would necessarily be a "messy process." Later, error checks would be built in. Some of the data were computerized, some were not. Sometimes the cost to develop special programs was considered to be too expensive; manual reports then had to suffice.[64]

On Thursday, Ashley and Copus talked on the telephone about the Affirmative Action Program, which had been reviewed with GSA but, as Ashley put it, "not yet set in concrete." He went on to describe how the program was the product of a task force and would be reviewed with each company by Easlick and Lilley. That, Ashley stressed, was "important." He admitted to Copus, "They're having a hell of a time with the companies." Ashley continued, "Lilley doesn't want to be in a position of letting the companies know that [the] program has been given to the FCC and EEOC. Lilley feels strongly that they won't give it until the end of April when all companies have viewed it [eight of the twenty-two companies had yet to do so]."[65]

Meanwhile, AT&T was suffering in the press. In the February 4 *New York Times*, Eileen Shanahan wrote an article on the Project on Corporate Responsibility. The project had announced a target set of nine companies, focusing on three principal target companies in 1972: GM because of its size, AT&T because of the EEOC hearings, and Warner Lambert because of drug labeling issues. Among its other recommendations, the project said that AT&T should put former EEOC commissioner and NOW president Aileen Hernandez on its Board of Directors.[66]

In March, *Time* magazine's special edition headlined "The American Woman" quoted Illinois Bell personnel supervisor Harriet White, "The major struggle is ahead of us."[67] Shanahan reported that the Equal Rights Amendment had passed the Senate on March 22 by a vote of 84–8.[68] The syndicated writer Nicholas von Hoffman wrote three columns in March with attention-grabbing titles: "A system designed by geniuses for execution by idiots"; "AT&T: no villains, only victims"; and "What's good for AT&T?" In an *AT&T News Bulletin*, the company fought back. First, the company complained, von Hoffman had used legal arguments (from the EEOC prehearing analysis) as if they were evidence. On the substance, the company argued, von Hoffman's quotes from the EEOC about the "horrendous" operator's job and so forth flew in the face of facts. "The operator's job is a good job—honorably and faithfully performed by fine employees."[69]

The company went on to describe its efforts to promote equal opportunity for women and minorities, but it was clear that AT&T was on a different wavelength from those who criticized its position. The critics would not accept what had been done in the past, and the company was too proud of its accomplishments to move on. At one level, AT&T wanted to defend its honor. At a more practical level, it wanted to settle this case and get rid of it. At a third, more professional level, it wanted to figure out how to do the EEO job and get on with it. Would it be fight or settle? Would professional personnel people be authorized to do the job?

AT&T had no rest on this issue. The New Orleans Chapter of NOW planned to devote the entire month of March "to promoting community awareness of unfair treatment of women employees in the Bell System." There would be pickets at the South Central Bell site on Barrone and Poydras Streets on March 8, a series of meetings with South Central Bell management and with the CWA, and pickets and leafleting again on March 29. Slogans used by NOW included, with artwork, "March on Bell," "Remember Mrs. Weeks," "Ask not for whom the Bell tolls . . . it tolls for she," "Dial 'O' for Oppression," and "Fight Discrimination NOW."[70]

Elsewhere across the country, NOW confronted AT&T. Women within AT&T asked tough questions of themselves and their employer.

7
SNAPPING AT THE HEELS

Wilma Scott Heide was firmly in charge of NOW, albeit in a less hierarchical fashion than John deButts was at AT&T. Sally Hacker took over the NOW AT&T task force, Judy Potter strategized for the EEOC, David Copus ran the hearings, Gene Kofke orchestrated the AT&T case, and George Ashley ran the AT&T side of the hearings. Heide wanted to reform corporate America, deButts wanted the case settled, and Copus wanted to change the world. The operating companies were still trying to defend the past; AT&T headquarters wanted to get on with it. Bob Lilley had a social conscience, Dave Easlick had an assignment, and Don Liebers had a profession. Everyone saw the case from a different perspective. By April, all were deeply engaged in the process.

NOW remained at the heels of AT&T throughout 1972. Hacker, who delved into the workings of AT&T far more than any other activist, wanted more than token women in management jobs; she hoped to change working conditions for union or working-class women and used what she called a Marxist analysis of AT&T's employment practices. To her, AT&T's implementation of technology intentionally targeted women workers. The network, she argued, was "put together by geniuses to be run by idiots . . . women are going to be the idiots . . . until they are all mated out and then there will be new idiots." To her, the coming together of technology and capitalism meant exploitation and oppression. At some levels, AT&T managers were not aware of the social impact of their systems, she admitted. But she felt that at the top, executives at AT&T headquarters and Bell Labs knew full well that women were cheap, expendable labor.[1]

In April, writing from her home in Vernon, Connecticut, to Hacker, at home in Roland, Iowa, Heide noted that "representatives of NOW are due to meet with AT&T President and Board *Chairone.*" She charged Hacker with setting up an appointment and insisted "the 'top' officer must be there." She thought those attending the meeting from NOW would include herself, Hacker, and others who were knowledgeable about affirmative action and the Bell System. Not content simply to throw out an idea, Heide listed fifteen dates she would be available in April and May, and she copied the others so they could get to Hacker quickly. Heide pushed NOW into action. Busy as she was with a myriad of NOW actions, Heide never let the AT&T case sit still. She coaxed and coached. When necessary she carried the message herself, facing up to Lilley and Brown, challenging each in his turn.

In the same letter, Heide told Hacker about the NOW stockholders' action that Marilyn Hall Patel, Charlotte Wolf (Colorado NOW), and Sue Dorthit were organizing for AT&T's annual meeting in Denver on April 19. She reminded Hacker that Whitney Adams, NOW's FCC coordinator, would be a source of progress reports on both AT&T's new policies and the EEOC case itself. "These, Sally, are some of the things that came to mind on how you might approach your exciting job," Heide concluded.[2]

Myers, in Illinois, also wrote to Hacker, apologizing in advance for being out of touch for the next month because she was working on a job in Kentucky. She passed on a copy of information Whitney Adams had summarized from various AT&T memos. Ann Scott and Adams suggested that the material be shared with the chapters, and Myers saw that it was done before she left. Myers also had a suggestion for Hacker: "I do think you might want to call Whitney or write to her very soon about your plans on AT&T. She has some very good input on this action."[3]

Hacker appreciated Adams's material and insight. She sent a note to the action-oriented task force, including members Collins-Robson, Dean, Heide, Myers, Scott, Hull, Patel, Linda Stults (Detroit), Adams, Hernandez, and Roberts. The group moved quickly and somewhat independently from idea to action. As part of the overall plan, local NOW chapters would move on specific targets.

Being in Iowa, Hacker worked directly with the NOW chapter in Des Moines, which tackled Northwestern Bell in a case before the Iowa regulators. In a note to the task force, Hacker wrote:

> *Carol Hayse, Des Moines NOW, who gave the testimony, managed a neat phrase or two on "domestic imperialism," then introduced "Unique Competence" into the record as evidence. You should have seen the reaction—*

the first sign of life in the well-oiled Bell machine. . . . A big argument ensued, that FCC had "serious reservations" about the quality of research in UC [A Unique Competence], that we couldn't introduce it as testimony since we hadn't been directly involved in the research, that in such case it was mere hearsay. . . . Those of you more knowledgeable can probably interpret all that better than I; apparently the scary part is where UC does document that Bell could well afford what it needs simply by more efficient and humane internal reorganization, rather than by rate increases.[4]

Hacker wrote to deButts, asking for a meeting with him and Lilley. Although he would find some of the letter's language upsetting, the tenor of the letter expressed sincere interest in working together to solve a problem: Hacker reminded deButts that NOW "is vitally concerned with eradicating oppressive, discriminatory policies based on sex. We want to bring about those changes which would allow equality of participation to men and women, in the responsibilities and opportunities in American Society." She suggested that in his new position at the head of "an extremely powerful corporation, a major employer of women," he would want "the best possible plan to redress the unfortunate condition of women workers there." NOW, she indicated, had "a similar interest" and, having "devoted much careful thought, research, and action to this question," wanted to discuss the matter with him personally and with Lilley and whoever he thought might add to or benefit by the discussion." Pushing for an appointment before the end of May, Hacker suggested specific dates and closed with, "We look forward with great anticipation to this opportunity, and to hearing from you, say, within two weeks time."[5] At no time did deButts or Lilley involve the AT&T Alliance for Women in the NOW meetings or correspondence. I suspect they had no idea we knew each other well.

NOW's stockholder action did take place at AT&T's Eighty-seventh Annual Meeting, held in Currigan Hall, Denver, Colorado. Over two thousand people attended.[6] And Catherine B. Cleary was duly elected to the board. When she arrived at the hotel in Denver the night before the meeting, she found no one in the AT&T suite but the helper. The next morning, deButts warned her that Evelyn Davis, a perpetual shareowner and annual meeting attendee, would ask, "Who's this woman?" DeButts advised her not to take anything Davis said personally. She was glad to be warned and was surprised that Davis would be opposed to women on corporate boards. Wilma Soss, another outspoken gadfly at annual meetings, also would voice opposition. Cleary suggested to deButts that she take Soss out to lunch, which she did. After the first question from Soss, "Who put you up to this?" was handled, the rest of the lunch was just lunch, and Soss did not complain about women on the board.[7]

Emily Dangel, a NOW representative from Englewood, Colorado, had proxies for three thousand shares of AT&T stock and thus had access to the shareowners' meeting. She made a statement about practices of sex discrimination and challenged the election of the Board of Directors and Auditors on those grounds. She did cast her votes for the woman nominee—Cleary.[8]

Responding to Dangel, deButts said he doubted the EEOC charges could be proved. He mentioned the four hundred male telephone operators now employed and the fact that women had jobs in installation and repair. He repeated his "confidence that the hearings before the FCC with the EEOC will demonstrate that the Bell System is a leader in equal opportunity."[9]

The AT&T board itself was cordial to Cleary, but not everyone was really comfortable with a woman on the board. The men would talk about how they tried to make equal opportunity work but "women didn't want the jobs." Nonetheless, Cleary thought the board members were men of integrity and goodwill in spite of their lack of understanding. She was "not a feminist" when she joined the board, although since law school, she knew women had to get over blocks that were just not there for men. She did not want to "speak for women," but that did not mean she was uninterested. Later, at General Mo-

Catherine B. Cleary, first woman appointed to AT&T's Board of Directors.

Reprinted with permission of AP/WWP.

tors, she would meet with women employees. Because of her own experience and because of her leadership responsibilities, Cleary had always been concerned about women in banking.[10]

As time went on, Cleary would be surprised at AT&T's "skimpy committee structure" compared with other boards she had experienced. Such a structure inhibited efforts of individual directors, at least the efforts of directors not close to deButts or geographically local. Another difference she noticed was that AT&T's board was not as "social" as others—fewer social events and trips, for example. Perhaps, she thought, that was related to the regulated environment or just the nature of the business. Cleary made it her business to ask questions about how women fared within AT&T, and she met annually with the personnel officers to find out where the women were.[11]

Catherine Cleary created "quite a stir" on the "twenty-sixth floor" (shorthand for executive offices at 195 Broadway), a top AT&T executive later recalled. However, Cleary had run a bank—had served in a "man's job"—and with confidence, talent, and personality, she eventually fit in with the board members and company officers.[12]

While the annual meeting went on in Denver, work on the case continued back east. Levy in his New York office and Copus in Washington continued to call back and forth to resolve data and document issues. In late April 1972 Copus was still waiting for collective bargaining agreements, which Levy promised were being collected and would be sent as soon as he checked them out. A model plan for affirmative action and a Transfer/Promotion Plan would also be available soon   by the end of the week, Levy promised.[13]

Two days later, Copus confirmed that the full package of company affirmative action programs had arrived. He reiterated that the proposal to GSA could not be approved without EEOC's consent, that "our modifications are nonnegotiable." Copus went on to say, "We will attack any plan which does not meet our 22 points."[14]

Meanwhile, what did the updated reports say about women in AT&T? While the hearings progressed, so did the numbers. The number of female district managers at AT&T headquarters would go up from 43 in 1968 to 81 by the end of 1972; across the system, there were 120 women in 1968, 288 by 1972. As table 4 shows, the percentage of change shows that women were beginning to catch up across the system.[15]

While there were more women in 1972 at higher levels than ever before, women still confided their concerns in safe places—in affirmative action com-

TABLE 4: GROWTH IN NUMBERS, 1968-72

Level	Bell System (AT&T Headquarters, Operating Companies, and Long Lines)		
	1968	1972	Increase
Third-level male	9,363	10,666	1,303
Third-level female	120	288	168
Fourth-level male	3,023	3,137	114
Fourth-level female	13	26	13
Fifth-level male	1,099	1,158	59
Fifth-level female	3	6	3
Above-fifth male	368	376	8
Above-fifth female	0	0	0

Source: *AT&T Answerback* no. 798 (June 5, 1973).

mittees, in approved organizations, or in private conversations. It was not always easy, and even "safe" places were not comfortable environments. The
AT&T Alliance for Women, the Women's Rights Committee at Bell Labs, and
other groups across the country spoke out on behalf of women. Individuals
provided information to NOW and the EEOC—organizations outside the
Bell System that were in a better position to bring about change.

Some women openly rejected the feminist and EEOC arguments. Some
were quiet, watching from the sidelines. I considered, for a time, running for a
NOW national office. In fact, I completed an application to run for the board
in 1971 and enlisted Hull, Collins-Robson, and Adams as my supporters, but I
never sent it.[16]

All of us had other lives, lives that had to be merged with our activism, lives
that one way or another had to support us through the times of frustration with
the "system." In time, consciousness raising would help me a great deal. One
of the alliance committees originally set up to run issues discussions turned
into a consciousness-raising group that met for four years—meeting at a member's apartment in New York or at the office, and then going out to dinner together. The women's movement had its intensely personal times and its
change-the-world times.

My NOW friends had personal lives and careers beyond NOW. For example, Lee Walker worked in technical publications for IBM. Ann Scott and Sally Hacker were university professors. Joan Hull worked for Celanese, Whitney Adams for the Federal Reserve, Mary-Ann Lupa at Scott Foresman, Bette Vidina for Metropolitan Life. In some cases, I did not know where my NOW friends worked—or much about their families. Most of us worked in three spheres, at least, trying to change our personal lives, our workplaces, and our world. Not many had their careers and their activism focus on the same company.

Whenever the opportunity arose in my work in corporate planning, I put "equal opportunity" on lists of important issues. Thus my work in equal opportunity consisted largely of taking advantage whenever I could, as part of my job, to do what I wanted to do in any case. Within a month after arriving in New York, I wrote in my journal about my goals with regard to "rights for Bell women": "maintain contacts, increase circle, possibly do a news sheet, investigate AT&T activities in this area as well as those activities of outside groups that affect Bell."[17] My friends worked with the company newspaper, public relations, business research; my "real" work and my alliance work built an extensive network within the business.

Women from all over the Bell System contacted the EEOC, NOW, the alliance, or the *Private Line*. They had stories to tell, information to provide, worries to talk about, or just wanted to make contact with others who shared their concerns. Management women often said they felt comfortable talking with women inside the business on women's rights but felt alienated from the women outside—the "feminists." When we talked about how difficult it was to change an organization from within, CWA leader and NOW founder Catherine Conroy told me about a center that Sister Austin Doherty ran at Alverno College in Milwaukee.[18] We talked about new lifestyle counseling—what should we be doing to help young women plan for meaningful lives. We worried about the consequences—in terms of time, health, energy, ideals, and ambition—of being wound up in the movement. If we had time, we would have liked to do a study in movement dynamics from an organizational psychology point of view. We would, if we had the luxury, study how leaders sustain themselves. We would investigate how organizations sometimes meet the psychological needs of their leaders and how those leaders would fulfill those needs when the organization disappeared.

When we had time to reflect, we pondered the source of greatness in a leader of the movement—was it ideas or simply the ability to continue working with energy, dedication, and spirit? We even asked ourselves if we were being realistic, and we wondered if we were really willing to give what it took without regret. There were barriers to "sisterhood." We tried to understand what it was that kept so many women from acknowledging common grievances. How could we bridge the gap? We understood why many were reluctant to challenge their bosses, but why were women who experienced discrimination at work so reluctant to join their sisters outside the company?[19]

Buying a button was a "safe" way to make contact. Maybe the button was never worn. The alliance supplied those union-made buttons with the Bell symbol modified to be a feminist symbol, but here, too, we were cautious—we used an old Bell logo. We even talked it over with the AT&T department having control of corporate identity, and we went along with its recommendation to avoid the newer logo.

At the time, we did not hear much news about the hearings, which had gone on the road. News was sporadic at best. The EEOC hearings became a participation sport for local groups as they went on the road to San Francisco, Los Angeles, New York, and Washington. Denniston had serious concerns about how the large crowds would be accommodated—they expected five hundred in New York City. He urged both the EEOC and the FCC to "stay within the bounds of the issues" so the hearings would not degenerate into a general investigation. He pleaded with the parties to "exercise your full influence."[20]

Denniston also worried that only 16 out of the 1,153 summaries that the EEOC had prepared had been agreed to by both the EEOC and AT&T. The FCC's Common Carrier Bureau was not ready with corrections to the transcript that were due, citing their heavy work load with the communications satellite case. AT&T did not have their comments ready either; their courier was "stuck at Allentown Airport." Some days went more smoothly than others.[21]

Knowing in advance about the California hearings, Ann Scott sent a letter to the presidents of NOW chapters in Los Angeles and San Francisco, providing draft copies of her testimony and urging them to file testimony on behalf of NOW. "It really is important for us to be represented at these hearings," she said. She suggested that their testimony develop information on discrimination in "your area" and warned it should not copy the language of her testimony; rather, they should express views in their own terms. She suggested they look for issues in the local company's "advertising in the media, in Bell System's own internal media, hiring into entry-level jobs, names of jobs, rotation

AT&T Alliance for Women buttons and other feminist buttons from the early 1970s.

Photograph by Jack Demuth.

through AT&T, the Initial Management Development Program, and child care."[22]

Public hearings were staged in California at the request of the Mexican-American Legal Defense and Education Fund (MALDEF) and the California Rural Legal Assistance (CRLA) groups. Chicanos and Asian American witnesses testified about their treatment by Pacific Telephone and Telegraph. Witnesses spoke of employment discrimination and inadequate telephone service, in that bilingual operation was not provided.[23]

At Pacific Telephone's 1972 annual meeting on March 24, just weeks before the hearings were scheduled for Los Angeles, President Jerome W. Hull announced plans and programs to improve opportunities for women and minorities. Reported in newspapers across the state, the big story was "Jobs for Latinos." Mario Obledo, the general counsel for MALDEF, praised the company action as "tremendous."[24]

Robert Gnaizda, a partner in Public Advocates, Inc., said he was "very excited" about the company's plan, especially the program to hire and train one thousand Spanish-speaking persons over the next five years.[25] Company spokespeople also praised the company's commitment to affirmative action. "Affirmative action is really an expansion of opportunity for everyone at Pacific Telephone and Telegraph, a program of inclusion rather than exclusion."[26]

Early on the day the FCC hearings were to start, the state leaders of Mexican American organizations held a press conference praising the new telephone company plan.[27]

When the hearings began, Obledo deferred to William L. Diedrich Jr. of Pacific Telephone, who lauded the new policy statement and read into the record the commendation given to the company by the Hispanic community. Obledo, Gnaizda, and Cruz Reynoso, leaders of the Hispanic community, stood up to congratulate Pacific Telephone. Surprised by the apparent agreement reached by the telephone company and the Hispanic community, FCC and EEOC lawyers questioned the enforceability of the pledge. Judy Potter, queried by the press over lunch, noted that there appeared to be a misunderstanding about the morning's discussion. She noted, "It seemed PT&T and certain members or representatives of the Chicano community negotiated a policy statement. The EEOC and the FCC have had no part of the negotiations to date. . . . This policy statement is unenforceable by law."[28] Denniston suggested to Diedrich that there was intense interest in the company's program and a sense of urgency about implementation. Diedrich reaffirmed Pacific Telephone's commitment.

The next day, the *Alhambra Post* reported, "Under the plan, PT&T plans to double the number of Mexicans it employs by 1975 and triple their number by 1980." Potter, EEOC counsel, was quoted as saying the company plan had "no teeth in it, which means it is in no way legally enforceable."[29] What upset the EEOC team was, first, not being made aware of the agreement, and second, the sense that the Hispanic community had sold out for a promise and not a legal commitment.

The hearings went on, with witnesses claiming that the company did not provide sufficient Spanish-speaking operators and thus did not meet the needs of the Hispanic community. After one particularly tense exchange, Denniston allowed the witness to make a test call to see if he could reach a Spanish-speaking operator. AT&T lawyers objected strenuously to such a spur-of-the-moment experiment. Nonetheless, a speakerphone arrangement was set up in Room 264 and the call was to be placed. The EEOC team supported the request, but Pacific's lawyer objected.[30] Diedrich feared they would be violating the Federal Communications Act, Section 605, by not notifying the receiving party that the call was being recorded. Copus interjected, "The caller could first announce in Spanish that the call is being monitored." Jim Juntilla, representing the FCC, which is responsible for the Federal Communications Act, offered that Section 605 would have nothing to do with this situation.

Denniston ended the discussion by stating that they needed to "observe the difficulty of the language barrier" and would make the call. He conceded that "if the company has any qualms about it, they may absent themselves," but he suggested they be present. Diedrich declined to participate; for AT&T, Ashley saw "no reason to be there." The call was made. It took six minutes and forty seconds to get the number requested.[31]

At the same hearing, Gene Kofke noticed less-than-savvy behavior on the part of his AT&T team. They arrived in limousines with black drivers. Fortunately for AT&T, they were not seen by the witnesses or the EEOC team, and Kofke passed the word on the need to avoid such blatant symbols of what the EEOC was trying to prove.[32]

The Center for United Labor Action (CULA) wanted hearings in New York, and testimony was heard there from "black and Spanish communities, women's groups, and other organizations such as CULA and the Suburban Action Institute . . . [which] opposed the relocation of AT&T's headquarters from downtown New York to suburban Basking Ridge, New Jersey," on the basis that the "move adversely affected the opportunity for black and Hispanic workers to either retain or obtain jobs at the new suburban site."

In New York on May 8, AT&T lawyers were joined by New York Telephone lawyers William R. Distasio and Raymond F. Scully. They met in an "ancient federal building," room 724 at 641 Washington Street, a long, dark, hot room with high ceilings.[33] Hearings went on through May 12. In addition to pandemonium inside, protesters outside passed out handbills claiming, "Let's Give Quigley the business." Doris Quigley, a chief operator who had been with the company for forty-seven years, would be the subject of much discussion in the hearings.[34] Randy Speck escorted EEOC witnesses by subway, but first he got lost—a "southern white boy from rural Texas" lost in a Spanish section of New York City.[35]

Adding to the confusion was the appearance of radical feminists from CULA, parties to the case but not represented by a lawyer; they were allowed to sit at the bench. Forced by Denniston to make room for them, AT&T and EEOC lawyers moved sideways to allow seating space for Mary Pirotti, Cathy Dennis, and Gavrielle Gemma.

AT&T and NYT had no respite from objections, chants, and pickets during the New York hearing. A telephone operator herself, Gemma pleaded with Denniston to call Chief Operator Quigley and AT&T vice president David Easlick to the stand, but he steadfastly stuck to the script of planned witnesses. Gemma confronted AT&T, charging the company with harassment from the day she started working on the hearings. The company, she argued, can spend six million dollars and have seven lawyers in the room while she and her friends put their jobs on the line to present their case. The audience broke out in applause, which Denniston quickly quelled. He did not mind her being enthusiastic, but he did not want the case to be delayed or made more complicated and difficult than it already was. He explained that, although it is customary for each party to have one spokesperson from the bench, the hearings were in New York to hear from individual employees and for that reason they could speak out. Gemma argued that the company should be on trial, not the employees. To her the situation seemed much more threatening to the employees.

Before the session erupted again, Potter brought up a point about the hearings in Los Angeles. Pacific had not provided their affirmative action program, claiming it would not be ready till May 1. She had heard, however, from Doris Wooten of the Department of Labor that Pacific had provided a sixty-page model program to a public conference during the same week as the Los Angeles hearing. Frustrated by the company's lack of forthrightness about the plan and about the surprise agreement with the Hispanic community, the EEOC argued strongly not to let Pacific out of the case as Pacific's lawyers requested.

Meanwhile, as the New York hearing continued amid the turmoil, Pirotti made an opening statement for CULA. First, however, she drew attention to the unpleasant and hard-to-find hearing location "practically in the river," observing that management usually holds its meetings in the "best hotels in town." CULA, Pinotta explained, is "a national organization for rank and file workers" and fought for the hearings so that AT&T would be tried by "the very people who suffered the most from their degrading policies, the operators and clerks. This is the woman's day in court." From her place with the lawyers, Pirotti explained that she wished to subpoena Chief Operator Quigley, who was, she said, well known for her harassment of employees. She wanted Easlick to take the stand because CULA suspected there was a "systematic policy . . . of racism and degradation of women." Applause and signs broke out again when she accused AT&T of giving the bosses money in their pockets that "working people don't take home in their pay check." "We will not be turned away," she continued. "We will not in the least be intimidated by the slick mellow mouth Wall Street lawyer sitting over there on our right."[36] And on and on it went.

Finally, Pirotti called CULA's first witness, Gavrielle Gemma, to the stand. A New York Telephone operator, Gemma formally testified to what she considered bad treatment, harassment, being treated with general disrespect, having filthy working conditions, no sick pay, and unbearable performance pressures in her litany of grievances. "Applause" (as the transcript calls it) interrupted the proceedings frequently. Denniston cautioned CULA women at the counsel table not to applaud along with the audience. Someone in the audience yelled out that the AT&T lawyer should applaud. It was a riotous scene. Gemma claimed that at her employment interview she was questioned on obedience to her parents, reasons for the breakup with her husband, and her plans for children. CULA's next witness, Cathy Dennis, cataloged what she saw as harassment on the job and lack of opportunities, while male managers with no experience were hired to supervise the women.37

AT&T attorneys intervened to limit the testimony. Gemma objected, saying that AT&T's objections showed what racists they were. Denniston interrupted that it would be simpler just to let the witnesses say what they wanted even if it was not strictly relevant. The crowd continued to interrupt with yells and signs, AT&T lawyers squirmed uncomfortably, unable to deflect the attack. Not paying any attention or even knowing procedural rules, Gemma objected to cross-examination by New York Telephone's lawyers, arguing that they should be on the stand for her to ask them questions. A voice in the audience called for evening hearings, arguing that most workers—except those fired—couldn't be there in the day.38

Larry Gartner, from the EEOC, called the next witness, William Floyd, a black switchman who had been fired by the telephone company for failing to list an arrest on an application. Floyd had begun an activist labor organization called Strike Back, which published a page attacking the company each month. Disillusioned by the union as well, Floyd had nothing good to say about the company. He argued that employees want to testify but are afraid; he proposed "protection" for them. Others latched onto the idea, though Morton M. Maneker, New York Telephone's lawyer from the Park Avenue firm of Proskauer, Rose, Goetz, and Mendelsohn, denied the company ever retaliated against anyone. The audience laughed.

Denniston agreed that witnesses should not be disciplined without a report to him. Copus suggested the EEOC get written notice of any disciplinary actions of the company toward any witnesses. Potter added that the EEOC should know when any witness is put on a disciplinary step—and, Gartner added, in advance of action. Although Denniston again agreed, AT&T and New York Telephone lawyers vehemently objected, claiming disruption to company operation. Pirotti and the audience found the company's position

insulting and made their opinion known loudly. Maneker complained about
the hearings getting out of control. And, in a sense, they were—the shouting
applause, hisses and laughter from the audience and big banners against the
company adorning the walls, all being filmed by TV news cameras.

Denniston expressed concern that Pirotti, Dennis, and Gemma were unable to maintain decorum. And on it went. Witness after witness told horror
stories, Gemma and Denniston traded words, and he cautioned her about
yelling at him. A training film called "Index" was shown, part of an explanation of how an operator's performance is rated. The film included a cartoon of
a shapely woman called Ms. Index with what appeared to be measurements
across her body. The film had a "frumpy, overweight female" to show poor
performance.[39] The parties argued about whether the film was humiliating to
women.

Witnesses presented by the EEOC included women in nontraditional jobs.
Elizabeth Ryan, a frameman in Troy, New York, loved her job. Others reported successes but still found limits to job opportunities. Eleanor Collins, an engineering associate, testified about the environment in Long Lines, the company's long-distance unit. In the parade of witnesses was Peter Johnson, one of
a group of Columbia University students who took telephone company jobs
specifically to work from the inside against what they saw as "wrongs."

New York Telephone tried to explain its operating procedures and its "absence control plan." The company ultimately complied with Denniston's order to provide advance notice of disciplinary action, but it also provided extensive rebuttal including statements by employees that contradicted CULA's
witnesses. The company provided background information on a contributing
factor—the bitter strike that lasted from July 1971 to February 1972 and left bad
feelings in its wake.

Next, the company filed affidavits from employees who knew and worked
with Gemma, Dennis, and the others. Colette Birnbaum, a service representative, union steward, and coworker with Dennis, stated that "most of Dennis'
testimony was absolutely false." Dennis, she argued, did not have the support
of her peers; in fact, Birnbaum claimed, they almost walked off the job because of her. Dennis, they felt, was being given "preferential treatment"
because of her involvement in the EEOC hearings. Carol Carter, a directory
assistance operator in the Times Square Bureau, where Gemma worked, said
that Gemma used the "everyday gripes of the operators" to imply that there is
"deep dissatisfaction and bitterness" among operators. An African American

herself, Carter did not believe that black operators were treated in a degrading, racist, or humiliating way, as Gemma claimed. And as for Quigley, Carter liked her "very much" and had at various times arranged to work in Quigley's office even though it meant a longer commute from her Staten Island home. "Quigley," she added, "has always been fair with the operators and she claims a great deal of respect from us." In her ten-page sworn affidavit, Carter charged that Gemma's attitude about her job was not shared and expressed the opinion that Gemma was going after publicity.[40]

Joan Hull, Lee Walker, and Judith Wenning represented NOW in New York. As education committee coordinator for NOW's New York chapter, Wenning directed her testimony to the career aspirations and employment plans of women of all ages. She introduced the "Virginia Slims American Women's Opinion Poll 1972" as proof that women support the "thrust for equality now." She argued that women are "interested in employment which offers advancement and high pay opportunities." Hull's testimony covered the "economic penalty of being female and working for the Bell System" and "atmospheric conditions at AT&T oppressive to female employees." Walker explained NOW's mission and, in particular, the work she was doing on employment and media-projected images of women. "The telephone company," she argued, "projects images of women that are stereotyped and thus limiting and restricting."[41]

The last field hearing was on May 31, 1972, in Washington, D.C., again with individuals and groups, such as NOW, testifying.[42] Glad to be back on familiar turf without the protestors, the teams were about to get started when in walked Gemma and the CULA team from New York. They had taken a bus to Washington so as not to miss the next action.[43] Having spent their own money and losing work time, they headed home a few days later.

At this point AT&T provided its list of witnesses to the EEOC. Denniston directed the company to distribute its direct case on or before August 1, with cross examination by the government lawyers to begin on or about October 2.[44]

While the EEOC case demanded time and attention, AT&T faced other challengers than Copus and Heide. To name a few of the problems AT&T faced in 1972: on the financial side, capital demands grew as annual construction expenditures—new plant—were going up 8 to 10 percent a year because of increased demand for telecommunications; service quality remained a time- and resource-heavy problem; the public opposed the company's effort to move to usage-sensitive pricing; increased competition, especially from specialized common carriers, forced pricing and provisioning policy changes; and the government had increased its interest in antitrust matters.

Twice a year, the Bell System presidents and principal officers of AT&T met to review major issues facing the business and to discuss policy decisions. The May 12, 1972, "Presidents' Conference" involved more discussion than usual and fewer presentations. Capital requirements, regulation, competition, and the image of the Bell System were the main topics.[45] That conference in Key Largo, Florida, was where deButts formally announced that AT&T would really compete.[46]

Hardly a conference or meeting went by, however, without reference to the equal opportunity issue. By mid-1972 a subtle shift could be detected in the content of internal publications, the speeches officers gave in private and public forums, and the company advertising—mostly in corporate ads but gradually in the operating companies' ads as well. More opportunities were structured for managers to hear talks by outsiders, including NOW members such as Lee Walker and Sally Hacker. The union began to talk seriously with management about how upgrade and transfer programs could be made to work. Professionals in the personnel departments were encouraged to put their skills to work defining ways to implement rather than to fight affirmative action.

Equal employment opportunity was going into the rule books, and that was not to be debated, though the particular implementation practices might be. DeButts wanted the EEOC case out of the way. It was taking too much time, too much money, and producing too much bad publicity; deButts faced Easlick with the simple question, "What will it take to settle?" The current negotiating team—Dan Davis, Clark Redick, and Lee Satterfield—ratcheted up its effort.[47] Money was still a key issue. It would cost money to continue and it would cost money to settle. "How much?" became a serious question.

A big corporation does not turn around easily. The May 19, 1972, issue of AT&T News promulgated a new policy accepting the use of "Ms.," but vestiges of the past would linger in many areas, not the least of which being the EEOC case itself.

While AT&T officers dealt with the annual meeting, the lawyers sparred over data, and NOW challenged telephone companies in the streets, the AT&T Alliance for Women moved ahead with its open and official organization. On May 4 the alliance had gone public with an after-work meeting in the third-floor assembly room at 195 Broadway. "The assembly room was full.

The audience was quite diversified, with an age range of about 18 to 60 and men accounting for about 35 percent of those attending," according to a company publication.[48] Liz Brydon, as group leader, explained the "voluntary" nature of the organization and its "interest in advancing the cause of equal employment opportunity for women within the company and a willingness to make an active contribution to constructive programs toward this end." An official recognition letter, dated April 26, 1972, from Easlick, then vice president of the Human Resources Department, was read, including a reference to personnel director Amy Hanan as "interface." Brydon, a "straightforward, crisp, and efficient leader with a sense of humor," introduced task forces on education, advancement, research, membership, upward mobility, and tracking. The AT&T Alliance for Women was official; news of the alliance would even hit the telecommunications industry trade magazine.[49]

Meanwhile, probably oblivious to the alliance activities and between their hearing dates, Copus and Levy kept talking, often exchanging memos to confirm telephone agreements. When an issue became contentious, such as delay in the provision of testimony or validation data on craft, clerical, or operator studies, Copus turned to paper. Also, by May 22 he wanted to document where things stood on collecting data by standard metropolitan statistical areas (SMSAs).[50] Copus was actually planning a vacation on the Colorado River around Memorial Day and did want the case under control.[51]

Meanwhile, another segment of AT&T seriously set about creating a "new line of career apparel" for Bell System women. For public-contact employees, the outfits would be provided at company expense. Any other employee could order through the catalog at her own expense.

Created by Leonard Fisher and Associates of New York and offered through Hart Schaffner & Marx, the "Belle Blu" collection of twenty-two garments (including a pantsuit) plus a coordinated group of accessories, reached the brochure and catalog stage before someone realized it might be the right idea at the wrong time. Research had been done on a line first designed by Saul Bass & Associates and tested in New York, Indiana, and New Jersey.[52] That research revealed that women employees would be interested if they had a wide range of choices, if the clothes were easy to care for, and if they were reasonably priced.

"Many outfits can be created through mix-and-match combinations," the brochure claimed, "but all have a distinctive similarity of appearance which can be further enhanced by wearing the Bell symbol jewelry offered in the

New Outfits Available Through Purchase Plan

These outfits are from the "Belle Blu" collection, a new line of career apparel created exclusively for Bell System women by Leonard Fisher and Associates of New York. Several items from the line in the corporate "stripe" colors of bright blue and yellow have been adopted for public contact employees already outfitted at company expense, such as exhibit guides and public telephone attendants. In addition, the entire collection of 22 garments plus a coordinated group of accessories is now available to every employee at her own expense on a mail order basis.

Designs Based on Research

The designs are based on the results of research conducted with groups of women employees, most of whom said they would be interested in career apparel if it provided a range of choice in styling and color, if the clothes were easy to care for, and if they were reasonably priced. The "Belle Blu" collection was then developed with

these criteria in mind—in addition to the corporate bright blue and yellow, most garments are also available in navy, beige, pink or green. Some are available in a specially designed print as well.

All items but the wool coat are machine washable and require little or no ironing. And the clothing and accessories are priced below retail items of equal quality. A complete week's wardrobe, including blazer, pants, skirt, jumper, dress and two blouses can be purchased for less than $150.00. Many outfits can be created through mix-and-match combinations, but all have a distinctive similiarity of appearance which can be further enhanced by wearing the Bell symbol jewelry offered in the collection.

Purchase Plan Is Voluntary

Any woman employee may buy as much or as little as she pleases from the collection—participation in the purchase plan is completely voluntary and each employee is free to make her own choices. A full color catalog, complete with

photographs, descriptions and ordering information will be sent to employees who fill out and send in the coupon below. In addition, presentations showing the clothing and accessories can be arranged at Bell System locations where 50 or more women express an interest in career apparel. The presentation includes a slide show, a set of sample garments and a live fashion show for large audiences. The presentation can be requested through your company's public relations department.

If the career apparel purchase plan meets with favorable employee reaction, new fashion items will be added to the collection every 12 to 18 months.

The clothing is made by Fashionaire, the career apparel division of Hart Schaffner & Marx, from woven and knitted 100% Dacron® polyester fabrics supplied by Burlington Industries. The accessories are produced by Etcetera, a division of Terner's of Miami, and the corporate jewelry is made by the Robbins Company.

"BELLE BLU" CATALOG

Send For Your Free Catalog

The catalog contains 20 full fashion color pages, photos and complete descriptions of each item, plus pricing and ordering information.

Simply fill in the coupon below and send it to Hart Schaffner & Marx to receive your very own "Belle Blu" catalog.

Name_____ Street_____

City_____ State_____ Zip_____

Company_____

Send To:

"Belle Blu" Catalog
Hart Schaffner & Marx, Fashionaire Division, 36 S. Franklin St., Chicago, Ill. 60606

Belle Blu, the Bell System's line of women's apparel.

From the author's collection and reprinted with the permission of AT&T.

collection." New items would be added every twelve to eighteen months, if employee reaction warranted. The twenty-page catalog was available upon request. I filled out the coupon for the catalog, but it never appeared.[53]

Writing to update Hacker on events in New York, Walker passed along the news about Belle Blu. "Sounds terrific for Switchones, Frameones, Lineones, etc. doesn't it? How about several NOW members buying the pants and wearing them to protest?" That would have been quite a photo opportunity for the press. Janet Kanter in Illinois kept a copy of a *Chicago Tribune* story on Belle Blu, affixing a note, "Why not 'Boy Blue' also? Or Blueboys?"[54]

In other news, Walker talked about her guest lectures at AT&T Long Lines and New York Telephone. The New York Telephone group had been a management development class of forty men. She was invited because a survey had shown that the top topic "these guys" wanted to hear about was women's liberation.

After that, Walker appeared with AT&T's Don Liebers on a New York talk show—Lee Leonard's *Midday Live* show. AT&T had contacted Channel 5 for an opportunity to discuss their affirmative action program. The TV station thought the show would be "enlivened" with a "few raving feminists." The telephone company backed away for a while but eventually agreed. Liebers felt that Walker talked nonstop; he had to interrupt her to say anything. Liebers offered to take Walker to any telephone company work site to see the situation for herself. Afterward, Walker described how "calls came in, all on my side." Liebers she saw as a "nice person" but one who now "knows this pressure from us will not let up."[55]

Liebers met with many outsiders. Walker, Hacker, Heide, Komisar, and others kept after him. Liebers traveled to Iowa to meet with Hacker. There, barefoot and relaxed, the academic Hacker chided Liebers about oppression in a classic campus-radical-meets-button-down-corporate-type scenario. Later Liebers and Heide met in Washington, D.C. Heide's firm handshake and nononsense conversation showed him a different side of NOW activism.[56]

Liebers understood he was dealing with a "people" issue, both in terms of the protagonists and in terms of the employees whose lives would be affected by the case. To him, they were people, not numbers, and he realized that lives were going to change significantly. Goals and timetables were necessary; affirmative action was the path to change though it raised the ire of many employees.[57]

The external pressures did not let up. NOW had several good reasons for pursuing the Bell System action. First of all, this case provided the opportunity for 2 percent of working women directly, and it would be a landmark case. Second, challenging AT&T would provide NOW with publicity, new members, and maybe even dollars. Third, and probably most useful, a win here would produce visible results.

As the case went on, more and more background information reached NOW and the EEOC. Individuals would identify opportunities for NOW interest, and Hacker would pass them along as ideas for chapter activities: evaluate Bell System child care projects; check Bell System advertising; suggest changes in materials the Bell System provides for school use; get the companies to modify white page listings in phone books, which provided only one listing per home, usually the man. Beyond these ideas, chapters could do some consciousness raising by meeting with Bell workers to read and discuss *A Unique Competence* together. The more formal NOW plan for AT&T action called for events throughout 1972–73, starting with NOW meetings with AT&T officers. Hacker was still stymied in her request to meet with deButts. Easlick offered to meet with NOW in his place on a phone conversation, but she insisted on meeting with deButts or Lilley.[58]

Then came plans for another nationwide NOW action at telephone company headquarters offices or business and switching offices in cities without headquarters. The tactics included pickets, posters, sit-ins, and pamphlets of information on the EEOC case for the public as well as employees.[59] Beyond that, NOW planned to put pressure on state public utility commissions, to increase pressure on local telephone company management, and to meet with union members and officials to build working relationships on joint goals.

NOW planned to build its EEOC testimony around five points: attitudes and their effects on opportunity for women, general social implications of Bell System practices, special problems of minority women, the need for the Bell System to inform employees, and the frequency of EEOC cases against the Bell System.[60]

On the witness stand Friday, June 9, 1972, Ann Scott presented NOW's interest in compliance—having corporations follow the government's rules for equal employment opportunity. Thoroughly prepared, Scott knew the rules and regulations. Judy Potter led Scott through her direct testimony, knowing at the time that Scott made a superb witness for the EEOC case. Potter had not met Scott until that very morning, and no one had written testimony from Scott in advance. Thompson Powers challenged Potter's approach, saying he expected witnesses to make statements, not be "led through a series of questions." Denniston allowed Scott to continue, telling Powers that rules facilitated matters but that in this case he would proceed without formally filed testimony. The FCC's Juntilla explained to Powers, who had not been at the field hearings, how they had tried to keep witnesses to remarks that were "relevant to the proceedings." Denniston, as he had many times before, expressed a desire to hear what the witnesses had to say and to "allow it in whatever form it is presented."[61]

Ann London Scott.

*Property of the Schlesinger Library,
Radcliffe Institute, Harvard University.
Reprinted with permission of the
Schlesinger Library and the photographer
Bob Adelman.*

Powers next pushed to know Scott's qualifications. Scott told the hearing of her work as consultant to the secretary of Labor regarding the Office of Contract Compliance's Revised Order 4, which required goals and timetables for women. She had also published articles on equal opportunity in professional journals, was a regular columnist for Ms., and gave speeches on the topic of compliance. In 1970 Scott had drafted for the State University of New York at Buffalo what she claimed was the first affirmative action program that ever existed for women.

Next, Scott commented on the Bell affirmative action programs she had reviewed—New York Telephone, Michigan Bell, Illinois Bell, South Central Bell, and Pacific Telephone and Telegraph. Scott explained the value of affirmative action as a whole and argued that "goals and time-tables are not an affirmative action program in itself. They are merely the means or tool . . . by which the ends of affirmative action are reached." Scott saw the end result as "rough parity in the employment profile of a company with the population." She recognized goals and timetable as "self-destruct" tools. "In certain areas," she continued, "men do not have goals set for them, and they should. The whole question of setting goals for male operators goes beyond the question of whether or not men should be represented in that job category. The real crime against women in employment in this country is sex stereotyping of jobs and it is sex stereotyping of jobs which keeps employment figures down, which keeps salaries down."[62]

Later, in referring to Illinois Bell, Scott described the Women's Advisory Committee on Affirmative Action, a group set up by Harriet White that "was comprised of women managers from all departments and all levels." And though the committee met with company officers to discuss upward mobility for women, Scott felt that they needed more responsibility and not just have "the right simply to talk to the President when he desires to see them." To be effective, the women needed freer access to information about the employment status of women in the company. As it was, she feared the committee had no power and could be dissolved at any moment.

Scott analyzed job and education levels more broadly, concluding that women in the United States in general are underutilized. She noted, "A woman with a college degree earns about the same amount on the average in this country as a man with an eighth grade education. While there is underutilization of this kind going on, we feel Bell as an employer of one out of every 56 women in this country, should do something about that."[63]

Other issues Scott raised were maternity policy, child care, using pregnancy tests as part of the hiring process, sex stereotypes, job advertising, and the use of the term "girl." She was upset that the affirmative action programs did not address the EEOC's new guidelines on "temporary disability." She praised Illinois Bell for its child care arrangements. Illinois Bell, she noted, maintains a list of licensed day home care center operators and provides guidance in establishing home child care centers. Illinois Bell consultants work with women who wish to take care of children and help them provide adequate facilities in their home. Scott suggested that programs like Illinois Bell's could be incorporated in local standard affirmative action programs.[64]

With her understanding of affirmative action and of Bell's management strategy, Scott tackled the issue of management training. She drew attention to the lack of telephone company women moving through the three-to-five-year rotational assignments at AT&T. "This route to top management must be open to women," she argued. She described how the initial management development program (IMDP) hires and trains men for this fast-track program. "In the future, NOW feels that at least 50 percent of the IMDP hires should be women." In conclusion, Scott suggested forcefully that the FCC review and enforce affirmative action programs for corporations they regulate and not grant rate increases "unless it is shown that the company is using good management." Scott did not consider discriminatory practices good management. Scott brought in Hacker's concern about technology's effects on the work force. "As part of their regulatory oversight," she added, "the FCC should look at affirmative action progress before granting the Bell System a license to expand into new areas."[65]

Powers asked Scott when she expected women to get work parity. Her personal opinion, Scott said, was 1985, based on how rapidly women were entering the work force, though she admitted there were other variables and that not all discrimination would be gone. Powers pushed her on whether there would be parity for women in building and construction jobs. He queried her on whether "parity can be achieved . . . by vigorous recruitment," and she responded, "No." Scott argued that "all society" needed to change. "We are trying to do that," she added. She did not see NOW going out of business by 1985, however.[66]

Double counting became a hot topic, as Scott accused AT&T of counting black women twice, and the parties debated how plans can measure progress toward both minority and female goals. Powers followed up on Scott's point about maternity testing and her view that it had no place in hiring procedures. Powers claimed if he were taking an opera company on the road for nine months he would want to know whether or not the female lead would fulfill the program. Juntilla objected to the irrelevancy of Power's question, but Denniston overruled the objection. Powers and Scott went back and forth on the question of pregnancy versus other disability.

> *Q. I am not sure you are saying pregnancy is never job-related or if you say it is, an employer should not inquire about it.*
>
> *A I am saying pregnancy should not be treated any differently from any temporary disability. If you asked about a heart attack from the point of view of temporary disability, then you could ask about any condition which would require temporary disability, but maternity should not be dealt with any differently.*
>
> *Q. But to the extent an employer had a policy of inquiring about physical disabilities which were related to job performance, it would be appropriate to include in that list of questions about pregnancy?*

A. *Only if he plans to treat pregnancy in the same way he plans to treat any other disability, but if he refuses to hire someone because she is pregnant or might become pregnant when he does not refuse to hire people who have conditions that might lead to a temporary disability, then he is treating men differently from women.*[67]

Another line of questioning delved into whether an employer had the right, as Powers put it,

Q. To inquire as to whether applicants, male or female, have marital or parental responsibilities that would limit their availability for work.

A. *Yes, I believe that that should not be asked. That is NOW's position that that information should not be asked. Our experience is that that has a bearing on the hiring potential for women.*[68]

At 3:05 P.M. that day the hearings were adjourned. Scott had proven an articulate witness. She personified the serious approach and dedication of NOW members that the press and public rarely saw. NOW mobilized street pickets, but it also pulled together facts, figures, and ideas on major issues and big cases such as this one. Often in her Baltimore home, Scott hosted strategy sessions with Heide and other leaders. While the intense workings of NOW were at times haphazard, there was an organizational framework.

Circulated within NOW was a list of contacts with comments about their connections to the AT&T case. The close working relationship of this task force and its prodigious output belied the fact that they were scattered across the country. Whenever NOW members met or whenever they talked on the phone, it was on their own time and at their own personal expense. By contrast, neither money, time, nor travel was a problem for the AT&T and EEOC teams.

The focus of the EEOC case returned to the New York–Washington axis. AT&T's policy direction came from the twenty-sixth floor of its headquarters at 195 Broadway in New York, but the legal team and its Kofke support apparatus settled into Washington, which, as usual, was warm and unpleasant in the summer heat. AT&T's testimony was due August 1, 1972, less than a month away.

8

PASSION AND ACTION

That summer in Washington, things were hot for AT&T, but I heard little in the news or in AT&T internal publications about the case. The lawyers continued their work. From his EEOC office in Washington, David Copus was still on the phone with AT&T's Hal Levy almost daily. On June 15, he pressed Levy on the delivery of data due to the EEOC; Levy replied, "Everything is in the process of being gathered. . . . People are awfully busy."[1] Not only was AT&T responding to data requests and reports, but its own filing was also due August 1.

Levy told Copus that the EEOC's request for forty sets of AT&T's filing was "really burdensome." Copus agreed to a delay of the delivery of the twenty-five copies he needed for district offices if Levy could provide fifteen copies on August 1. Two of the sets would have "everything," including glossy prints and printed material. In return, Copus promised wage data to Levy by the next Monday.[2]

At AT&T headquarters I heard more about "interconnection" than affirmative action. The FCC had established a joint federal-state board to consider how customers could safely attach non-Bell equipment to the telecommunications network (Interconnection Docket 12174). Only equipment made by Bell could be plugged into AT&T's network at that point, and the company sensed a real threat.

Internally, the word of affirmative action did spread throughout the company, and NOW willingly provided guest speakers. In June, Judith Lonnquist, a NOW lawyer, spoke on sexual discrimination to a Bell Labs affirmative action committee in Illinois; Judy Bell, a local NOW president, spoke to a similar committee in Columbus, Ohio; NOW's Irma Diamond spoke to AT&T Long Lines in White Plains, New York.[3]

Though the unions steadfastly refused to become parties to the EEOC's case, they did not ignore the issues. Delegates to the Communications Workers of America (CWA) annual convention and the CWA Women's Activities conference in Los Angeles, June 12–14, 1972, discussed women's issues. The convention adopted a resolution supporting the ERA; an amendment to the resolution called for more women to be appointed to responsible union positions. The keynote speaker was Joseph Beirne, CWA president. He was introduced by Valerie C. Howard, head of the women's activities and consumer affairs staff at CWA headquarters. I never met Howard, but she knew what we were doing and helped us connect with sympathetic Bell System women in the union. Beirne claimed that AT&T management took duties out of men's jobs and gave them to women at a lower pay. He said he warned AT&T about "antifemale policies and practices." Claiming that progress had been made in the 1971 negotiations, Beirne "pointed out CWA's cooperation with the EEOC and its investigation of charges against the Bell System so that the Union may become the charging party on behalf of an entire class of employees affected by any discriminatory practices."[4]

Glenn E. Watts, then CWA secretary-treasurer, told the women to "address themselves to their grievances with the same spirit and vigor they displayed when they fought for—and won—the right to vote."[5] Others on the CWA convention program included Elizabeth Duncan Koontz, deputy assistant secretary of Labor and director of the Women's Bureau, and Aileen Hernandez, NOW officer and former EEOC commissioner.

Meanwhile from Michigan, NOW coordinator Linda A. Stults reported to Sally Hacker, "The first state-wide meeting of all NOW chapters in Michigan was held June 11 and action against Michigan Bell was made one of the priority issues." She added she had her "very own copy of Michigan Bell's Affirmative Action Program," noting, "It *stinks!*" Another action item for Michigan was a meeting that Detroit NOW held with women from Michigan Bell. NOW attorneys indicated that "at least three cases are good enough to go into court with." NOW's plan was "to find as many cases as possible in different parts of Michigan and file them all on one day."[6] NOW planned a three-pronged program in Detroit: schedule organized and well-planned approaches to offices of Michigan Bell throughout the state, treat the project as a priority item for Michigan NOW, and, importantly, open communications lines and solicit the support of the CWA.[7]

Illustrative of the circle of information surrounding AT&T, Stults told Hacker about the alliance: "I don't know if you're familiar with the newly formed AT&T Alliance for Women, so I'm enclosing an article which was sent to me by Lois Kerkeslager. You can contact her at 20 W. 64th St., Apt. 23H, New York City, 10023. She works for AT&T and gave me some good tips on how to organize Bell women." Copies of the letter went to Ann Scott, Mary Lynn Myers, and Whitney Adams.[8] Of course, Scott, Myers, and Adams knew full well what we were doing.

In July, my friends in Chicago NOW testified against Illinois Bell in its rate case, Illinois Commerce Commission Docket 56831. Chicago NOW had filed a petition to intervene in May, much as the EEOC had filed in AT&T's rate proceeding. NOW based its filing on hiring, promotion, and wage issues, using the EEOC's A Unique Competence as substantiation.[9] Chicago NOW's Janet Kanter published a series of Telegriefs, reaching out to Illinois Bell women in a publication taking off on the company's Telebriefs. Telegriefs gave Bell women "food for thought" with pointed questions about job openings and advancement probabilities, facts and figures, as well as information on how to receive their own copies of A Unique Competence, an update on NOW actions against Illinois Bell, and suggestions about how to take action themselves.[10]

From both his EEOC network and his personal friendship with Adams, Copus knew about the Illinois and Michigan actions. Particular cases, however, were at that moment less useful to him than indications of systemwide behavior, as he suspected he would find in AT&T's testing procedures. Copus called Levy "to needle him" about testing information. In his notes, Copus observed, Levy did "bitch" but did not really complain about getting the testing data. Levy apologized for the delay and hoped all three reports—craft, clerical, and operator—would be in by the end of the month. The "force loss studies" had not been received, though Levy had talked to most of the companies. If anything comes in, "He'll call," Copus noted. Later, in a conversation he initiated, Levy said he questioned the rationale for the EEOC's requests but would still try to obtain the data.[11]

As Copus kept after Levy, Hacker kept after Bob Lilley, who finally responded on July 13, 1972, indicating he would meet with NOW "to discuss feminist issues." Hacker was asked to call Miss Ann Lowes, his secretary, to set up a "mutually agreeable date."[12]

AT&T's testimony, filed on August 1, 1972, included eight witnesses from AT&T headquarters, nine outside experts, and representatives from each of the operating companies and Long Lines. AT&T provided a "summary memorandum,"[13] and Gene Kofke called the outside witnesses to an education session and "rally" in Denver. Not all the experts knew enough about the Bell System, he thought, to be effective, and he hoped his meeting at the Brown Palace Hotel would help them get ready for the hearings.[14]

AT&T issued a press release: "The Bell telephone companies are 'fully committed' to equal employment opportunity and have been unjustly maligned by the Equal Employment Opportunity Commission." The release extolled Bell's progress and cited arguments from John Kingsbury's filed testimony. It reiterated that the company is committed "unequivocally to the elimination of discrimination on the basis of race, religion, sex, or national origin in its employment policies." Kingsbury's testimony admitted the company has "further to go" but argued "to brand actions in 1965 or 1966 as discriminatory because they are not consonant with 1971 views is unfair and improper." He went on to say that the EEOC failed to realize the company's primary function is "to provide communications service to the American public, not merely to provide employment to all comers, regardless of ability." The company already has affirmative action programs, the release emphasized, plans that have specific goals and timetables for minorities and women. "The goal is to achieve a work force that approximates the percentages of minorities and women in the relevant labor market." The release included charts, graphs, a list of key points, a chronology, and photos. The photos showed Quayne Gennaro, a female traffic staff supervisor in New Jersey; Don Taylor, a California directory assistance operator; a California installer, Benita Knight; Illinois Bell's installer-repairman Juan Cuellar; and Michigan Bell's truck driver Mary Jo Hanlin.[15]

The next day, the *New York Times* headline read, "AT&T Contends Government Exaggerates Job Discrimination Charges"; the *Wall Street Journal*'s headline was "AT&T Says Bias Charge Is 'Monstrous Hyperbole.'"[16] AT&T's in-house newspaper, *AT&T News*, focused on the flurry of activity prior to the filing:

> *When Al Kunberger of federal relations took the plane to Washington, D.C. the morning of Aug. 1, he carried with him a brief that amounted to untold hours of work in research and preparation and had touched hundreds of employees at AT&T and the operating companies.*
>
> *Preceding him the night before was a truck that carried some thirty cartons of material destined for the EEOC, in addition to two to three cartons for the other parties involved in the case.*
>
> *The final filing consisted of over 10,000 sheets of paper, Kunberger*

explained, that included some 2,000 pages of written testimony and an-
other 8,000 pages of exhibits, charts and tables.

"Although this was a logistics problem of major proportions, our people
went right to work on it," Kunberger said.

Mrs. Kay Horn of the service center in Room 2312 supervised the typing
which took 18 typists approximately 1,250 hours to complete.

Then it was back to federal relations to the proofreaders and editors co-
ordinated by Mary Churchill.

Kay Strickler of administrative services supervised the printing of some
three-quarters of a million sheets that comprised well over 2,000 man
hours of work.

When all was done, the filing measured 48" in height and over 50 lbs.
in weight.

Not a bad day's work.[17]

While the EEOC case demanded attention and hours of work, it still was
not the biggest issue for AT&T's executives. From my vantage point in corporate planning, I knew about policy presentations to the Executive Policy Committee (EPC). On August 9, 1972, Henry M. "Hank" Boettinger explained
how issues flowed through a sixteen-step process from preliminary identification to policy implementation and tracking for the EPC. He listed current issues as network access protection, interconnection, station equipment, certifi-
cation, sale of inside wiring, picturephone, and private line pricing.

Equal employment opportunity did not make this list. Perhaps he saw it as a
nonissue. His test of an issue was to state its inverse—if no one would defend
it, it wasn't an "issue," it was a platitude. Boettinger identified nine key concerns for the Bell System's future: corporate structure, interconnection, R&D
policy, number services policy, separations, organization, two-way visual network, interbusiness relationships, and regulatory policy.

Again, equal employment opportunity did not make the list. AT&T had no
real policy difference with the EEOC or quarrel with the objectives of equal
opportunity. The case was a public relations problem and an administrative
nightmare, but it did not require the level of policy attention that these other
issues did.[18] Given its size and structure, AT&T faced complex issues and
challenges to its way of doing business. The telecommunications industry itself had started to change significantly, and AT&T had fundamental problems
to solve. Nonetheless, for the legal and negotiating teams, the case had top priority.

After appeals and comments were in, the administrative law judge presiding—Frederick Denniston—agreed to a delay in cross-examination of AT&T's witnesses from October 2 to 30.[19] In the interim, Copus and Levy continued to talk about the seemingly endless data requests each had made of the other. At one point AT&T seemed reluctant to provide data supporting the testimony of Kingsbury, its first witness; Copus called George Ashley and threatened, "We go to Denniston for everything" or AT&T gives the EEOC the data Kingsbury used. Within three days Ashley called back, agreeing to send the tape in two weeks or less.[20]

Planning for the next phase, the FCC and EEOC lawyers divided the responsibility for cross-examining the AT&T witnesses.[21] With witness testimony to review in advance, Copus dug into details and studied statistics for his cross-examination of Dr. Robert M. Guion, a luminary in industrial psychology and a formidable witness, and Kingsbury, AT&T's first corporate witness. With Guion, the issue came down to whether tests were valid indicators of performance. Copus did not try to refute the statistical evidence but did find a way to disassociate the witness's claims from the issues of sex. A friend in another agency had found for Copus a statement from Guion that similar study results could not be extended to sex because there were no women in the jobs to study. Reading testimony prepared for Kingsbury, Copus leapt up from his chair when he saw a flaw in the logic Kingsbury used to explain the growth of minorities in the company work force. The data did not account for turnover, and without that, growth figures told only part of the story.[22]

Back at AT&T, we read the company's version of the hearings, mostly summations of filed testimony. The case itself seemed important but distant—with more of a long-term effect than our day-to-day actions. Lee Walker of NOW returned for a speaking engagement with Long Lines. Larry Glynn hired her for four talks at $150 per talk—a fortune for the low-budget NOW team. She discussed the women's liberation movement, NOW, feminism, and the future.[23]

Somehow we had energy to burn. In addition to our day jobs and our action projects, members of the New York City Chapter of NOW got together a softball team called the Sisters: we played ball in Central Park. More seriously, NOW activities surrounding the 1972 anniversary of the right to vote included a day (August 23) designated for "Employment and the Bell System."

Hacker's real passion was sociology. During the summer, she circulated a four-page AT&T status report entitled "AT&T 'Safeguards' Women's Rights!!"

"Safeguard" was a reference to a major defense contract AT&T held and a not-so-subtle indication of a Hacker conspiracy theory.[24] She updated NOW members on AT&T's filing and other actions, such as AT&T's placement of a full-page color ad in Ms. showing a male operator. The text of the ad: "The phone company wants more operators like Rick Wehmhoefer." "This is interesting," she wrote, "especially since NOW members who have examined AT&T on local phone company affirmative action plans . . . report such plans included *no affirmative action for male operators.*" AT&T also placed an ad showing a female installer.

Union people were telling Hacker that men would not want operator jobs or would not stay for long. Hacker surmised, "Further, 'too many' men are thought to inevitably create pressure for better wages in that job." Northwestern Bell, she noted, had sought college men for the operator job, and, "Yes, they do pay more money for college experience." She speculated, "One wonders what kind of college experience better qualifies a person to be an operator." "Perhaps such 'premiums,' and such ads as those in Ms., are less expensive than raising the salaries of *all* operators, as they would have to do to hold many men on the job." Hacker analyzed the recent testimony of Northwestern Bell in the EEOC case filing. AT&T still challenged the terms of the EEOC complaint, calling it "hyperbole of monstrous proportion," and argued that the agency leapt to conclusions by "inference illogically derived from statistics improperly applied." Reviewing Northwestern Bell's statement, Hacker wrote,

> The spookiest thing about this memo is the way this corporation—largest employer of women in the U.S.—divorces itself from society. They say EEOC "ignores the realities of the labor market." Who helped create those realities? They say progress is good, measured against "relevant" standards. What about moral responsibility, moral leadership in the community, on the part of this largest private corporation in the world? They have, they say, with "effort and dedication," "adopted affirmative action programs to help speed that progress." Sure. But not until they were forced into it by law and protest, and then only after years of flagrantly violating the law itself.
>
> The testimony in the August 1, 1972, AT&T bulletin pleads for time, and charges the EEOC with "operating outside the traditions of a society undergoing radical changes. . . ." Job discrimination has been illegal since

AT&T advertisement prepared by N. W. Ayer and used in print media during the case. This ad was autographed by AT&T attorneys and presented to Judy Potter, EEOC attorney.

Property of Judy Potter. Reprinted with permission of AT&T.

the 1964 Civil Rights act; where has Bell been? . . ."And how quickly men and women will take the opportunity to move into jobs traditionally held by the other sex, only time will tell. Well, Bell, the time is NOW."[25]

A good example of the information NOW chapters should pursue was in the action challenge Hacker wrote:

Have you checked with Bell employees in your area? What kind of pre-natal care do pregnant women employees get? Paid maternity leave? Parental leave? What about child care beyond pre-natal care? What programs for child care has Bell developed for all its employees in your area? Have you read your local Bell company's affirmative action plan? Is it easily accessible to company employees? Are there specific goals and timetables to hire more male operators? Is 50 percent a goal for women employees at all levels? (operators, secretaries; why not?) What are procedures for reviewing progress? Frequency of review? I'm sure for satellites and ABM's they are fully aware of the need for close review toward meeting goals. What does a statement like "vigorously pursue" mean, specifically? Do they encourage formation of women's groups, such as the recently formed Women's Alliance at AT&T? Do contracts with CWA still say workers at a low pay rate can be transferred to a higher base-pay job, but kept at a lower salary for a year? . . .

For immediate relief, we can calculate for each company what back pay is owed to women. Linda Stultz and others in the Detroit NOW chapter did this for Mich. Bell, and came up with $91 million dollars, since the law against discrimination went into effect years ago. We plan something coordinated, nationwide, for a couple of months from now, but would prefer no advance publicity for the moment. Keep October in mind, however.[26]

In the summer of 1972, women at AT&T banded together in the alliance and in consciousness raising. We had a feminist party in two apartments at One Lincoln Plaza—apartments 23H and 21A rang with laughter and good times on August 25 as we celebrated a bit early for the next day's commemoration of the right to vote. The alliance's newsletter, *On Board*, carried cartoons drawn by Ed Smith, of Management Sciences and Corporate Planning, proving the women's movement had both a sense of humor and an appreciation for men's work.[27]

By August 7 there were ninety members in the alliance and $11.50 in the

AT&T Alliance for Women cartoon drawn by E. E. Smith and reprinted with his permission.

treasury. Our official company liaison assured us she would provide support "in the $100 to $200 range" but told us not to expect AT&T to "officially fund Alliance activities."[28]

The alliance stayed focused on headquarters issues and never tried to intervene in any aspect of the EEOC case, though individual alliance members played important roles in the company's public relations department and did their share of wordsmithing press releases and stories. The case preparation moved along without us. Brown and Lilley had a private lunch at 195 Broadway on Tuesday, September 5.[29] Then, in the midst of preparation for cross-examination of AT&T's witnesses, NOW, the EEOC team, and even members of the AT&T legal team were stunned by an announcement. On September 19 GSA and AT&T told the world they had agreed on an affirmative action program and upgrade and transfer plan. Arthur F. Sampson, the acting administrator of GSA, and AT&T president Lilley signed the agreement. All operating companies would modify their affirmative action plans by October 1, 1972, and introduce an upgrade and transfer plan by January 1, 1973. Ed Mitchell from GSA and AT&T's negotiator Lee Satterfield felt they had successfully finessed the EEOC case. AT&T supported the agreement in part to show that it could negotiate and in part hoping to resolve the issues. AT&T thought it had successfully gone around the EEOC to the agency directly responsible for the Bell System's compliance with the regulations governing federal contracts. And they got a deal they liked, with none of the insults, penalties, or back pay that the EEOC wanted. On the government side, the GSA was happy, but other government agencies were not.[30]

Laurence Silberman, undersecretary of Labor, called Satterfield to tell him the deal would die. Internally, AT&T attorney Ashley was furious as well, mostly because the end run created chaos. Because Satterfield had kept the Congressional Black Caucus up-to-date, they did not object, but in general the agreement rattled almost everyone.[31]

Following a press conference, Eileen Shanahan covered the deal for television news. She called AT&T's personnel office and talked with Don Liebers just as he was ready to leave his office for vacation. Demanding specifics, she queried Liebers about how many women and minorities were going to be promoted as a result of the new agreement. When, surprised by events, he could not give her the data, she assumed he was withholding it and accused him of lying.[32]

Before the day was out, Copus was on the line with Levy demanding details. He learned that the goals for males were 5 percent of new hires for operators and 8 percent for clericals. For outside plant, the deal was for 10 percent of new hires to be female. Questions still remained about tests and maternity leave, according to a page of notes Copus labeled "AT&T negotiations."[33]

Specifically, the model affirmative action plan and the upgrade and transfer plan moved toward the following goals: moving 50,000 qualified women into higher-paying jobs, 10 percent of which would be in management; moving 6,600 qualified minority male employees into better jobs, 12 percent of which would be in management; seeking 6,000 qualified women to fill vacancies as installers, line workers, frame workers, and so on; and trying to fill 4,000 vacancies in operator and entry-level clerical jobs with men who qualified. The plan required annual progress reviews and modifications of goals as appropriate. "The agreement stipulates that two issues—the validity of Bell System testing procedures and the issue of sickness disability or other payments for pregnancy and childbirth—will be left for resolution in other forums."[34] AT&T internally reported on the GSA approval, concluding that "the agreement does not relate directly to the EEOC–Bell System case now in progress, but obviously gives further witness to Bell System efforts to comply fully with equal employment law."[35]

NOW, the IBEW, and the NAACP objected immediately to the GSA agreement. NOW's press release, put out on September 20, quoted Ann Scott on six "significant deficiencies" in the AT&T/GSA plan. Specifically, the plan failed in the following ways: no special relief, such as back pay, to women and minorities subjected to discrimination in the past; no "meaningful goals and timetables for the employment of females in outside craft jobs"; no "meaningful goals and timetables for the employment of males in operator and clerical jobs"; failure to adopt the EEOC maternity leave guidelines; failure to change testing practices that have an unfair impact on minorities; and failure of Bell companies in the South and Southwest—those with the worst records—to adopt accelerated goals and timetables for blacks and Spanish-surnamed Americans. Scott called the GSA's approval of the plan "nothing short of a sham."[36]

From her East Seventy-seventh Street apartment in Manhattan, Joan Hull got off a letter to Sally Hacker suggesting task force members write to Philip Davis, the acting director of the OFCC, demanding the AT&T plan be rejected. She told Hacker also about a task force member from Richmond, Virginia, who visited C&P Telephone Company offices to review their affirmative action plan. When she saw that the company listed four female executives, she asked for details, only to find out that those "executives" were chief operators.[37]

NOW joined with NAACP, MALDEF, and the Women's Legal Defense

Fund to hire David R. Cashdan of Berlin, Roisman, and Kessler to protest formally the "adequacy and lawfulness of the GSA agreement." Specifically, Cashdan argued, the agreement was not in line with Executive Order 11246 and Revised Order No. 4. Issues brought up were the absence of "relief" or back pay, wage transfer policy problems, the lack of advanced entry opportunities, low goals, disregard of barriers caused by invalid employment tests, lack of programs for the Chicano community, and the failure of the agreement to follow the EEOC's maternity leave policies.[38]

While the GSA did have the contract compliance role for government contractors on behalf of Labor's OFCC, it could be overruled by the Labor Department—and it was. After a meeting on Monday, September 25, with Richard Grunewald, assistant secretary for employment standards, Richard Schubert, then solicitor of Labor, and Phil Davis, William J. Kilberg, then associate solicitor for labor relations and civil rights, pulled the case into the office of the solicitor over the objection of Labor's own OFCC. Phil Davis wanted to support Ed Mitchell at GSA. Kilberg, based on his experience and input from his own civil rights network, felt more could be done. WEAL activist Bunny Sandler had come to talk with him about the case, arguing that GSA did not have a good agreement. He had to admit that the agreement did not go far enough.

If Kilberg could get Justice involved, the agencies together would have enough clout to truly transform business practices away from gender-specific jobs. That to him was the way to break barriers for women. Kilberg got David Rose at Justice to agree to bring an action in federal court and to work together with Labor and the EEOC to get a governmentwide agreement with AT&T. The OFCC participated, unhappily at first because of their frustration over the breakdown of the GSA agreement.[39]

Dave Easlick, in the midst of his presentation of the GSA deal to AT&T's board, was interrupted. The deal had died. How, he wondered, did the EEOC manage to derail such a carefully planned agreement?[40]

On September 29 Labor's OFCC formally notified Lilley that the affirmative action plan agreed to by GSA did not conform with Revised Order no. 4. The OFCC claimed jurisdiction henceforth for AT&T compliance.[41]

Ultimately Easlick issued his own orders to his negotiating team to settle the case once and for all. On October 17 Copus received a letter from AT&T requesting that negotiations resume.[42] By that time the coalition of government agencies was ready. The Department of Labor joined in weekly negotiations. Copus, Charles Wilson, and Jack Pemberton from the EEOC and the AT&T team sat at the table with, from Labor, Richard Schubert, William J. Kilberg, and Ronald M. Green from the Solicitors Office; Carin Ann Clauss, an associate solicitor for the Fair Labor Standards Office; and Karl W. Heckman, a counsel from the Fair Labor Standards Office.

Copus and Kilberg continued to try to get the CWA and IBEW unions involved in the settlement. Coming from a construction background and still carrying a union card, Kilberg had close connections with the unions. After the daily negotiation sessions, he would meet in the evening with Elihu Leifer and others from the IBEW to talk about how the proposed settlement terms might work.[43] Their entreaties for union participation paid off, with the IBEW petitioning to intervene on September 29. IBEW, however, limited its interests to "conditions, practices, programs or proposals of the New England Telephone Company which may affect collective bargaining agreements."[44] Denniston granted IBEW's petition. Copus continued to lobby the CWA by sending John Morgan, CWA's assistant to the president, a copy of the "EEOC analysis of Bell System plans approved by the GSA."[45]

Unaware of the intense fight between government agencies over the GSA agreement, Joan Hull and I had lunch together on September 29, cooking up more ways that NOW could influence the AT&T affirmative action plan. We talked about how the upgrade and transfer plan looked good on paper but might be difficult in implementation if all employees did not buy into it.[46] Ever mindful of NOW's budget and the personal costs, Hull suggested that Hacker try to hop on an AT&T company plane to fly east for her meeting with Lilley, which was then scheduled for October 25 at 2 P.M.[47] In October, NOW committed more funds to the AT&T project—Chicago NOW authorized expenses of $23.99 for their Bell Action Committee.[48]

AT&T's Public Affairs officers spent a lot more than $23.99 at their next meeting at the Marriott Camelback Inn in Scottsdale, Arizona. There for a week in October, the company's public affairs officers from all the Bell companies talked about the EEOC case, among many other issues. Lilley and Satterfield attended. Tom Scandlyn, assistant vice president for AT&T Federal Relations, reported on the EEOC case, providing key points and statistics from AT&T's testimony. He forecast what Bell's witnesses might say on the stand, what areas the EEOC would probably cover, and what they would try to establish. He expected the EEOC would challenge AT&T on BFOQs, employee benefits, training and upward mobility, affirmative action goals, the numbers of women in management, and other key issues.[49]

Scandlyn thought the EEOC would try to establish evidence of past discrimination in violation of the law. The EEOC could also be expected to argue the existence of affected classes, for example, female operators. AT&T would probably be accused of having plans that did not measure up to intent of the law. EEOC claims might reach to top Bell System executives' not being skilled or sensitive in equal employment matters or to an intentional failure to implement EEO plans. Looking ahead, Scandlyn estimated the case would drag on to an initial decision in December 1973 and an FCC order in the fall of 1974, quite possibly resulting in a detailed set of guidelines to insure compliance. When the discussion later covered pending legislation, the conference heard Washington Office staff updates on bills that would enhance the power of the EEOC. Senate Bill 2453 would give EEOC "cease and desist" enforcement powers. EEOC chairman William Brown had supported a different version, preferring to have power to apply for court enforcement orders. The conference reviewed the FCC Equal Employment Rules from August 1970 and discussed a range of Bell System employment practices in the context of affirmative action.[50]

During the fall of 1972, others interested in the case maneuvered to influence its outcome. NOW was especially active. On October 6 Whitney Adams attended a meeting in Washington for Ann Scott—a meeting between the EEOC task force on AT&T and the IBEW. The meeting covered an IBEW proposal regarding the transfer plan and "open bidding" for jobs. Adams felt the most beneficial part of the day was meeting Pat Cote, a union member in local 2307 representing all accounting employees in New England. Adams reported that Cote "is very much interested in working with NOW."[51] Another contact.

From Hacker in Iowa on October 6 came a long missive, a two-page NOW AT&T newsletter to the AT&T task force and other interested NOW leaders. Along with the newsletter was a raft of attachments and material to support events, especially a national fall action against the Bell System.[52] At its Everett, Washington, meeting in October, the National Executive Committee of NOW upped the ante, putting one hundred dollars more into the AT&T action proposed by Hacker.[53]

NOW representatives Heide, Scott, Hacker, Hull, and Betty Harragan finally met with Bob Lilley and Dave Easlick on October 25 at Lilley's twenty-sixth-floor office at 195 Broadway. Heide introduced her colleagues professionally—Shakespearian scholar Dr. Ann Scott, sociologist Dr. Sally Hacker, business manager Joan Hull, and herself as mother, Girl Scout leader, nurse, and teacher. Lilley listened intently. Easlick found the meeting confrontational, and he leaned forward aggressively.[54] Eventually Lilley would excuse Easlick from the office and talk alone with the NOW members.[55] This was no idle conversation. NOW had planned for months and had a firm agenda. They wanted answers from Lilley. They planned to bring up a relatively new threat—involving the Defense Department because of Bell Labs, Western Electric, and Sandia contracts. And they would press again for goals and timetables, maternity leave, child care, job posting and transfer/upgrading policies, and maybe, just maybe, presenting their bill for $4 billion.[56] Hacker had done her homework and provided the rest of the team with background information, including speeches from Chairman H. I. Romnes. She wanted to present demands to Lilley in writing and have the company respond.[57]

NOW issued a press release about their meeting with the AT&T officers, highlighting NOW's intent to "enlighten the corporate officers on the philosophy and goals" of NOW. The press release, which listed as contacts Ann Scott, Wilma Scott Heide, and Betty Harragan, described the two-hour meeting as the setting for NOW to denounce the GSA and AT&T agreement. When Heide demanded a "point-by-point" response from AT&T, Lilley pointed out that AT&T held a "firm position on the issue of back pay," adding that the company has an "emotional hang-up" on that matter. The press release points out that Scott replied to that, "So do we." Heide apparently told Easlick "the AT&T solution was part of the problem as long as men set up and try to implement affirmative action programs for women."[58]

Hacker drafted a letter to Lilley after the meeting and sent it on to the NOW national office to be typed and sent; the organization did have some staff support. In addition to reviewing the meetings, Hacker asked for specific responses regarding what she saw as deficiencies in the company's affirmative action program and upgrade and transfer plan. Also, she asked for specific data to do an analysis of the implications for women of changes in communications technology.[59]

In a self-assessment written for a NOW national action review, Hacker criticized herself for not using the regional and state structure of NOW for getting information out on the AT&T task force actions. She had discovered that two of the four regional directors did not know about an AT&T action until two days before it was to take place. NOW had grown so large it could no longer be organized on an ad hoc basis.[60] In spite of Heide's plan for a coordinated national organization, which she had discussed with me the year before, events demanded faster action than NOW could manage effectively. Much of NOW's efforts remained entrepreneurial.

At this point, Hacker was personally beginning to formulate a different charge against AT&T—that the company planned to phase out the very jobs women and minorities held. She researched the Iowa area of Northwestern Bell and believed the company planned "to phase out a good many women and minorities." She determined this by viewing the "changing occupational structure" of the company and the plan it had to "increase the number of jobs at the management, craft, and other skilled levels, while the actual number (not proportion) of jobs at entry-level-clerical, or as operators will be decreased." She determined also that "the faster increase in women in management positions than other jobs" that Iowa claimed "is due to the fact that the number of management positions are increasing faster than the jobs women usually hold which are in fact decreasing, not increasing in numbers." Hacker analyzed the data, claiming that AT&T only presented the data that made the company "look good."[61] Later (December 13) she would send a copy of her analysis of Iowa data to Copus.[62]

In her large mailing to the task force and local NOW chapters, Hacker included "leaflet material," providing content and useful statistics to the local chapters: she reminded them that in 1970, there were 31 million women in the labor force and 550,000 women in the Bell System. Thus one of every fifty-six working women worked for the Bell System.[63]

Only a few days later, on October 30, Kingsbury took the stand as AT&T's first witness. On the same day, Heide, Scott, and Hull were in Washington to meet with EEOC chairman Brown to talk about having sex discrimination a part of all charges and to urge him to issue a statement to his staff "that participation in civil rights activities by staff is a plus." From Brown's office, Heide, Scott, and Hull walked over to meet with members of the U. S. Commission on Civil Rights. The AT&T case was just one of their concerns.

Throughout November, AT&T witnesses flew to Washington, D.C., to testify in the EEOC case. NOW people were all over the country as well. Scott was in Seattle, where she described the plan AT&T filed with the GSA as a "whitewash" and "tokenism at its best." The plan was dead, but it showed to her that the company and some parts of government would settle for less than she thought was right. The *Seattle Post-Intelligencer* went on to quote Scott on the GSA's action, "The GSA's approval of the Bell System's program is nothing short of a sham." *Seattle Post-Intelligencer* writer Diana Montgomery claimed the GSA retracted its approval for further study after the criticism. Scott promised, according to the article, "NOW is going to keep watching the Department of Labor, the White House and AT&T to make sure they don't sneak anything past us."[64]

Hacker had not received a response from Lilley to her letter, so she called Don Liebers on November 14. He claimed to have been very busy and that his colleague Dan Davis had tried to reach her in New York. They discussed EEO data and how those data might be made available to her; the notes end with a "rushed off to catch a plane," but it isn't clear which of them was the one to head off so quickly—it could have been either.[65]

Other letters flew back and forth. From all over the country Bell women wrote to Hacker and Scott, describing their experiences with sex discrimination. Hull wrote to Brown at the EEOC as a follow-up to their meeting on October 30. Pointing out their common cause and general agreement, Hull urged the EEOC to be even more aggressive on several matters pending— sex-segregated advertising, for example, that was being pushed by Gerald Gardner in Pittsburgh. Hull praised the EEOC for its new guidelines on maternity leave and offered support for the coming budget hearings before the House Appropriations Committee. She reminded him that Heide's October 18 letter addressed to Brown and Roberta Romberg requesting EEO-1 data on the EEOC itself had not been answered; NOW again asked that "the EEOC give priority to the hiring, upgrading and better utilization of females."[66]

The EEOC's AT&T team found itself working hard on the case, supporting negotiations, and now having to respond to queries from other companies. On November 18 at the New York University Student Center just off Washington Square, Randy Speck discussed the AT&T case at a workshop on aspects of sex discrimination. The session was hosted by the New York City Commission on Human Rights, headed by Eleanor Holmes Norton. Liz Brydon attended, bringing her interest as an AT&T manager, AT&T Alliance for Women president, and a woman.[67]

In a tangentially related work, the futurist Alvin Toffler explained to AT&T how "movements" operated, "given to spontaneous, hard-to-predict surges of passion and actions." He described the structures of movements as "loose and adhocratic rather than bureaucratic and permanent." When it comes to tactics, Toffler advised, movements like the new consumer movement have "no strategy-making center and thus cannot easily concentrate all its energies on a single selected target." A movement "has the enormous advantage of being everywhere at once . . . is capable of harassing, applying social karate, and then vanishing only to appear again a few days later in some other part of the field."[68]

Writing in 1972, Toffler forecast for AT&T a world where old structures were replaced by a "highly novel" new environment. The routine would no longer be routine, and employees would be faced "with situations in which the implementation of an existing policy or procedure could lead to disaster. The individual is faced, in short, by situations in which he must *invent* a response." Changes in expectations and family structures led Toffler to predict "major changes in the needs and expectations of Bell's female employees, as is already apparent in their demands for more day care facilities and increased promotional opportunities."[69]

On November 19 Gene Kofke took the stand. Technically he represented New Jersey Bell as assistant vice president for personnel, but he was as knowledgeable a witness as any, having shepherded the case in his special assignment at AT&T. Extolling Lilley's actions as a previous president of New Jersey Bell, Kofke explained Lilley's action plans. He reiterated AT&T's good intentions as he reminded Denniston of the company's initiative in studying sex discrimination through internal task forces well before the case. He referred to his own 1971 memorandum outlining the work of the committee and promulgating guidelines on sex discrimination in the company. Under questioning he admitted that the committee's recommendations were not entirely accepted.[70]

On December 4, following Kofke, Wes Clarke represented Bell of Pennsylvania. Clarke reviewed personnel research, the impact of labor laws, and Bell of Pennsylvania's implementation of the Initial Management Development Program, which had its first woman in 1971.[71] Illinois Bell's Jack B. Gable, who had previous experience dealing with both internal feminists such as Harriet White and activists from Chicago NOW, testified.[72] One by one, the operating company vice presidents of personnel flew to Washington, were briefed by the legal team, coached by Satterfield, and escorted to the FCC hearing room. They came from all parts of the country to defend the Bell System.

9

CLOSING THE DEAL

With just two Bell witnesses remaining, Frederick Denniston recessed the hearings for the holidays, scheduling the next session for January 15, 1973. Behind-the-scene negotiations became intense.

NOW took no holiday, with a major action against AT&T in the works for January 3, 1973. On December 2 Sally Hacker and Toni Carabillo sent out an "AT&T Action & Press Kit." The intent? "Present NOW's bill on behalf of current and past women employees of Bell Telephone for back wages amounting to $4 billion." Heide and several other NOW leaders went to 195 Broadway again to meet with AT&T on January 5, 1973.[1] Nationally, NOW encouraged each local chapter to make an appointment with a local Bell official to discuss the company's affirmative action plan and gave details about what to look for. NOW members were encouraged to work with other activist groups—"union members, minority organization, peace groups"—but to keep the NOW identity and purpose. Street demonstrations and pickets were recommended. One suggestion was to find copies of the new AT&T ads portraying a woman on a telephone pole and a man as an operator, paste them on picket signs, and add, "Advertise less and *do* more." Hacker reminded her readers that AT&T expected record earnings for the year and that they operated "107 million telephones or 80% of all the phones in the nation."[2]

Meanwhile, AT&T and government negotiators huddled in Suite 712–714 at the Sheraton-Carlton at Sixteenth and K Streets in downtown Washington.[3] Bob Lilley himself had many reasons to be on hand in Washington—George Shultz, now secretary of the Treasury, appointed him chairman of the U.S. Industrial Savings Bond Committee on Thursday, December 7, 1972, and the two had a meeting on the next Monday.[4] On two or three occasions when talks with the EEOC stalled, Lilley met with Bill Brown alone, then they got their people together to tell them to go back and work things out. AT&T accepted the inevitability of back pay but still held out on certain changes in the business. Brown and Charles Wilson (EEOC general counsel) realized they could not be obstinate on every issue—they had to set priorities and sometimes to give in. Copus was not so ready to negotiate, believing strongly in their case's prospects. NOW pressured Brown to let them participate in the negotiations, but he refused. He felt there were too many areas in which people could disagree, and with too many negotiators an agreement would never be reached. He would have liked to have the union involved but could not convince them to participate.[5] Both the EEOC and AT&T's labor relations department kept the union informed about the negotiations.[6]

In New York, AT&T's top executives met in their "cabinet" to discuss progress on the case at 10 A.M. on Wednesday, December 18. At 9 A.M. on Thursday, Lilley had a private meeting with Gene Kofke, his hand-picked coordinator of the case.[7] AT&T wanted a settlement. On the government side, Copus never tired, but the rest wearied of the case. Negotiations moved from the Sheraton-Carlton to government offices, usually at Labor. Often Wilson and Lee Satterfield would walk back to their offices together, developing what would become a long-term friendship. As the negotiations stalled again, Wilson suggested that AT&T's agreement would constitute compliance with all the agencies involved. After other negotiation sessions, Wilson walked back to the EEOC with Copus, trying to make him see the value of a consent decree over continuing the case.[8] A trained negotiator, Wilson kept the process moving; Jack Pemberton, with his calm demeanor, kept discussions on track. Copus focused on content, consulting when he needed to with NOW and other civil rights leaders.[9]

On what turned out to be the last day of negotiations, Lilley asked Satterfield to call Brown. Lilley wanted to know if Brown had set a deadline and how serious he was. Lilley was having a difficult time with the Bell company presidents and wanted to push off the decision until he could get more support. Lilley told Satterfield he had met with Brown enough to know that if Brown said this was his cutoff date, it was. Brown told Satterfield that they'd gone back and forth enough. If the settlement didn't go through this time, he meant to take the case back to Denniston. Agreement was reached on December 28, 1972.[10]

After working day and night for months, the EEOC team could relax. Marjanette Feagan, a secretary and partner in the project, invited the team to a Superbowl VII party at her home in Washington. There in the Feagan's finished basement, with food and beer, they watched the Washington Redskins lose to the Miami Dolphins on January 14, 1973.

Some doubted Copus would stick with the deal, but he did. In general, Copus felt AT&T negotiators were motivated to settle because the company wanted "to do the right thing."[11] AT&T had agreed ultimately to the most contentious points—goals and timetables for men in operator positions and back pay. Maternity leave, however, did not make the final agreement, though it had been an issue Copus and Lilley both supported.[12]

The teams from AT&T, the EEOC, the FCC, and Justice sent copies of their proposed agreement to IBEW and CWA officers. The CWA still wanted no part of the agreement; Richard Hackler, the assistant to the president of CWA, told Solicitor of Labor Richard Schubert that the CWA wished no active involvement with any government agency; they wanted to negotiate with AT&T directly. The CWA board would meet on January 12 and then allow Hackler to meet with Schubert again—the date set was January 15. Even then, the CWA would hold firm, willing to negotiate only with AT&T. When word of a settlement reached the CWA, they wanted the settlement held up pending their negotiations with AT&T. The CWA's leader, Joseph Beirne, sent a letter to Rex Reed, head of labor negotiations at AT&T, asking for "immediate negotiations" on the transfer program and other settlement issues.[13]

Once the negotiating teams reached an agreement in principle, AT&T called in outside counsel Thompson Powers to put it into its final legal form. William Kilberg, associate solicitor for Labor, and Carin Clauss, associate solicitor for the Fair Labor Standards Division, joined the group in composing an interagency press release.[14]

With minimal time to actually write the agreement, Powers called on two colleagues, Jim Hutchison and Nick Cunningham, at Steptoe and Johnson.[15] The final version was reviewed by Levy, Ashley, Garlinghouse (by this time AT&T's chief counsel); Justice; Labor; and the EEOC. Powers knew Brown wanted a settlement that established a process, and he built that into the document. AT&T's board met on January 17 and its executive policy committee on January 18; after those meetings, Easlick joined the group in Washington, where a Memorandum of Agreement was signed, with ceremony, by Easlick for AT&T, Brown for the EEOC, and Schubert for Justice.

Up to the last minute, Powers and the AT&T staff worked on the consent decree documents at 2000 L Street. Powers handed a copy of the drafts to David Rose, the Justice Department attorney, who made last-minute changes.

Signing the Memorandum of Agreement. Front row, left to right: David K. Easlick, AT&T; William H. Brown III, EEOC; Richard F. Schubert, Department of Labor; back row: Lee A. Satterfield, AT&T; William J. Kilberg, Department of Labor; Karl W. Heckman, Department of Labor.

Rainstorms pelted the airport and commercial flights were delayed. Both AT&T and the government team flew to Philadelphia together on AT&T's plane.[16]

In Philadelphia, the complaint, answer, proposed consent decree, and Memorandum of Agreement were presented to the Honorable A. Leon Higginbotham Jr., U.S. District Court for the Eastern District of Pennsylvania. Technically, charges had been filed in three federal jurisdictions—New York, Philadelphia, and Washington; Bernard Segal, Bell of Pennsylvania's counsel, suggested Philadelphia as the site for the decree.[17] Higginbotham granted judicial approval of the agreement, and the settlement was announced. The judge's review was not perfunctory, however, and Higginbotham lived up to his reputation as a careful and thorough judge who raised many questions.[18] He kept the lawyers in conference until well after five o'clock, when the air conditioning shut off and the room became warm. It was warm for the government lawyers, especially, as they thought about the press release that even then was hitting Washington ahead of the court's action.[19]

The transcript of the proceedings notes that David Rose, who represented the Justice Department that day before Judge Higginbotham, commended the EEOC and the Labor Department, as well as AT&T and its subsidiaries, for their "large step forward" in what he perceived was the first time a private company and all relevant government agencies worked together.[20]

Ashley noted that after "extensive and intensive negotiations," AT&T has "what we believe will be a very equitable settlement of our responsibilities, and we are anxious to advance the cause of equal opportunity through our affirmative action programs."[21] In his closing remarks, Higginbotham thanked all involved for their cooperation and commended them on their "very, very significant effort," then commented particularly on the role of those in government service:

> I want to commend all of the lawyers for what appears to have been Herculean efforts to reach a rational agreement on a difficult problem with an assurance that the past errors of deprivations will be eradicated. Particularly to those lawyers and similar employees in the government service, I know that when accepting the choice of working in the public sector they sometimes forego the more lucrative financial options available in the private sector. From personal observation I also know that the life of a government lawyer in the human rights field often is not one of total joy and occasionally consists of substantial grief because of frustration in reaching these goals with promptness and substance. Yet, you must know that your concern for improving the quality of life in our society for all, where the variables of race, religion, national origin or sex will not be a deterrent, constitutes an important mission.
>
> I commend chairman William H. Brown III, and all of his associates and those other persons of the public sector as well as the parties in the private sector for any efforts which they have made there and will make elsewhere to see that the lofty dreams of equal opportunities for all become an immediate reality.[22]

The next day, the EEOC went through the formality of filing a motion to terminate proceeding in Docket 19143, and on January 25 Denniston postponed the hearings indefinitely.[23] Not every party agreed with the settlement—

CULA and the Harlem Consumer Education Council filed opposition based on the fact that no "party representing the interest of Bell workers was allowed to negotiate."[24] The CWA filed a motion to intervene, which Higginbotham denied on October 5, 1973, outlining all the opportunities the CWA earlier had to get involved.

AT&T, at this point having committed itself to the settlement, took on the defense of the consent decree.[25] AT&T's Easlick, queried by *Telecommunications Week* about the cost of the decree, indicated that the settlement would not lead to additional rate cases. "In his prepared statement, the AT&T official said that the Bell companies will carry out their affirmative action programs, and the 'more precise understanding of what the law requires in the employment opportunity field,' including the provision of 'equity payments to selected individuals, in a sound, business-like way.' "[26]

In a statement to the Bell company presidents, AT&T chairman John deButts stressed:

> *Two aspects of last week's agreement need to be clearly understood:*
> *—First, we have committed ourselves to nothing beyond what is right and what the law requires.*
> *—And second, qualifications remain the fundamental criteria for advancement in our business, as they must if we are to continue to fulfill our service responsibilities to the public.*
> *Having said that, however, I would like to emphasize my personal conviction that firm and fair implementation of our commitments under this agreement will make us a stronger business as a consequence. What I am sure you recognize is that we have committed ourselves in good faith to goals that will require not only good faith but hard work to accomplish. Therefore, now is not too soon to undertake the programs of practical action that will insure those goals are fulfilled.*
> *It has been a point of pride with us that what the Bell System sets out to do it does. This tradition applies no less to our equal employment undertakings than to any other aspect of our business. Thus I am sure I can count on your readiness and that of your colleagues in Bell System management to do all you can to assure that we meet not only the letter of last week's agreement but its spirit as well.*

The back pay cost of $15 million translated to less than two cents per share, since there were more than 549 million AT&T shares outstanding among more than three million shareowners at the time of the agreement. The company intended to cover the approximately $23 million promotion pay plan and other adjustments through earnings growth.[27]

Easlick feted Clark Redick, Dan Davis, and Lee Satterfield—the AT&T negotiating team—and their spouses with dinner in New York at the Four Seasons and gave them Steuben bowls to commemorate the occasion. The case was settled, the mission accomplished.[28] The EEOC had its own celebration, at which team members received "superior performance awards" and "a little cash" for their efforts.[29]

In its January 18 press release, NOW expressed "mixed" feelings. NOW found unacceptable the less-than-"equitable" back pay settlement, the lack of compliance with maternity leave guidelines, and the less-than-"adequate" goals and timetables. The $15 million in back pay was termed "chicken feed." The issue in maternity leave was AT&T's refusal "to treat employee disabilities caused by pregnancy as temporary disabilities under any health or temporary disability insurance or sick leave plan." Still, NOW applauded the agreement as better than the earlier GSA agreement, noting that the agreement "signals the beginning" of AT&T's move to become "a model employer in equal employment opportunity." NOW promised to continue its "creative actions and monitoring."[30]

In Scott's personal notes, she recorded a discussion she had with Hull, Stults, Copus, Conroy, and Hacker. Among the ideas for follow-up were pursuing state attorney general actions, encouraging fifty thousand women to apply for the new opportunities at Bell companies, working with Bell women to take advantage of settlement provisions, getting information out about the decree, working with the union, and figuring out how to organize "fearful women."[31]

On January 19 Lilley headed to Washington for a different event—Richard M. Nixon's second inauguration.[32] Meanwhile, Satterfield hosted a party in his mostly finished basement for both the AT&T and the government teams. At the party Copus was given one of NOW's recent ads—featuring a pregnant man—and asked if he was finally satisfied. AT&T's lawyers gave the EEOC lawyers autographed copies of the famed female installer and male operator ads.

Though they could enjoy each other's company that night in Washington, the AT&T team found that when they returned to normal life in the company, they were not welcomed back as conquering heroes. When Easlick and Satterfield described the settlement to deButts and the Bell Company presi-

The EEOC's AT&T team. Lawrence J. Gartner, Marjorie Feagan, David A. Copus, Randall L. Speck, William O. Wallace.

Photograph property of Randall L. Speck and reprinted with his permission.

dents, they initially received a strong negative reaction. With the chief counsel, Mark Garlinghouse, speaking for the agreement, however, the deed was done.[35]

NOW and government representatives went on the speakers' trail. A panel of the major players appeared at the NOW national conference in Washington, and NOW celebrated its victory. NOW members who were also Bell System employees gathered at the conference to talk about the implications of the decree. There for the first time I met Lorena Weeks, the Southern Bell woman who won the switchman job. Joan Hull coordinated a workshop on AT&T that included Copus, Conroy, Hacker, Stults, and Israel.[34] In a newsletter to the NOW Compliance and Enforcement Task Force, Hull summarized what was discussed and followed up with employment sex discrimination strategies so the chapters could continue their efforts.[35]

Back in Manhattan at 195 Broadway, Easlick met with our AT&T Alliance for Women leaders in March, preparing for Lilley's formal meeting with the alliance membership on March 28, 1973.[36] Another major alliance program was the slide show on women in advertising that had been suggested at the party months before. Alliance president Barbara J. Colbert reported to the members on alliance projects in the works with the company, including an extensive research project on employee attitudes about women in the work environment.[37]

NOW's Task Force on AT&T set new priorities, including "fighting sexism at Bell Labs and Western Electric."[38] In a letter to Lilley soon after the settlement, Heide reminded him of the promise he made to her in the October meeting: "If I can be of any help to you, let me know." She asked him to "educate the American public" through national public affairs programming on the topics of the ERA, affirmative action, and child care.[39] Letters continued to go back and forth—Hacker to Copus, Liebers to Heide, Heide to Liebers, and so on. Heide was asked to write an article on "what is a feminist" for the Bell Telephone corporate magazine.[40]

On March 12, 1973, Denniston called the parties back once more to the FCC hearing room at 1919 M Street. With him that day were Copus (EEOC), Levy and Powers (AT&T), James M. Paulson and Elihu Q. Leifer (IBEW), and Jim Juntilla, Daniel Morper, and Giovanna Longo (FCC). After handling details, such as getting official copies of the actual agreement, Denniston wanted to discuss the monetary effect of the agreement. Copus summarized the three key elements of the agreement—the affirmative action program, the upgrade and transfer plan, and the back pay/financial restitution section. The amounts involved, he noted, were only estimates—it was not yet known how many individuals would receive payments or how large those payments would be.[41] Copus drew attention to a few unresolved issues—working conditions, for example—that were "not amenable to civil rights legislation." On maternity leave, he noted that AT&T was in compliance on the matter of when leave would be taken and for how long; what AT&T did not agree to was the disability provision.

Denniston raised a question related to the original intervention—the question of whether discriminatory practices of a company affect revenues or expenses or otherwise affect rates. Juntilla replied that witnesses who testified on that matter had not been rebutted and thus the record could stand. He admitted, however, that the record was probably "not definitive" on the matter. All agreed the issue had been discussed in a hypothetical or illustrative way.[42] In closing the case, Denniston stated:

> I do think it is appropriate to make the comment that my personal observation was that there was a very high degree and high caliber of cooperation between counsel in the case, and certainly it was a case that had sufficient counter views that if there had not been that full cooperation, it could have been a very sticky proceeding. I want to thank everyone associated with it.[43]

In his order issued April 9, 1973, Denniston closed the record. At this point he released New York Telephone from its obligation to report on disciplinary actions regarding witnesses who testified or were scheduled to testify, and formally accepted the settlement. The order (FCC 73M-434) reviews the entire case in detail and describes the terms of the settlement, the parties to the agreement, and the extent to which AT&T could rely on the plans and provisions of the agreement as compliance with the relevant laws. "The present settlement, or Memorandum of Agreement, brings Bell into complete harmony with the present requirements of EEOC and of the OFCC, with one minor exception." (That exception had to do with an "area of disagreement" over testing and training, but AT&T ultimately accepted it.) The FCC's findings were that, "upon implementation of the agreement," Bell System companies would be in compliance "with the Civil Rights Act of 1964, as amended, and with the requirements of Revised Order No. 4 of the Office of Federal Contract Compliance, Department of Labor, and existing regulations." And, importantly, Denniston wrote, "The extent to which past practices of the Bell System Companies have been in violation of applicable equal employment requirements cannot be determined, but, while denying any violations, those companies have agreed to make retroactive payments, estimated to total $15 million."[44]

In its first section, the AT&T and EEOC consent decree detailed the required affirmative action and upgrade and transfer programs, goals and timetables, transfer promotion, layoff and recall procedures, employee information, testing, promotion pay plans, treatment of female college graduates hired into management, and pay adjustments. The decree went on to establish reporting and compliance procedures. Officially, the term of the decree was six years. The EEOC provided a document, "How Women Can Take Advantage of the AT&T Settlement," to alert Bell System women nationwide of the "significant elements" of the settlement and to tell them how to get further information.[45]

NOW provided a detailed, annotated summary of the settlement, with "reactions, report from the National Conference, and The Long, Hard Road Ahead."[46] A victory in such a large case would reward the volunteers and keep up the energy level of the chapters across the country. Local NOW chapters would build on success and use the experience to challenge other companies.

Not long after the decree, Brown met with Lilley and the president of Western Electric. Western was on the EEOC's list, and Lilley warned the Western president to have a good look at the agreement.[47] By September 1974 Western Electric would also agree to a settlement involving back pay.[48]

In 1974 reviews of AT&T's performance indicated that some goals were not being met, though overall the Bell companies met over 90 percent of intermediate targets. With much less sound and fury the negotiations led to a supplemental agreement between the EEOC and AT&T, an agreement that on May 13, 1975, was entered at the U.S. District Court in Philadelphia.[49]

This second decree, with a term of five years, established a management promotion pay plan and granted back pay awards. The *Wall Street Journal* interpreted the decree as setting aside "$7 million in back pay to 7,000 management employees" and adjusting wages "by $23 million over the next year to compensate for pay discrimination."[50] Oversight of the decree's implementation would be handled by a government coordinating committee including the EEOC, Labor, Justice, and the GSA.[51] The supplemental agreement established a different method for evaluating progress based on the first year's experience and emphasized the need for application on the "affirmative action/override," to be used in certain cases to select "basically qualified candidates."[52]

The case was settled; AT&T had started on the long road of implementation, and women and minorities were beginning to take advantage of new opportunities.

The "cause" of equal opportunity was not over, however, and NOW pressed on. Hacker communicated with local NOW chapters and with women inside AT&T on several issues: helping women file complaints if the company did not live up to its commitment, working to resolve maternity leave, and reviewing the occupational structure of the telecommunications industry. As a follow-up to the AT&T workshop at NOW's 1973 national conference, Hacker wrote, "The consensus of the AT&T workshop was to turn efforts now toward helping women at Bell gain strength and solidarity within caucuses at the workplace, in the union, or professional/technical organizations."[53]

In the early weeks of April, both Copus and Heide found time in their travels to stop in Des Moines to see Hacker. Soon thereafter, Hacker reported to Copus that she had received a grant from the Ford Foundation to study automation's effects on women workers in four major Iowa industries, including the telephone company. The case was over, but not the cause. She noted that AT&T's Don Liebers had written to Heide, asking if NOW wanted to meet with him.[54]

On the same day as her letters to NOW chapters and to Copus, Hacker wrote to me suggesting that I write about organizing management women. She asked also for information that would help her understand AT&T's plans for new technology. She was beginning to look at satellite communication, fiber optics, and the impact of automation on jobs and people.[55] To Hacker, automation was important. In her view, "technological changes happen a hell of a long time before unions or the law or anybody else gets around to dealing with the effects."[56]

The *Wall Street Journal* continued to cover the story of women in management, reporting on the New York Telephone settlement with the state's Division of Human Rights.[57] Other companies came into the *Journal's* spotlight — Exxon, Chrysler, General Motors, and Dow Chemical. In a front-page story on April 18, 1974, staff reporter Mary Bralove covered success stories but noted that "few women are progressing beyond the middle level." Women represented less than 1 percent of the officials, managers and professionals in twenty major corporations studied. And the number of women graduate and doctoral business students had only risen to 5.5 percent from the 3.1 percent it was five years before.[58]

In May *Business Week* covered "a flurry of job bias cases." Brown at the

EEOC credited the AT&T settlement as the "single most powerful goad toward corporate housecleaning of biased policies."[59] After interviewing those of us involved, Lisa Cronin Wohl, in November's *Ms.* magazine, wrote "Liberating Ma Bell," reviewing the AT&T case. She put the $15 million settlement into perspective by comparing it with AT&T's earnings that year of $2.5 billion. Brown, Copus, Scott, Kilberg, Heide, Hacker, Lilley, Kofke, and Liebers all added to her story.[60]

On January 30, 1974, Lilley spoke to the National Press Club in Washington about AT&T's position given that large institutions were being challenged on almost every front. As he focused on issues such as monopoly, competition, and the public interest, he noted, "Surely no other organization—public or private—has been more carefully scrutinized on a continuing basis than has the Bell System." And, he noted, "the company welcomed the scrutinizing but did not necessarily enjoy it." As an example, he described the EEOC case. That charge did not seem fair to AT&T at the time; "when the smoke had cleared, however—when time had tempered and assuaged our bruised feelings—we reached an agreement with the EEOC that meets its objectives and our objectives because it was simply right and proper."[61]

10

POSTSCRIPT

G raidually after January 1973 the entangled lives of AT&T officers, NOW activists, and government lawyers separated.

With the decree signed, AT&T set about implementing the decree in the same organized, systematic way it implemented any policy. John deButts and the lawyers turned to other serious issues, and the work of equal opportunity fell back into the hands of human resources staff and managers throughout the business. Headquarters groups focused on staffing programs, such as upgrade and transfer, that would become the structured paths for employees to take advantage of opportunities created by the decree. Staffs assumed measurement and monitoring responsibilities. Headquarters communicated with the Bell companies, as they always had, through conferences, letters, and "Bell System Practices." The requirements of the decree became part of normal operations. Don Liebers knew that people would not always be positive about these programs and that some people might "get hurt." Nonetheless, he saw "no other way."[1]

Units of the Bell System settled local cases. For example, New York Telephone agreed to terms with New York State's Division of Human Rights, promising to promote women from 20 percent to 57 percent of management vacancies. At the time of settlement, only 30 of New York Telephone's 1,008 district managers were female, one of its 280 division levels, and one of the 80 department heads above that.[2]

The "delayed restitution" part of the EEOC settlement meant continued efforts to identify women affected by discrimination. The idea that a company would have to make payments to those who did not seek promotion because of known barriers was a new approach.

Reactions from other businesses varied. "There's a lot of teeth-chattering going on around here," a retail business executive told *Newsweek* just after the settlement. And Ruth Bader Ginsburg, then a Columbia professor and ACLU lawyer, noted, "Most companies will take guidelines a little more seriously now." Barbara Boyle discussed the AT&T case in a *Harvard Business Review* article entitled "Equal Opportunity Is Smart Business" and launched her own company to help the business world adapt.[3] NOW's Ann Scott continued to call the settlement "chicken feed" and put business on notice that NOW would be vigilant.[4]

NOW turned to other targets, though Sally Hacker would personally continue to investigate AT&T. The NOW Compliance and Enforcement Task Force coordinated by Joan Hull sent out a newsletter in March 1973 that provided updates on the AT&T consent decree and strategies for chapters to use locally. Included was a list of "not NOW corporations" that NOW was pursuing either directly through lawsuits or by supporting those who had filed. The list included Brandeis University, Celanese, Gulf Oil, Hofstra University, Montgomery Ward, Pillsbury, Sperry Rand, the IBEW, and Xerox.[5]

After the consent decree, the government coordinating committee (EEOC, Labor, Justice, and GSA) reviewed progress annually with AT&T's human resources development department. In 1973 alone, they found a 25 percent increase in women at second-level management and above, a 34 percent increase in blacks, and a 27 percent increase in Spanish-surnamed employees at that level. Women in craft jobs increased 78 percent, blacks 13 percent, and Spanish-surnamed 22 percent. AT&T reported an 81 percent increase in males in clerical and operator positions. Though the percent growth seemed large, the actual numbers were still small, however, and "interim targets were not met for many job classifications in many companies."[6] Implementing a decree for a national business with about 800,000 people was by its nature a slow, difficult process.

After the 1973 numbers were reviewed, the government committee determined that an "affirmative action override" needed to be encouraged, and a letter signed by all the relevant government agencies was sent to AT&T and the Bell operating companies requiring "seniority provisions of applicable collective bargaining agreements be overridden where necessary to meet intermediate targets." The 1974 review showed "substantial improvement," and the government chose not to do onsite reviews that year; instead they developed a detailed supplemental action program with AT&T.[7]

Gradually the AT&T numbers would change at even the higher levels. Between 1968 and 1982 the numbers of women increased, though not reaching goals at all levels and in all jobs. In 1982 growth at fourth and fifth levels was even more significant because the total number of employees actually decreased as cost-cutting measures were introduced. I tracked progress at higher levels by using the company's "Answerback Program," which allowed an employee to ask questions about the business. Periodically from 1971 until 1983 I would ask about the numbers and even the names of women at fifth level and above and the names of female board members; the company dutifully provided them. Table 5 shows growth in numbers from 1968 to 1982.

TABLE 5: GROWTH IN NUMBERS, 1968-82

Level	Total Bell System						
	1968	**1972**	**1975**	**1977**	**1978**	**1980**	**1982**
Third-level male	9,363	10,666	10,622	10,892	11,186	11,678	9,685
Third-level female	120	288	633	953	1,240	1,593	1,579
Fourth-level male	3,023	3,137	3,031	3,097	3,138	3,251	3,256
Fourth-level female	13	26	37	56	80	116	168
Fifth-level male	1,099	1,158	1,098	1,131	1,156	1,189	1,080
Fifth level female	3	6	6	10	13	21	23
Above-fifth male	368	376	372	393	405	434	396
Above-fifth female	0	0	2	2	3	5	5

Source: *AT&T Answerback* no. 9051 (April 20, 1983).

In 1984, as the result of yet another consent decree, this one to settle an antitrust case, the Bell System units parted company. Bell Laboratories and Western Electric ceased to exist as separate wholly owned subsidiaries of AT&T. Components of these organizations and AT&T headquarters were retained in a newly organized AT&T or spun off into a newly created Bellcore.[8] The Bell companies were spun off into seven regional companies, which have since been involved in a variety of divestitures, mergers, and acquisitions. The entire telecommunications industry exploded, forming and reforming corporate entities with tremendous impact on workforce composition. Thus, numbers cannot easily be compared; the AT&T of today is not the AT&T of 1970.

Not all corporations were happy that AT&T had settled its case with innovative personnel practices. Over time, however, many corporations adopted the new practices either because they saw value in set procedures or because they wished to avoid the public embarrassment AT&T had endured.

Brown left the EEOC chairmanship late in 1973. Before he left, the EEOC filed suit against twenty companies, including General Motors, General Electric, Sunshine Biscuits, the Metropolitan Life Insurance Company, and Phillip Morris. Having garnered new respect within government and in the private sector, the EEOC was a much stronger agency than it had been in December 1970, when the AT&T case began. Nearly four hundred lawyers and support people had been hired for regional litigation centers.[9] In addition, the process of settling with AT&T had broken new ground by promoting coordination within government of the agencies regulating equal employment. A new era of enforcement had begun.

In local settings, NOW chapters kept their contact with Bell companies, continuing to monitor the implementation of affirmative action.[10] Nationally, NOW went through intense leadership challenges and internal fights over priorities. No other corporate target caught the imagination or fury of a full NOW attack.

Women inside AT&T increased their feminist activities for a while, emboldened by the company's acceptance of the decree. The AT&T Alliance for Women prospered until 1977, when it was structurally weakened by AT&T's move of a large portion of its staff out of New York City to Basking Ridge, New Jersey. Women's groups formed and dissolved within the company, paralleling the external women's movement. The alliance also suffered from the chaos created by growing competition in the telecommunications industry and ultimately by the divestiture that resulted from the antitrust case. During its prime, the alliance had pushed the company into job posting for management positions, held career fairs to educate women on available career paths inside the business, sponsored outside speakers to help the education process, served as a visible reminder of women's issues, and most important, created a support network for women.

Immediately after the case, women's rights groups expanded elsewhere in the Bell System. At Bell Laboratories alone there were nine groups in six locations. In addition to providing a support system for the women involved, these groups analyzed personnel polices regarding career mobility, child care, and maternity leave, still unresolved issues in business. One group of managers at Bell Labs documented how it felt to be a woman in the affirmative action meetings and shared some of the "negative climate" in which they found themselves. Candidly they described the burdens and risks pioneer women carried.[11]

Though we still talked about discrimination, many of us were determined to succeed. We knew we had the structural support of the law, but that did not solve all our problems. Day in, day out we had to find our way through a maze of old and new behaviors. We made some careless assumptions after the case that barriers were down and that all we had to do was work on our own careers. I went to Washington as part of an Executive Exchange Program, which I saw as a launching pad for a plan to take me to the executive suite by 2000. While in Washington, I did not contact NOW or any of the other activists from the case. I was too caught up in the glamour of the "executive" exchange. On a cocktail napkin there in Washington, I plotted my ambitious path to CEO.

I underestimated the barriers and overestimated my ability, though I did successfully pass through several assignments in New York City telephone plant operations, a finance position at AT&T, a management role in executive seminars, and several key positions in sales and marketing. I was encouraged to soft-pedal my feminist rhetoric, and I did. Then, in 1984, divestiture split apart my experience base and cut me off from many of my mentors. Still, I reached fourth level before taking an early retirement of my own free will in 1990.

Women continued to join together in formal and informal groups. New York Telephone's Women's Network, formed in 1980, would become the NYNEX Women's Network when the Bell System was split, and later would evolve into another organization to which I belonged, the Association of Management Women (AMW) In 1987 the NYNEX company publication covered "Changing Corporate Attitudes" regarding women in the workplace, noting that women were dispelling myths and taking advantage of new opportunities. The greatest change was seen at third level and above, where the numbers had doubled since 1977, and in crafts, where the number of women had tripled. Still, the company acknowledged, "there is room for improvement, especially at or near the top."[12] In the 1990s, after NYNEX merged with Bell Atlantic to form Verizon, AMW became WAVE — Women's Association for Verizon Employees.

Telecommunications industry trade publications also noticed changes, and in June 1988 *Telephony* reported that women were "confident, comfortable in powerful new roles." Telling the stories of leading women in the increasingly competitive industry, the article credits not just the "landmark agreements" but also divestiture itself as having "spurred dramatic changes." Bell Atlantic reported its first female corporate officer—Carolyn S. Burger. Pacific Bell reported women in "seven of the 62 senior management posts." Ameritech had 11 women out of "187 senior people." NYNEX had 13 of 173, and Bell South reported 14 percent of its "1,495 senior managers."[13]

The changes in the business were not ignored by scholars. Phyllis Wallace published a thorough review of the case itself and dedicated the book to "William H. Brown III and all who worked with him on the AT&T case. Their work resulted in a 'quantum jump' for equal employment opportunity."[14] In a study done at Wharton, Herbert R. Northrup and John A. Larson reviewed the impact of the decree and results through 1979. Northrup and Larson describe "radical shifts in the manner in which the Bell System handled its employee relations" and studied the impact of the decree on "quality of the workforce, organizational structure, the role of the supervisor, discipline, employee attitudes, and union relations." While acknowledging the company's success in implementing the decree, the study claims resultant problems, conflicts, and costs.[15] No stranger to the case, Northrup had been hired in 1973 by the National Association of Manufacturers when they built their case against affirmative action on the basis of the cost and its impact on industry.[16]

Thirty years have passed since NOW's witness Ann Scott responded to Frederick Denniston's queries about the future. When she testified, "affirmative action" was still an untried concept. If "the aim of the affirmative action is a rough parity in the employment profile of a company with the population," as she claimed, the Bell companies did make progress over the years. Scott viewed goals and timetables as "self-destruct" tools to reach parity. Scott said she expected parity by 1985, though she believed all discrimination would not be gone by then and NOW would still be in business. Scott died of cancer in 1976, never able to see the results of her efforts. She chose to fight for women's employment rights on a national scale. She could have stayed in academia or confined her fight to changing academic opportunities for women. But she chose the larger fight. At Scott's memorial service, Representative Pat Schroeder described how Scott's "political strategy for feminism was founded on a profound faith in the power of women when they are organized and an abiding belief that the freedom of women is indivisible from economic and social freedom for all people."[17]

Bob Lilley, from his established position of power as president of AT&T, quietly and firmly chose to deal with the issues of the 1970s, including race and sex discrimination. At a memorial service for Lilley in 1986, Michael I. Sovern, then president of Columbia University, said that Lilley "built bridges of understanding." Sovern continued, "Bob Lilley approached every problem and every challenge with modesty, with compassion, with patience, devotion, wisdom, courage, and absolute intellectual integrity." Lilley's son Robert Mc-Gregor Lilley said of his father, "He brought dignity to the things he touched, and he conferred it on those with whom he dealt. His power was subtle, almost oriental, in his care to save the face of others." William J. McGill, president of Columbia during the tumultuous 1970s, relied on Lilley, a trustee, for his skill at "conflict resolution" and noted at the memorial service, "Because of his innate decency and his stability in crisis, Mr. Lilley had an intuitive power not only to solve problems but to evoke grudging admiration from those who deemed themselves his adversaries. Accordingly, in the kind of struggle I am describing [student riots], he emerged almost immediately as a leader, bridging differences that no one imagined could be compromised, and managed to heal wounds where most of us saw only ugly scars. . . . He was the soul of reason and patience. I never met a more determined man."[18]

Bill Brown, at the EEOC, had a personal style similar to Lilley's, but there the similarities ended. Brown led an underdog agency in the highly charged political environment of Washington during Nixon's administration. A Philadelphian by birth, Brown served in the Army Air Force in the Pacific before getting his bachelor's degree from Temple and his law degree from another Philadelphia school—the University of Pennsylvania. Starting out as an associate attorney with Norris, Schmidt, Green, Harris, and Higginbotham, Brown moved to the Philadelphia district attorney's office and from there to the EEOC. More visible than Lilley, Brown lobbied for his cause—before the House and Senate, on television and radio, in press interviews and conferences. Brown watched over the AT&T case, sometimes frustrated that he could not step in and argue the case himself, especially since he had more trial experience than his staff. He played a different role, however, and became a counterpart to Lilley—confident, knowledgeable, and savvy.

Lilley for AT&T, Brown for the EEOC, and Scott for NOW brought reason, determination, and savvy to their roles as enablers. Aggressive action on the part of Heide, Copus, Hacker, and hundreds of other individuals made it happen.

The women's liberation movement of that era distrusted individually strong leaders, preferring a collective approach. Scott, Heide, and Hacker had to work within that framework, constantly communicating with NOW members across the country. With these leaders were individuals willing to dedicate extraordinary resources, time, and effort to the cause. Women who did not know Lorena Weeks or work for the Bell companies, or work for any corporation for that matter, came out to the rallies and protests.

The AT&T case also took over the lives of innocent bystanders—Ashley, Levy, Denniston, and others—to the point that they too became indistinguishable from the cause-driven in their dedication of time and personal commitment to the case. For many it would be the most memorable, most meaningful work they ever did.

Neither NOW nor the EEOC began this case with formal power. NOW activists created power—out of information, from their creative use of dispersed coordinated actions, through their persistence, and with audacity. Both NOW and the EEOC leveraged power through affiliations with individuals and other groups. After the case, the EEOC wielded more power than before, and NOW was known as a force to be reckoned with. This was not their only collaboration, but it was the one with the most far-reaching implications for affirmative action.

The intent of the architects of affirmative action, as evidenced in this case, was to structure the personnel practices of business to help corporations achieve a goal of equity. Specifically for the case, the goal was to ensure that equal opportunity existed within AT&T and to make sure the company lived up to the law. Within AT&T, goals and timetables were set, as they would have been for any business project, and a measurement system was set up to evaluate progress and redirect efforts as necessary. AT&T already had management systems in place—the overlay of affirmative action, though painful to some individuals, was perhaps easier than it would have been in a less structured operation.

The impact of the case can be debated, as can the question of how fundamental change occurs. What is apparent is that a major corporation was forced to change significantly. That change would not have happened without all of the players—internal agents for change, external activists, and government pressures. Perhaps over time or after other examples, AT&T would still have adopted the strong affirmative action program it did, but change could not have been so quick, so comprehensive, or so influential.

The case and its aftermath touched millions of lives—employees, managers, families, friends, shareowners, and others. In dollars, the case cost millions and caused more millions to be spent. Did the EEOC prove that discrimination cost telephone ratepayers, as was originally claimed? Not really, though it was not disproven either. What is clear is that women and minorities ultimately got better jobs.

The conflict was peacefully resolved. No one in the case was a public figure, and at the time the world was watching Nixon and Watergate. The press paid little attention, and aside from a few reactive press releases, AT&T did not make a big fuss about the case. Once the decree was signed and implementation was under way, AT&T's management style did not allow external argument or internal opposition. Results were gradual; no sudden stars were created, principally because most promotions were from within. Importantly, bigger problems surfaced for management—competition and antitrust.

Equal opportunity became a part of the routine, and therein lies the power of the case. What was radical became routine. As part of the settlement, some individuals faced new opportunities, perhaps even received a few settlement dollars. For others, the changes meant new competition for jobs, new rules to play by. As the affirmative action plan went into effect, a certain amount of turmoil and backlash developed. Not every adjustment was painless, but the system worked. The wave washed over AT&T. When it was gone, the landscape had changed.

The advocates of equal rights in this case benefited from a unique combination of events and an unusual constellation of people, but similar situations can arise or be created to deal with more current problems. We learn by example. Here's a case where intervention, pressure, and persistence worked. The world has not run out of creative, active, and courageous people, and thus is likely to see new coalitions and challenges. The journey from awareness to massive social change to taking advantage of that change is indeed a difficult road. Over the past few years, feminists from the 1970s have reconvened to celebrate their victories. What comes out of those celebrations, however, is the desire to reenlist, to engage again with what matters, to make a difference, and to talk with young women about their experiences. We have questions about how the system works now. We are surprised that discrimination still exists; they are amazed that we had to fight so hard.

Not all the employment problems facing women and minorities are gone, but enough has changed to give women and minorities a better chance, and many of those who followed us proved the case by their success. What we argued for was, after all, just an equal opportunity.

NOTES

PREFACE

1. Caroline Bird, *Born Female* (New York: Pocket Books, 1969), 199, 705.

2. www.lucent.com/press/0102/020107.coa.html.

3. Dick Kelsey, "AT&T Accused of Sexual Harassment, Discrimination," reported by newsbytes.com, http://www.newsbytes.com, November 29, 2001. Original source: *Washington Post*.

CHAPTER 1

1. Frances J. Chessler, e-mail to author, January 22, 2001.

2. Frank Goetz, interview with author, Wheaton, Ill., July 13, 1996.

3. Chessler, e-mail.

4. Werner Ulrich, interview with author, Naperville, Ill., July 13, 1996.

5. Chessler, e-mail.

6. Beth Eddy (a.k.a. Chilton), e-mail to author, August 29, 2001.

7. *New York* magazine introduced *Ms.* as an insert in its December 20, 1971, edition.

8. "Feedback," *Bell Labs News*, December 30, 1971. Author's copy.

9. Carol Kleiman, "You Won't Find Any Protective Laws Here!" *Chicago Tribune*, n.d.

10. Lois Kerkeslager to Morgan Sparks, August 26, 1970. In testimony provided for EEOC hearings on May 3, 1967, AT&T explained its policy: "Death benefits under our plans are mandatory in the case of a male employee leaving a widow with whom he was living at the time of death. The widower of a female employee is a mandatory beneficiary under the plans only if physically or mentally incapable of self-support and actually supported in whole or in part by the deceased female employee at the time of her death." Testimony of Harold H. Schroeder, classified file relating to litigation against American Telephone and Telegraph Company, 1971–73, series 2, exhibit 50, records of the Equal Employment Opportunity Commission (EEOC), record group 403 (RG 403); National Archives Building, College Park, Md. (NACP).

    Two months to the day after my letter to Sparks, Bell Labs' top executive on benefits, he replied: Differences in treatment of men and women in the field of benefits have developed rather broadly over the years. They exist elsewhere in the Bell System, other telephone companies, many other industries, the federal Social Security system, and other government retirement systems. When the bill that resulted in the Civil Rights Act of 1964 was under consideration in Congress, statements were made on the Senate floor to the effect that the proposed law was not intended to prohibit such differences in treatment in benefit plans, including earlier retirement options for women. This has led to a general state of confusion and uncertainty with respect to long-established differences in treatment based on sex. (Morgan Sparks to Lois Kerkeslager, October 26, 1970. Author's personal copy.)

Sparks concluded by referring to two pending lawsuits in the federal courts and by indicating that the company would wait for decisions in those cases before making changes in its plan. Change would not be quick. Just pointing out inequities would not make them go away. And it was not just other companies, not just stories in the paper or on the news. This was not a hypothetical discussion; those were our benefits we were talking about. By February 1971 we presented a petition on the benefits issue to the top executive at our location, Ray Ketchledge. He saw our logic and agreed to pass it up the line. We heard also that the major telecommunication workers' union—the Communications Workers of America (CWA)—was going to ask for equal death benefits in their next contract negotiations.

11. *Frontiero v. Richardson* 411 U.S. 677 (1973), as discussed in Barbara Allen Babcock et al., eds., *Sex Discrimination and the Law: History, Practice, and Theory*, 2d ed. (New York: Little, Brown, 1996), 167–68.

12. NOW flyer, August 26, 1970. Author's copy.

13. Eddy, personal notes.

14. Author's personal notes.

15. Harriet White, telephone conversation with author, February 9, 2001.

16. Eddy, personal notes.

17. Eddy, e-mail to author, August 29, 2001.

18. Ibid.

19. Author's personal notes, June 8, 1971.

20. Ulrich, telephone conversation with author, October 22, 1996.

21. Author's personal notes, June 21, 1971.

22. Author's personal notes, n.d.

23. Author's personal notes, June 8, 1971.

24. Ibid.

25. Ibid.

CHAPTER 2

1. *Washington Post*, November 18, 1970, A1.

2. The FCC regulates interstate and international communications in the public interest. Within the FCC, the Common Carrier Bureau administers regulation of communication by telephone, telegraph, radio, and satellite. Dockets are assigned to administrative law judges, who conduct evidentiary adjudicatory hearings, as would be the case with Docket 19143, the investigation into AT&T's employment practices. Traditionally, the FCC's "continuing surveillance" of AT&T and the close interaction between the government and the company produced reasonably low rates and high-quality service with little or no consumerist intervention. By the late 1960s, however, the process had become more formal, with public hearings established in 1965, according to Fred W. Henck and Bernard Strassburg in *A Slippery Slope: The Long Road to the Breakup of AT&T* (New York: Greenwood, 1988), 110. AT&T rates fell as the result of a 1969 negotiation, but economic conditions changed, and by November 1970 AT&T requested an increase (123).

3. David Copus, interview by author, Washington, D.C., August 13, 1996.

4. Alvin Toffler, *Social Dynamics and the Bell System* (New York: AT&T, 1972), 55.

5. Allen T. Demaree, "The Age of Anxiety at AT&T," *Fortune*, May 1970, 272.

6. 195 *Management Report*, June 11, 1970, AT&T Archives 391 02 03.

7. Demaree, "Age of Anxiety," 156.

8. William H. Brown III, interview with author, Philadelphia, December 12, 2000.

9. William C. Oldaker, interview with author, Washington, D.C., June 17, 1998.

10. Created by Title VII of the Civil Rights Act, approved July 2, 1964, the EEOC is administered by five commissioners appointed by the president. The EEOC chairperson at the time of the AT&T case, William H. Brown III, had considerable authority, but the commission did not have the power to levy sanctions until 1972. Within the EEOC, the General Counsel's Office and a specially created task force handled the AT&T case. The Department of Justice enforced federal laws and represented the government in legal matters; the Civil Rights Division litigated equal employment cases and in the AT&T case officially represented the U.S. government. Charged with implementation of laws, rules, and regulations covering employment matters, the Department of Labor included, under the assistant secretary for employment standards, the Office of Federal Contract Compliance (OFCC) and the Wage and Hour Division, both integrally involved in the AT&T case. The Department of Labor implemented executive orders of the president, including those related to this case: 11246 (Johnson) and 11375 (Johnson). Responsible for the legal activities of the department, the Solicitor's Office directed litigation and provided oversight of the legislative program. The solicitor took control of the AT&T compliance effort in September 1972 and became actively involved in negotiating the agreement. The General Services Administration (GSA) provides management services to the U.S. government. As part of its responsibility for overseeing contractors, GSA is charged with ensuring compliance of government contractors, such as AT&T, with rules and regulations regarding nondiscrimination in employment. GSA follows the guidelines established by Labor's OFCC as it reviews contractor bids and performance.

11. Leonard Garment, Crazy Rhythm (New York: Random House, 1997), 151, 220–21.

12. Bernard Strassburg to Dan Emerson, Washington, D.C., November 14, 1969, series 2, EEOC RG 403, NACP.

13. Henck and Strassburg, A Slippery Slope, 38–39, 64–65, 102–3.

14. George P. Sape, telephone conversation with author, August 5, 1998.

15. FCC, Memorandum Opinion and Order, p. 5, Docket no. 18742, August 11, 1970, quoted in Phyllis A. Wallace, Equal Employment Opportunity and the AT&T Case (Cambridge, Mass.: MIT Press, 1976), 244.

16. Copus, interview.

17. A Texas minister, Holcomb had been working for racial justice and equal employment in Texas. On November 22, 1963, he had been scheduled to give the invocation at the Dallas luncheon for President Kennedy and was in the fifth car of the motorcade. Instead, he was the one to announce the assassination to the waiting crowd. "Recollections of Luther Holcomb," http://www.eeoc.gov/35th-voices, accessed August 20, 2001.

18. Ann Scott, "Feminism vs. the Feds," Issues in Industrial Society 2, no. 1 (1971): 37.

19. Brown, interview. After delays tied to the confirmation debate over Abe Fortas's nomination as chief justice of the Supreme Court, Brown finally got a call from Senator Hugh Scott that he would have an unheard-of interim appointment.

20. Susan Deller Ross, interview with author, Washington, D.C., June 26, 2000. East, one of the few women with a government position having to do with women's issues, served as the hub of a huge wheel connecting a wide circle of activists. Few in number, the women leveraged their influence by working together and developed tactics as they went along. Bernice Sandler, telephone interview with author, November 7, 2001.

21. John Harmon Florer, National Organization for Women: The Formative Years: The National Effort to Require Federal Action on Equal Employment Rights for Women in the 1960s, prepared for Manpower Administration, December 18, 1972, U.S. Department of Commerce, NTIS, Report no. DLMA 91-34-69-26-1.

22. Equal Employment Opportunity Commission, A Unique Competence (Washington, D.C.: GPO, 1971), and Ross, interview.

23. Petition for Intervention, cover letter, 2, and C.F.R. Section 23.55 as printed from http://squid.law.cornell.edu index. The EEOC claimed that AT&T violated the following specific laws and

regulations: (1) Sections 201(b), 202 (a), 214, 501, and 502 of the Federal Communications Act of 1934, 47 U.S.C. (common carriers forbidden "to make any unjust or unreasonable discrimination in charges practices, classification, regulations, facilities or services . . . or to subject any particular person, class of persons, or locality to any undue or unreasonable prejudice or disadvantage," 47 U.S.C. 202 [a]); (2) 47 C.F.R. Sections 23.49 (a), (b), and (c) revised as of October 1, 2000, and incorporated as Section 23.55 (requirements for equal employment, including policies, programs, responsibilities, and reviews related to recruitment, selection, training, etc.); (3) Sections 703(a) and 703(d) of Title VII of the Civil Rights Act of 1964, 42 U.S.C. Sections 2000c-2(a) and 2000e-2(d); (4) the Equal Pay Act of 1963, 29 U.S.C. Section 206(d) (1); (5) Executive Order 11246, 30 F.R. 12,319 (1965), as amended by Executive Order 11375, 32 F.R. 14303 (1967); (6) the Civil Rights Act of 1866, 42 U.S.C. Section 1981; (7) the fair employment practice acts of approximately thirty states and the District of Columbia; (8) the fair employment practice ordinances of numerous large cities; and (9) the Fifth Amendment to the Constitution of the United States (this amendment imposes upon the U.S. government and its regulatory agencies a duty not to discriminate against anyone because of sex, race, or national origin through its charge that "no person shall be deprived of life, liberty, and property, without due process of law"); see p. 32 of Petition for Intervention.

24. Ibid., cover letter.

25. American Telephone and Telegraph Company, New England Telephone and Telegraph Company, the Southern New England Telephone Company, New York Telephone Company, New Jersey Bell Telephone Company, the Bell Telephone Company of Pennsylvania and the Diamond State Telephone Company, the Chesapeake and Potomac Telephone Company, the Chesapeake and Potomac Telephone Company of Maryland, the Chesapeake and Potomac Telephone Company of Virginia, the Chesapeake and Potomac Telephone Company of West Virginia, Southern Bell Telephone and Telegraph Company, South Central Bell Telephone Company, the Ohio Bell Telephone Company, Cincinnati Bell, Inc., Michigan Bell Telephone Company, Indiana Bell Telephone Company, Inc., Wisconsin Telephone Company, Illinois Bell Telephone Company, Northwestern Bell Telephone Company, Southwestern Bell Telephone Company, the Mountain States Telephone and Telegraph Company, Pacific Northwest Bell Telephone Company, the Pacific Telephone and Telegraph Company, and Bell Telephone Company of Nevada (Western Electric and Bell Telephone Laboratories were not parties to the case).

26. Petition for Intervention, 12, 4.

27. Ibid., 47.

28. Potts v. Flax, 313 F.2d 284, 289 (5th Cir. 1963), as cited in Petition for Intervention, 47.

29. P. Wallace, Equal Employment, 244, and "AT&T Chronology," February 11, 1971, AT&T Archives 86 10 02, 5 Reinman Road, Warren, N.J.

30. NOW Legal Defense and Education Fund Petition, 3.

31. George P. Sape, interview with author, New York, May 16, 2000, and handwritten comments on an April 10, 1970, memorandum from Hugh Sloan to Leonard Garment, April 16, 1970, box 3, folder 9, Leonard Garment Papers, Manuscript Division, Library of Congress, Washington, D.C.

32. Garment, Crazy Rhythm, 151.

33. Memo from Director of Compliance to Staff Director, April 11, 1967, series 2, EEOC, RG 403, NACP.

34. William O. Wallace, e-mail to author, August 3, 2001.

35. Chris Roggerson to Gordon Chase, November 3, 1967, series 2, EEOC, RG 403, NACP.

36. Draft, "Bell Consolidation," N. Leventhal, February 28, 1968, series 2, EEOC, RG 403, NACP.

37. Stephen J. Pollak to Alexander, July 29, 1968, series 2, EEOC, RG 403, NACP.

38. Employment Analysis, "Bell System," n.d., series 2, EEOC, RG 403, NACP.

39. Mercer to Alexander, October 4, 1968, series 2, EEOC, RG 403, NACP.

40. Bob Randolph to Gordon Chase, October 7, 1968, series 2, EEOC, RG 403, NACP.

41. Chase had help from Mike Blumenfeld, Bill Wallace, Nat Leventhal, Bob Randolph, Dan Steiner, Bob Harris, Bill Enneis, and Fred Abramson. Randolph memorandum on the "Bell Project," November 1, 1968, series 2, EEOC, RG 403, NACP.

42. Gordon Chase, memorandum to P. Wallace et al., October 22, 1968, series 2, EEOC, RG 403, NACP.

43. George W. Drape II to Dan Steiner, "Proposed Commission Visits to Bell System Companies," March 21, 1969. David Copus's name appeared on an April 4, 1969, memorandum to Daniel Steiner on the subject of "Prohibition by Southern Bell against Women with Illegitimate Children." Another memorandum on the topic was sent by Frederick B. Abramson to William Oldaker. "Miller vs. Southern Bell and Wilcher vs. Southern Bell," June 17, 1969, series 2, EEOC, RG 403, NACP.

44. Bernard Strassburg to Daniel E. Emerson, November 14, 1969, series 2, EEOC, RG 403, NACP.

45. Emerson, series 2, EEOC, RG 403, NACP.

46. Burch to Romnes, March 19, 1970, series 2, EEOC, RG 403, NACP.

47. Romnes to Burch, March 26, 1970, series 2, EEOC, RG 403, NACP.

48. AT&T Transmittal no. 10989 in the Matter of AT&T, Long Lines revisions of Tariff F.C.C. no. 263, rates for Long Distance Message Telecommunications Service, series 2, EEOC, RG 403, NACP, 1, 3, 4.

49. Ibid., Exhibit 1, 11-13.

50. William Chapman, "AT&T Outraged at U.S. Bias Charge, Claims Leadership in Minority Hiring," *Washington Post*, December 12, 1970.

51. "H. I. Romnes of AT&T: Running the World's Largest Company," *Nations Business*, April 1971, 736ff, AT&T Archives 11 10 03 01.

52. At sixty-three, Romnes had spent his entire career with the Bell System, working as an installer with Wisconsin Telephone for a summer and, when he graduated from the University of Wisconsin, accepting an offer from Bell Telephone Laboratories in New York. Over the years, he served at Bell Labs, AT&T, Illinois Bell, Long Lines, and Western Electric, and he learned the technical and personnel sides of the business. Romnes established a position at the level of executive vice president for "human affairs" and included an innovative department within it for "environmental affairs." That group was charged with dealing with "the impact of our business on the community we serve and vice versa." In an interview for *Nations Business*, Romnes reported, "We are looking into many things, like whether we could attract more competent women to work for us if we had day care centers for children," 195 *Management Report*, AT&T, no. 14, March 17, 1968, p. 1, author's copy.

53. 1970 annual meeting pamphlet, April 15, 1970, AT&T Archives 183 02 01.

54. *Long Lines Magazine*, AT&T Archives, vol 5, 43-45, 1964-65.

55. "Current Information," no. 11, July 6, 1964, AT&T Archives 391 02 02.

56. 195 *Management Report*, November 25, 1966, AT&T Archives 391 02 02.

57. "Gilmer: Urban Crisis Demands Action 'NOW,' " 195 *Management Report*, AT&T Archives 391 02 02.

58. William H. Brown III, interview with author, Philadelphia, July 31, 1998.

59. George P. Sape, interview with author, New York, May 16, 2000.

60. P. Wallace, *Equal Employment*, 247.

61. Randall L. Speck, interview with author, Washington, D.C., July 10, 1998.

62. Copus, interview.

63. Well respected in the telecommunication industry, Denniston came to the FCC after a career as a GSA trial lawyer. At GSA he had represented the government in a case involving rates for AT&T's dedicated private line service. In that setting, Denniston had been AT&T's antagonist,

but AT&T's legal staff regarded him as capable and solid. George E. Ashley, telephone interview with author, November 30, 2001.

64. Sape, telephone interview.

65. N. Thompson Powers, interview with author, Scottsdale, Ariz., February 19, 2001.

CHAPTER 3

1. In the first wave of female executives, Liz would retire in 1991 at the vice-presidential level. M. Elizabeth Brydon, recollections, June 1991, duplicated, 5.

2. John W. Kingsbury, response to author in AT&T Answerback no. 798, June 5, 1973.

3. AT&T News 5, no. 8, June 5, 1970, AT&T Archives 383 03 06.

4. R 1289, series 2, EEOC, RG 403, NACP.

5. The diagnosis and evaluation team included V. Becker, S. Gael, M. B. Gillette, E. Mahler, and J. L. Moses, chairman. Their report, "The Utilization of Women in the Management of the Bell System," became EEOC exhibit R-1289 and figured prominently in the EEOC's filing. Ibid.

6. Edward Mahler, interview with author, Bridgewater, N.J., July 13, 2000.

7. Demaree, "Age of Anxiety," 158.

8. Harold W. Burlingame, interview with author, Basking Ridge, N.J., June 27, 2001.

9. Mahler, interview.

10. Donald Liebers, interview with author, Dennis, Mass., December 5–6, 1998.

11. Mahler, interview.

12. Kingsbury, response to author.

13. Susan Brownmiller, "Liberty for Women," Bell Telephone Magazine, 48, no.5 (September/ October 1970): 15.

14. Ibid., 20.

15. Illinois Bell Bulletin, April 7, 1971.

16. William C. Mercer to all company presidents and AT&T vice presidents, December 15, 1970, series 2, EEOC, RG 403, NACP.

17. William C. Mercer, "Business Looks at Itself," reprinted in "Women in Industry," Industrial Relations Department, National Association of Manufacturers, 227 Park Avenue, New York, N.Y. 10017, December 1970, 29.

18. Ibid., 34.

19. Ibid., 28.

20. NOW files, Schlesinger Library, Radcliffe Institute, Harvard University, Cambridge, Mass.

21. Mercer letter, May 12, 1965, series 2, EEOC, RG 403, NACP.

22. Woods letter, San Francisco, February 16, 1966, R-1025, series 2, EEOC, RG 403, NACP.

23. "Compliance with Title VII, Civil Rights Act of 1964," R-1046, series 2, EEOC, RG 403, NACP.

24. William C. Mercer, "System Public Affairs Conference Remarks," 11-13, R-542, series 2, EEOC, RG 403, NACP, p. 14.

25. Glenn M. Ziegler to Mr. Pollard, San Francisco, October 23, 1969, R-1029, series 2, EEOC, RG 403, NACP.

26. S. A. Sawyer to All General Data Processing Division Employees, Illinois Bell, September 28, 1970, series 2, EEOC, RG 403, NACP.

27. Priscilla J. Tooker to All Service Bureau Employees, November 19, 1970, series 2, EEOC, RG 403, NACP.

28. District Commercial Manager to L. B. Harper et al., San Jose, December 18, 1970, series 2, EEOC, RG 403, NACP.

29. Robert J. Samuelson, "AT&T Seeks Higher Long Distance Rates," *Washington Post*, November 18, 1970, D1.

30. Liebers, interview.

31. Demaree, "Age of Anxiety," 266.

32. Robert D. Lilley, 1971 and 1972 calendars, in box 9, Lilley Collection, Columbia University Rare Book and Manuscript Library (CRBM), New York.

33. Liebers, interview.

34. Eugene Kofke, interview with author, June 26, 1997.

35. Kim Armstrong (a.k.a. Manna), telephone conversation, July 13, 1999.

36. Bell Telephone Laboratories, *Management Topics* 6, no. 53, December 15, 1970, 1–2, author's copy.

CHAPTER 4

1. Mary Jean Collins (a.k.a. Collins-Robson), interview with author, July 7, 2001.

2. Aileen C. Hernandez and Letitia P. Sommers, *The First Five Years: 1966–1971* (Chicago: NOW Publication, 1971), 3.

3. Aileen C. Hernandez, "Equal Employment Opportunities for Women: Problems, Facts, and Answers," *Contact*, fall 1973, 12, Avon Collection, Hagley Museum and Library, Wilmington, Del.

4. Eleanor Humes Haney, *A Feminist Legacy: The Ethics of Wilma Scott Heide and Company* (Buffalo: Margaretdaughters, 1985), 9.

5. Ibid., 159.

6. Bunny (Bernice) Sandler, e-mail to author, November 9, 2001. In 1969 Sandler initiated the first class-action charge of sex discrimination in higher education by challenging the University of Maryland and every other college and university in the country. Educational institutions had been excluded from coverage in Title VII in "educational activities." This action and the friendship between Sandler and Scott provided the basis for Scott's use of the contract compliance argument with its requirement for affirmative action. Sandler, an activist with the Women's Equity Action League, was chair of their Action Committee on Federal Contract Compliance.

7. Bunny (Bernice) Sandler to Ann Scott, March 29, 1970, Ann London Scott papers, 91-MI32-93-MI, folder 57, Schlesinger.

8. Joan Hull to Ann Scott, December 15, 1970, Scott papers, 91-M132-93-MI, folder 57, Schlesinger.

9. Lucy Komisar, "The NOW Phone Company Anti-Discrimination Affirmative Action Kit," 1970, duplicated, 1–4. In great detail, Komisar gave pointers on what to look for. She encouraged meetings with company officials and gave suggestions on how those meetings should be run. Other local organizations and the union were to be invited to join in the discussion. Noting that NOW had filed in support of the EEOC petition to the FCC, she suggested that NOW could do the same thing with local phone companies, "and we leave other tactics to your imagination."

10. On the ad hoc committee then were Evansgardner, Eliza Paschall, Marilyn Hall Patel (coordinator of the stockholder action committee), Maggie Quinn (Cincinnati), Sylvia Roberts, and Lee Walker (New York). Paschall was a government insider, Roberts was the NOW attorney who worked on the *Weeks* v. *Southern Bell* case, and Walker was an IBM technical writer who would later testify in the EEOC hearings and meet with corporate leaders. As was common with NOW calls to action, the letter included four pages of detailed suggestions and information. Gardner included suggestions from NOW's Washington-based attorney David Cashdan on what types of information "would be useful to those accumulating evidence for the hearings." Over a dozen pages of supporting material followed, including Roberts's statement before the Special Subcommittee on Education Hearings on Section 805 of H.R. 16098: "To prohibit discrimination against women

in federally assisted programs and in employment in education; to extend the equal pay act so as to prohibit discrimination in administrative, professional and executive employment; and to extend the jurisdiction of the U.S. Commission on Civil Rights to Include Sex." Hearings held in Washington, D.C., June 17, 19, 26, 29, 30, 1970. In that statement, Roberts described the Weeks case.

11. EEOC case 6-5481, decision March 1967, as amended February 1967.

12. Aileen C. Hernandes to Frank M. Malone, February 18, 1971. Author's personal copy.

13. Aileen C. Hernandez to William H. Brown III, January 4, 1971, Scott papers, 91-MI32-93-MI, carton 2, folder 59, Schlesinger.

14. Eliza Paschall to Hernandez et al., February 23, 1971, Scott papers 91-MI32-93-MI, carton 2, folder 59, Schlesinger.

15. Testimony, exhibit 12, series 2, EEOC, RG 403, NACP.

16. Hernandez to Brown, March 15, 1971, NOW files, Midwest Women's Historical Collection, Special Collections Department, University of Illinois at Chicago (UIC).

17. Ann Scott to the Honorable Bella Abzug, March 9, 1971, Scott papers, 91-MI32-93-MI, carton 2, folder 59, Schlesinger.

18. Act NOW 3, no. 2 (March 13, 1971), author's copy.

19. Midwest Regional Conference Resolution, March 28, 1971, NOW files, UIC.

20. NOW press release, Midwest region, March 29, 1971, NOW files, UIC.

21. Harriet White, telephone conversation with author, February 9, 2001.

22. NOW leaflet, author's copy.

23. Illinois Bell Bulletin, April 7, 1971, NOW files, UIC.

24. Chicago Daily News, March 29, 1971 (copy provided by Kathy Rand).

25. Kathleen McElroy to Ann Scott, March 29, 1971, Scott papers, Schlesinger.

26. Pittsburgh Post-Gazette, March 30, 1971.

27. JoAnn Evansgardner, interview with author, November 11, 1996.

28. Act NOW, undated page, NOW files, UIC.

29. Lorraine Hardt, LaGrange (Ill.) Citizen, May 26, 1971.

30. Patricia Stemper, Chicago Tribune, May 19, 1971.

31. AT&T News, April 30, 1971, 6.

32. Chicago Sun-Times, May 11, 1971.

33. Ibid.

34. Ann Scott and Toni Carabillo, "National Actions: Report [to the NOW Board]," n.d. (approximately July 1971), NOW files, UIC.

35. Act NOW 3, no. 6 (July 1971): 5.

36. Eliza Paschall to Ann Scott, August 1, 1971, Scott papers, 91-MI32-93-MI, carton 1, folder "67-n.d," Schlesinger.

37. Act NOW, special edition, August 9, 1971.

38. Aileen Hernandez speech, tape recorded, personal copy.

39. Conference Implementation Committee notes, November 20–22, 1971, duplicated, NOW files, Schlesinger.

40. Mary Lynn Myers, e-mail to author, August 20, 2001.

41. Mary Lynn Myers to Ann Scott, October 13, 1971, Scott papers 91-MI32-93MI, carton 2, folder 62, Schlesinger.

42. Mary Lynn Myers, Report to Compliance Task Force et al., December 20, 1971, duplicated.

43. Ibid.

CHAPTER 5

1. EEOC, *A Unique Competence* (Washington, D.C.: GPO, 1971), 4.

2. Copus, interview.

3. David Copus, annotated letters and notes, series 2, EEOC, RG 403, NACP.

4. Ibid.

5. Randall L. Speck, interview.

6. Bob Kutter, "Still No Lady Repairmen, but a Few Lawyer-Freaks," *Village Voice*, December 9, 1971.

7. Copus, interview.

8. Bill Wallace, e-mail.

9. Speck, interview.

10. Bill Wallace, e-mail.

11. Phyllis Wallace had been chief of technical studies in the research department of the EEOC from 1966 to 1969. In *Equal Employment Opportunity and the AT&T Case*, her 1976 book, she expanded on the testimony of the EEOC and FCC witnesses, putting the specific testimony into a broader context of workplace equity, (2).

12. EEOC expert witnesses included Judith Long Laws, Ph.D., asst. prof. of sociology, Cornell University, *Causes and Effects of Sex Discrimination in the Bell System*; Sandra L. Bem and Daryl J. Bem, Ph.D., asst. prof. and assoc. prof. of psychology, Stanford, *Do Sex-Biased Job Advertisements Discourage Applicants of the Opposite Sex?*; and Susan B. Leake, asst. director of placement, Simmons College, *College Recruiting by New England Tel.*; among others.

13. Bill Wallace, e-mail.

14. Civil Action 73-149, opinion, Judge A. Leon Higginbotham, October 5, 1973.

15. 195 *Management Report*, May 13, 1971.

16. 195 *Management Report*, April 15, May 13, 1971.

17. *Bell Labs News*, July 9, 1971.

18. Brown, interview.

19. "Unvarnished Nixon c1971: Bigotry revealed in tapes," *Chicago Tribune*, June 3, 2001.

20. Brown, interview.

21. "Power versus the People: A Look at Job Discrimination in Houston," William Greaves Productions, 230 West 55th Street, New York, N.Y., July 13, 1970, videocassette.

22. Brown, interview.

23. P. Wallace, *Equal Employment*, 247.

24. Sape, interview.

25. Speck, interview.

26. Lee Satterfield, interview with author, Washington, D.C., November 9, 2000.

27. P. Wallace, *Equal Employment*, 248–49.

28. Copus, interview.

29. Satterfield, interview.

30. Ibid.

31. Speck, interview.

32. Copus, interview.

33. Ibid.

34. EEOC, *A Unique Competence*, ii.

35. AT&T chronology, AT&T Archives 615 02 13.

36. EEOC, *A Unique Competence*, 29–30.

37. Ibid., 33, 39, 45.

38. Ibid., 46, 47, 50.

39. Ibid., 58, 61–62.

40. Ibid., 102–4.

41. Ibid., 148–50, 152.

42. Ibid., 153.

43. Ibid., 173.

44. Ibid., 176, 178.

45. Ibid., 203.

46. Ibid., 241, 259, 272. For further study of the issues of race, see Venus Green, *Race on the Line: Gender, Labor, and Technology in the Bell System, 1880–1980* (Durham, N.C.: Duke University Press, 2001).

47. Rodolfo Gonzales, "I Am Joaquin," quoted in Stan Steiner, *La Raza: The Mexican American* (New York: Harper and Row, 1969), 240–41, quoted in EEOC, *A Unique Competence*, 289.

48. EEOC, *A Unique Competence*, 275.

49. Speck, interview.

50. Liebers, interview.

51. AT&T news release for A.M. papers of Wednesday, December 1, 1971, duplicated.

52. Southwestern Bell, *Management Report* 28, no. 21G (December 2, 1971).

53. Invitation in Speck personal files.

54. Author's personal notes.

55. George E. Ashley to author, November 17, 2001.

56. Author's personal notes, January 16, 1972.

57. Author's personal notes.

58. Ibid.

59. "Women in Management: Pattern for Change," *Harvard Business Review*, July August 1971, as quoted in an internal document written by the author, February 1, 1972. The same document referred to other studies: Dr. Margaret Henning (Simmons College), "Career Development for Women Executives," and Warren Farrell (New York University), "Resocialization of Men's Attitudes."

60. David K. Easlick, telephone conversation with author, July 1999.

CHAPTER 6

1. *NOW Compliance and Enforcement Task Force Newsletter* no. 4, February 1972.

2. P. Wallace, *Equal Employment*, 249.

3. *Detroit News*, January 21, 1972, 3-C.

4. *Detroit Free Press*, February 24, 1972, 1-C.

5. Robert D. Lilley, speech before a seminar of the Federal Mediation and Conciliation Service, as reported in the *AT&T Management Report*, February 13, 1972.

6. AT&T chronology, AT&T Archives 615 02 13; Liebers, interview.

7. Judy Potter to Lois Herr, Cape Elizabeth, Me., May 21, 1997.

8. Ross, interview.

9. Potter, interview.

10. Sape, interview.

11. Kofke, interview.

12. Ibid.

13. Speck, interview.

14. Ashley, telephone conversation.

15. Eventually the summaries were filed. The final version was agreed to by AT&T as "fairly reflecting information contained in said document on that point" and in many cases there was an "AT&T addition," which the EEOC agreed to, summarizing the portions of the document considered by AT&T to be pertinent. In doing this, neither "sponsored" the data or waived any evidentiary objection rights. Hearing transcript, series 2, EEOC, RG 403, NACP.

16. Ibid., 277.

17. Ibid., 294.

18. Transcript, vol. 12, 689–90, series 2, EEOC, RG 403, NACP.

19. Transcript, vol. 13, series 2, EEOC, RG 403, NACP.

20. Speck, interview.

21. Transcript, 1061-3, series 2, EEOC, RG 403, NACP, 1064–65.

22. Ibid., 1057–74.

23. Potter, interview.

24. Wallace, e-mail.

25. Whitney Adams to Joan Hull, Washington, D.C., February 2, 1972, NOW files—Hull, Schlesinger.

26. *New York Times*, February 2, 1972.

27. Reflections on the conference provided in a memorandum from the author to S. H. Rokos, AT&T, February 29, 1972.

28. "1971 Meeting of Shareowners," AT&T, Thursday, April 22, 1971, 15. A third nominee from the floor was Paul Gorman, former president of Western Electric; he received 23,238 votes. AT&T Archives 183 02 01. This O'Connor is also known as Sandra Day O'Connor and is now a Supreme Court justice.

29. Personal notes.

30. Catherine Cleary to author, Milwaukee, Wisc., June 2, 2000.

31. *Fortune*, April 1973, 80–89.

32. Cleary interview, April 7, 1997.

33. Mary-Ann Lupa's notes on an agenda, February 20, 1972, NOW files, 83-27, UIC.

34. Personal notes, February 18, 1972.

35. W. L. Lindholm, remarks at Bell Telephone Laboratories directors meeting, January 28, 1971, 11.

36. Mary Lynn Myers to Sally Hacker, March 2, 1972, Hacker papers, Schlesinger.

37. "Power versus the People: A Look at Job Discrimination in Houston," William Greaves Productions, July 13, 1970, videocassette.

38. Wilma Scott Heide to Editor, *Saturday Review*, February 26, 1972.

39. *AT&T News*, March 29, 1972, 4.

40. John D. deButts, Human Affairs conference, March 8, 1972, author's copy of informally printed document, 4.

41. *Womankind* 1, no. 6 (February 1972): 3, 20–21.

42. Author's personal notes, February 28, 1972.

43. Author's personal notes, February 4, 1972, and luncheon, February 10, 1972.

44. Author's personal notes, February 4, 1972.

45. Author's personal notes, February 1, 1972.

46. Author's personal notes, December 16, 1971.

47. Author's personal notes, n.d.

48. *Private Line*, New York, August 1972, duplicated.

49. Author's personal notes, n.d.

50 Draft, "NOW Corporate Equal Opportunity for Women: Bill of Rights," n.d.; Lois Kerkeslager (a.k.a. Herr), "External Realities: Social Activists and the Corporation," n.d.; Elisabeth Hogan to author, Brookline, Mass., May 7, 1972.

51. Author's personal notes, June 1, 1972.

52. Author's personal notes, December 1971.

53. "Image of Women at Bell Labs," draft of a Holmdel AAC letter, n.d.

54. *Private Line*, fall 1972.

55. *Private Line*, March 27, 1972.

56. David Copus, personal notes, March 27, 1972, series 2, EEOC, RG 403, NACP.

57. Bob Lilley, 1972 calendar, March 22–April 7, CRBM, op cit.

58. Kofke to author, August 10, 2001.

59. Kofke, interview.

60. Burlingame, interview.

61. Kofke, interview.

62. Ibid.

63. Copus, personal notes, March 28, 1972, series 2, EEOC, RG 403, NACP.

64. Ibid., March 29, 1972.

65. Ibid., March 30, 1972.

66. Eileen Shanahan, *New York Times*, February 4, 1972.

67. "Slow Gains at Work," *Time*, March 20, 1972, 82.

68. Eileen Shanahan, *New York Times*, March 23, 1972.

69. *AT&T News Bulletin*, May 14, 1972.

70. Flyer distributed by New Orleans NOW, New Orleans, La.

CHAPTER 7

1. Sally L. Hacker, *Doing It the Hard Way: Investigations of Gender and Technology* (Boston: Unwin Hyman, 1990), 24; 109, 129.

2. Wilma Scott Heide to Sally Hacker, Vernon, Conn., April 3, 1972, Schlesinger.

3. Mary Lynn Myers to Sally Hacker, Chicago, April 6, 1972, Schlesinger.

4. Hacker, "Brief Note," April 25, 1972, Schlesinger.

5. Hacker to deButts, April 24, 1972, series 2, EEOC, RG 403 NACP.

6. AT&T News, April 28, 1972.

7. Catherine Cleary, interview.

8. Sally Hacker, mailing to NOW AT&T Committee et al., June 1972.

9. 1972 Annual Meeting of Share Owners, booklet, April 19, 1972.

10. Cleary, interview.

11. When Virginia Dwyer's promotion to treasurer was to be announced, Lilley hinted to Cleary that he had "good news for you." Much later, with Brown as the chairman, Cleary looked at the binder of pictures and biographies of managers with top executive potential and saw no women. When she pointed that out, Brown seemed to be somewhat embarrassed. Cleary, interview.

12. Fifteen years later, when Cleary retired from the board, AT&T's chairman, James Olson, established the Catherine Cleary Management Award to be given to an AT&T woman each year. Al von Auw, telephone conversation with author, March 31, 1997.

13. David Copus, notes from telephone conversation, April 25, 1972, series 2, EEOC, RG 403 NACP.

14. David Copus, notes from telephone conversation with Pat Johnson, April 27, 1972, series 2, EEOC, RG 403 NACP.

15. AT&T Answerback, no. 798 (June 5, 1973).

16. "Revised Standard Informational Form for Candidates for NOW National Elections," author's personal files.

17. Author's personal notes, December 27, 1971.

18. Conroy, a founder of NOW, was the highest-ranking woman in the Communications Workers of America, the major union representing Bell System workers.

19. Author's personal notes, December 9, 1971.

20. Transcript, vol. 29, April 7, 1972, series 2, EEOC, RG 403 NACP.

21. Ibid.

22. Ann Scott to NOW, Los Angeles and San Francisco presidents, n.d., Schlesinger.

23. AT&T case chronology, AT&T Archives 615 02 03 02.

24. San Francisco Examiner, March 24, 1972, 1.

25. Oakland Tribune, March 24, 1972, 11.

26. R. D. Middleworth, quoted in the Delano Record, March 28, 1972, 1, 2.

27. Los Angeles Herald Examiner, April 17, 1972, A-3.

28. Transcript, 2802-03, series 2, EEOC, RG 403 NACP.

29. Alhambra Post, April 18,1972, B-3.

30. Speck, interview.

31. Transcript, 3397–3402, series 2, EEOC, RG 403 NACP.

32. Kofke, interview.

33. Sanford L. Jacobs, "Women Employees Call Bell System Duties Boring, Oppressive," Wall Street Journal, May 12, 1972, 4; transcript, vol. 35, series 2, EEOC, RG 403 NACP; Speck, interview.

34. Transcript, vols. 35–39, series 2, EEOC, RG 403 NACP.

35. Speck, interview.

36. Transcript, series 2, EEOC, RG 403 NACP, 3598–99, 3602–3.

37. Ibid.

38. Ibid., 3569 75.

39. Jacobs, "Women Employees."

40. Affidavit of Carol Carter, series 2, EEOC, RG 403 NACP.

41. Testimony of Judith Wenning, May 1972, series 2, EEOC, RG 403 NACP; testimony of Joan Hull, May 1972, series 2, EEOC, RG 403 NACP; testimony of Lee Walker, FCC staff exhibit 10, series 2, EEOC, RG 403 NACP.

42. P. Wallace, *Equal Employment*, 249–50.

43. Potter, interview.

44. AT&T case chronology.

45. *AT&T Management Report*, May 18, 1972.

46. John D. deButts, *Cloving Remarks* (New York, 1979), limited edition, copy 65 of 100 (excerpts from talks at Bell System Presidents' Conferences and Meetings, 1972–78).

47. Liebers, interview.

48. *RRC By-Line* 11, no. 11 (June 1972).

49. *Telephone Engineer and Management*, June 15, 1972, 33.

50. Copus to Levy, May 22, 1972, series 2, EEOC, RG 403 NACP.

51. Copus, interview.

52. R. S. Calvert, general letters 70 10 038 (October 1, 1970) and 71 05 01 (May 10, 1971), AT&T Archives 299 11 02.

53. Brochure, "New Outfits Available through Purchase Plan," n.d.

54. Janet Kanter personal files.

55. Walker to Hacker, September 18, 1972, Schlesinger.

56. Liebers, interview.

57. Ibid.

58. Hacker to Easlick, June 6, 1972, Schlesinger.

59. Hacker, "Re: The largest oppressor of working women in the United States," memorandum to NOW AT&T committee et al., June 1972, Schlesinger.

60. Ibid.

61. Transcript, series 2, EEOC, RG 403 NACP, 4956.

62. Ibid., 4970.

63. Ibid.

64. Ibid., 4973. Scott noted innovative aspects of the Illinois Bell program: "Additionally, home day-care operators are given two half-day seminars at the Erickson Institute for Childhood Development to help them have some background in early childhood development. Illinois Bell pays for these seminars and retains the Institute as a consultant for Illinois Bell's staff who work continuously with the home daycare operators. Currently, it has provided daycare arrangements for 462 female employees."

65. Ibid., 4980.

66. Ibid.

67. Ibid.

68. Ibid.

CHAPTER 8

1. David Copus, notes, June 15, 1972, series 2, EEOC, RG 403, NACP.

2. Copus, notes, June 30, 1972, series 2, EEOC, RG 403, NACP.

3. Author's personal notes.

4. *CWA News*, June 1972, 15; provided by Janet Kanter.

5. Ibid.

6. Stults to Hacker, June 25, 1972, Hacker papers 88-M13, carton 2, "NOW AT&T, 1972," Schlesinger.

7. Ibid.

8. Ibid.

9. Michael H. Tonry to Michael Fultz, ICC, with attached petition, May 1, 1972, in files of Janet Kanter.

10. *Telegriefs*, August 1972, duplicated.

11. Copus, notes, July 26, 1972, series 2, EEOC, RG 403, NACP.

12. Robert D. Lilley to Hacker, July 13, 1972, Hacker papers, 88-M13, carton 2, "NOW AT&T, 1972," Schlesinger.

13. Summary memorandum, AT&T, series 2, EEOC, RG 403, NACP.

14. Kofke, interview.

15. AT&T news release, August 1, 1972.

16. *New York Times*, August 2, 1972, and *Wall Street Journal*, August 2, 1972.

17. *AT&T News*, August 11, 1972, as reprinted in *Private Line*, September 1972, duplicated.

18. "Annual Report of the Principal Activities of H. J. McMains Section," August 1972–August 1973. Author's personal copy.

19. *AT&T Management Report*, no. 39 (August 31, 1972): 1.

20. Copus, notes, August 18, 21, 1972, series 2, EEOC, RG 403, NACP.

21. Ruth Bader (FCC) took King and Cohen; Jennie Longo (FCC) had Pick and Tyler; Jim Juntilla (FCC), Glazer, Coss, and Fergeson; Copus (EEOC), Bray, Grant, Baxter, Guion, O'Leary, Hunt, Kinsgbury; Gartner (EEOC), Perl, Folk, Oppenheimer.

22. Copus, telephone interview, September 27, 2001.

23. Outline of presentation by Lee Walker, NOW, for AT&T Long Lines guest speaker program, September 14, October 12, and December 7, 1972, NOW files, Schlesinger.

24. The use of the word "Safeguard" in the title is a direct reference to AT&T's contract for the antiballistic missile (ABM) project known as Safeguard. Hacker included in the memo a challenge to AT&T in "social obligations," directly pointing to the defense contracts the company had won, such as the ABM, satellite systems, and ADSID (air-delivered seismic intrusion detector). ADSID, she reported, is "disguised as a tropical plant and dropped in Viet Nam" to "register footsteps and transmits the information to a computer which helps decide whether or not to bomb the person attached to the foot." Hacker concluded: "ABMs and ADSIDs and all the rest are valid concerns of feminists who are told we simply have to wait, that change takes time and money, that innovations don't happen overnight. If AT&T can 'do' an ABM, why haven't they 'done' good health care and child care, if only for their own employees?" Hacker memorandum, August 1972, Hacker papers, 88-M13, carton 2, "NOW AT&T, 1972," Schlesinger.

25. Ibid.

26. Ibid.

27. *Private Line*, August 1972.

28. J. K. Mullen, board minutes from September 7, 1972, distributed September 10, 1972.

29. Lilley, 1972 calendar, Lilley papers, box 9, CRBM.

30. Satterfield, interview.

31. Ibid.

32. Liebers, August 26, 1998.

33. Copus, notes, September 19, 1972, series 2, EEOC, RG 403 NACP.

34. *AT&T Management Report* no. 43 (September 20, 1972).

35. Ibid.

36. AT&T case chronology, AT&T Archives; NOW press release, n.d.

37. Joan Hull to Sally Hacker, September 24, 1972, Hacker papers, 88-M13, carton 2, "NOW AT&T Lists," Schlesinger.

38. Ibid.; Cashdan to Philip Davis, September 29, 1972, Hacker papers, 88-M13, carton 2, "NOW AT&T, 1972," Schlesinger.

39. William J. Kilberg, telephone interview with author, September 26, 2001.

40. Easlick, interview.

41. Kilberg, interview.

42. Series 2, EEOC, RG 403 NACP.

43. Kilberg, interview.

44. Cashdan to Philip Davis, September 29, 1972, Hacker papers, 88-M13, carton 2, "NOW AT&T, 1972," Schlesinger.

45. A. Leon Higginbotham, *Opinion*, October 5, 1973, in Civil Action 73-149, 14.

46. Author's personal notes.

47. Hull, letter to Hacker, September 29, 1972, Hacker papers, 88-M13, carton 2, "NOW AT&T, 1972," Schlesinger.

48. Chicago NOW Financial Report for October 1972, NOW files, 83-27, 7-125, UIC.

49. Bell System Public Affairs Conference documentation, AT&T Archives, 615 02 03 02.

50. Ibid.

51. Adams memorandum to Scott, Hacker, Hull, Heide, October 6, 1972, Hacker papers, 88-M13, carton 2, "AT&T printed, 1971–72," Schlesinger.

52. Hacker memorandum, October 6, 1972; Hacker papers 8 8-M13, carton 2, "NOW AT&T 1972," Schlesinger.

53. NOW executive committee meeting minutes, Everett, Wash., October 9, 1972, 78-34, 1-8, UIC.

54. Joan Hull, telephone conversation with author, September 22, 2001.

55. Easlick, interview with author, November 2000.

56. Hacker, October 6, 1972. NOW based its claim on *A Unique Competence*, pp. 174–75, where $500 million per year is estimated, accounting for age, education, etc. Given eight years of "illegal unequal pay" since the Civil Rights Act of 1964, NOW calculated $4 billion. Sally Hacker and Toni Carabillo, "Action against AT&T, January 3, 1973," memorandum to chapter president et al., Los Angeles, December 2, 1972, UIC.

57. Hacker, notes for NOW National Action Review, late 1972, Hacker papers, 88-M13, carton 2, folder "NOW AT&T, c1973–77, n.d.," Schlesinger. Lilley did not respond until January 23, 1973, per Hacker's notes.

58. NOW press release October 25, 1972.

59. Hacker, notes to task force, November 3, 1972, Schlesinger.

60. Hacker, notes for NOW national action review, Schlesinger.

61. Hacker memorandum, October 2, 1972, Schlesinger.

62. Hacker memorandum to Copus, December 13, 1972, Schlesinger.

63. Hacker memorandum, October 6, 1972, Schlesinger.

64. Ibid., with article included from the *Seattle Post-Intelligencer*, November 12, 1972, C4.

65. Hacker, handwritten notes addressed to Heide and attached to her notes for NOW national action review, late 1972, Hacker papers, 88-M13, carton 2, folder "NOW AT&T c1973-77, n.d.," Schlesinger.

66. Hull to Brown, December 4, 1972, NOW files 72-8-82-M211, carton 18, folder "NOW/EEOC," Schlesinger.

67. Invitation letter, October 1972, with Brydon notes, personal copy.

68. Toffler, *Social Dynamics*, 62–63.

69. Ibid, 67, 76.

70. Transcript, vols. 56, 57, series 2, EEOC, RG 403, NACP, 6589, 6604, 6895, 6642, 6715.

71. Ibid., 59:6988.

72. Ibid., 62:7417.

CHAPTER 9

1. NOW press release, January 5, 1973, lobby of AT&T, 195 Broadway, New York. Present at the meeting for NOW: Heide, Scott, Hacker, Jacqueline Ceballos (Eastern regional director), Judith Lightfoot (Southern regional director), Karen DeCrow (head of the political task force), and Dorothy Crouch (president of the New York City NOW chapter). Hacker papers 88-M13, carton 2, "Notes on Compliance & National Action," Schlesinger.

2. Hacker to chapter presidents et al., Los Angeles, December 2, 1972, UIC.

3. Satterfield, interview.

4. Lilley, calendar, 1971, box 9, CRBM.

5. Brown, interview, December 12, 2000.

6. Robert J. Williams, AT&T, to Hackler, CWA, December 14, 19, 1972.

7. Lilley, calendar, 1971, box 9, CRBM.

8. Satterfield, interview.

9. Copus, telephone interview, September 27, 2001.

10. Satterfield, interview.

11. Copus, telephone interview, September 27, 2001.

12. Kofke, interview.

13. A. Leon Higginbotham, *Opinion*, October 5, 1973, in Civil Action 73-149, 16–17.

14. Carin Clauss, telephone interview with author, July 19, 2001.

15. Powers, interview.

16. Rose, telephone interview with author, March 7, 2001.

17. P. Wallace, *Equal Employment*, 252, and Brown, interview, December 12, 2000.

18. Rose, interview.

19. Clauss, interview.

20. Proceedings before Honorable A. Leon Higginbotham Jr. in the matter of the EEOC, James D. Hodgson, Secretary of Labor, U.S. Department of Labor, and United States of America versus AT&T et al., Philadelphia, Pa., January 18, 1973, series 2, EEOC, RG 403, NACP, 12.

21. Ibid., 15.

22. Ibid., 23.

23. Denniston called a conference on March 12, 1973, to cover the details of closing the case. Then, on May 30, 1974, a second consent decree covering $30 million in back pay and wage adjustments for twenty-five thousand Bell management employees would follow as Civil Action 74-1342. AT&T case chronology, AT&T Archives.

24. In the matter petition filed by the Equal Employment Opportunity Commission et al., Docket No. 19143 before the FCC, "Brief in Opposition to Equal Employment Opportunity Commission to Terminate This Proceeding," Harlem Consumer Education Council, series 2, EEOC, RG 403, NACP, 2.

25. Powers, interview.

26. Telecommunications Week, January 23, 1973, as quoted in Private Line, February 1973, duplicated.

27. Southwestern Bell, Management Report 30, no. 1G (January 30, 1973), author's copy.

28. David Easlick, telephone conversation with author, December 2000.

29. Randall L. Speck to author, Washington, D.C., September 11, 1998.

30. NOW press release, Chicago, January 18, 1973, Hacker papers 88-M13, carton 2, "Notes on Compliance & National Action," Schlesinger.

31. Scott, handwritten notes, Hacker papers 88-M13, carton 2, "Notes on Compliance & National Action," Schlesinger.

32. Lilley, calendar, 1973, Lilley papers, box 9, CRBM.

33. Satterfield, interview.

34. Hacker, "AT&T Workshop," proposed schedule and suggestions, NOW National Conference, Washington, D.C., February 18, 1973, author's copy.

35. NOW Compliance and Enforcement Task Force, Newsletter, March 1973, author's copy.

36. "Lilley Addresses Alliance," On Board 1, no. 5 (March 23, 1973), author's copy.

37. Barbara J. Colbert (a.k.a. Evans), "An Open Letter from the Alliance President," December 4, 1972.

38. Hacker to Valerie Kuck, President, Women's Rights Association at Bell Labs, Murray Hill, February 1973.

39. Heide to Lilley, Vernon, Conn., January 30, 1974, Heide papers, Schlesinger.

40. Heide turned in her manuscript in January 1974, but it was never used. Heide to Leonard Moran, January 25, 1974, enclosure; twenty-page manuscript, Heide papers, Schlesinger.

41. Transcript, in the matter of petitions filed by the EEOC et al., Docket 19143 before the FCC (Conference), March 12, 1973, vol. 68, series 2, EEOC, RG 403, NACP, 8173.

42. As they discussed materials accumulated in the case, Levy observed, "We are a long way apart from having anything that would be reliable information for any scholar or anyone else who is seeking to utilize this material." Denniston revoked the protective order he had issued May 18 concerning witnesses in New York. Transcript, series 2, EEOC, RG 403, NACP, 8185, 8191, 8201.

43. Ibid., 8204.

44. FCC 73M-434 memorandum opinion and order, Hacker files, 88-M13, box 2, folder "AT&T Printed, 1971-73," Schlesinger; also exists in series 2, EEOC, RG 403, NACP.

45. EEOC document, 1973, author's personal files.

46. Sally Hacker, AT&T Newsletter no. 4, Des Moines, n.d., personal copy.

47. Brown, interview, December 12, 2000.

48. *Wall Street Journal*, September 30, 1974, as quoted in P. Wallace, *Equal Employment*, 282.

49. Supplemental agreement, EEOC, James D. Hodgson, Secretary of Labor, U.S. Department of Labor and United States of America, May 13, 1975, Civil Action No. 73-149, as quoted in P. Wallace, *Equal Employment*, appendix D.

50. *Wall Street Journal*, May 31, 1974, 5.

51. P. Wallace, *Equal Employment*, 280.

52. Supplemental agreement, EEOC.

53. Hacker to Judith G. Stowes, Chairperson, Eastern Massachusetts Chapter, Des Moines, April 14, 1973, Hacker papers, Schlesinger.

54. Hacker to Copus, Des Moines, April 14, 1973, Hacker papers, Schlesinger.

55. Hacker to Kerkeslager, Des Moines, April 14, 1973, Hacker papers, Schlesinger.

56. Hacker to Naomi Weisstein, Des Moines, April 27, 1973. In this letter, Hacker describes herself as the "Iowa grandmother who 'witched' with you at the AAAS meeting in Chicago." Weisstein she described in another letter: "psychologist, author of 'Psychology Constructs the Female,' 'Woman's Nigger,' etc., pianist for Chicago Women's Liberation Rock Band, and one of the most 'together feminists I have ever met' . . . doing research at Bell Labs this year." Hacker to Midge Corasick, Des Moines, April 27, 1973.

57. *Wall Street Journal*, April 24, 1973, A1.

58. *Wall Street Journal*, April 18, 1974, A1.

59. *Business Week*, May 26, 1973, 30–31.

60. *Ms.*, November 1973, 52–54, 92–97.

61. Lilley, *The Last Word*, AT&T internal publication, author's copy.

CHAPTER 10

1. Liebers, interview.

2. The New York case arose before the AT&T settlement, having been instigated by NOW's New York chapter. NOW activists worked with the union to find women from Bell who would testify about their experiences and with the state's attorney general to get the case filed. Joan Hull, e-mail to author, October 15, 2001.

3. M. Barbara Boyle, "Equal Opportunity for Women Is Smart Business," *HBR*, May–June 1973, reprint no. 73303, Avon Corporate Records, box 129, Hagley.

4. "Ma Bell Agrees to Pay Reparations," *Newsweek*, January 29, 1973.

5. NOW Compliance and Enforcement Task Force, *Newsletter* 8 (March 1973), author's copy.

6. EEOC Interim Report, March 12, 1975, author's copy, 2, 3.

7. Ibid., 4, 5.

8. Bellcore focused on local exchange support, the numbering plan, national security issues, etc.

9. "Job Bias Agency Pushes Law Suits," *New York Times*, April 6, 1973.

10. Hacker to Copus, April 14, 1973, Hacker papers, Schlesinger.

11. J. B. Baron, J. A. Lindner, and D. C. Troppits, "Perspective on Indian Hill Affirmative Action Meetings," Naperville, Ill., August 12, 1977; Anne M. Anderson, memorandum to Fran J. Chessler, "Meeting with Mr. F. E. Wetzel, Corporate EEO Officer," Murray Hill, N.J., April 9, 1979; A. M. Anderson, "Wetzel Meeting Follow-up with Mrs. E. M. Watson," memorandum to Fran J. Chessler, Murray Hill, N.J., May 8, 1979; E. M. Watson, memorandum to F. J. Chessler, Murray Hill, N.J., November 14, 1979; Jane M. Herron and Fran J. Chessler, letter to Anne M. Anderson, Naperville, Ill., February 22, 1979.

12. *Exchange* 4, no. 7 (New York, July 1987).

13. Carol Wilson and Larry Lannon, "Women Confident, Comfortable in New Roles," *Telephony*, June 20, 1988, 38–44.

14. *Equal Opportunity and the AT&T Case* (Cambridge, Mass.: MIT Press, 1976).

15. Herbert R. Northrup and John A. Larson, *The Impact of the AT&T–EEO Consent Decree*, Labor Relations and Public Policy Series, no. 20 (Philadelphia, Wharton, 1979).

16. "NAM Action on Current Issues" in NAM files, "NAM Policy/Program/Legislature Group," box 189, ACC 1411, Hagley.

17. Scott papers, 91-M132 93 MI, carton 1, folder 6, Schlesinger.

18. Memorial service, New York, November 24, 1986, Lilley Collection, box 11, CRBM.

Chronology of Case-Related Events

YEAR	U.S.GOVERNMENT	AT&T	FEMINISTS
1963	Equal Pay Act.	Plan for Progress implementation.	Betty Friedan's *The Feminine Mystique.*
1964	Civil Rights Act.		
1965	EO 11246 bars discrimination by construction contractors, specifies affirmative action, and establishes the OFCC.	Full-scale study of telecommunications launched by FCC.	Sex-segregated want ads debated. Civil rights and antiwar protests.
1966		Lorena Weeks bids for job as switchman.	NOW founded.
1967	EO 11375 amends 11246 to include "sex." EEOC builds file on AT&T.	AT&T programs address urban racial and employment problems.	NOW provides legal counsel for Weeks. NOW demonstrates against EEOC.
1968	OFCC Guidelines for 11246 (race). EEOC negotiates with AT&T.	Five-month telephone strike. Carterphone decision allows customer-owned equipment to be connected to AT&T's network.	Caroline Bird's *Born Female.* NOW holds White House "rights not roses" protest.
1969	OFCC Guidelines for 11246 (sex). EEOC Guidelines. OFCC Order #1 requires compliance reviews. FCC proposes guidelines on nondiscrimination.	Court rules sex is not a BFOQ for switchman. MCI granted private line for Chicago–St. Louis route. Bell System suffers major service problems.	Matina Horner's "Women's Will to Fail."
1970	OFCC Order #4 extends coverage to non-construction contractors. OFCC issues Guidelines for 11375. FCC orders common carriers to provide affirmative action plans. EEOC files petition for intervention in AT&T rate case.	AT&T creates task force on women. Women's Rights Committee starts at Bell Labs. AT&T files for first general long distance rate increase in 17 years.	NOW has 3,071 members, provides a phone company anti-discrimination kit, and holds first Women's Strike Day, August 26.

YEAR	U.S.GOVERNMENT	AT&T	FEMINISTS
1971	FCC establishes Docket 19143 to investigate AT&T employment practices. OFCC Revised Order #4 requires goals and time-tables. EEOC files *A Unique Competence*.	Lorena Weeks gets switch-man job. Specialized common carriers allowed to compete with AT&T. Longest national strike of telephone workers. First black elected to AT&T board. AT&T Alliance for Women founded.	NOW pickets Bell companies and issues business and industry antidiscrimination kit.
1972	EEOC AT&T hearings begin. Equal Pay Act extended to cover administrative and professional employees and outside sales. GSA approves AT&T affirmative action plan, but Justice assumes jurisdiction. Equal Employment Opportunity Act gives EEOC enforcement powers.	AT&T submits model affirmative action program to GSA. First woman elected to AT&T's Board.	NOW bills AT&T for $4 billion back pay, designates AT&T as a "National Action," and sets August 23 as "Employment and the Bell System Day."
1973	AT&T consent decree. *Frontiero* v. *Richardson* benefit case decided by Supreme Court.	AT&T implements requirements of decree including $15 million back pay, assessment, upgrade and transfer programs.	NOW stages National AT&T Action Day. NOW national conference builds strategies for business compliance and government enforcement.
1974	Second AT&T consent decree involves $30 million back pay and wage adjustments. Justice files antitrust suit against AT&T.	Western Electric makes back payment of $800,000 to women.	
1975	Supplemental agreement between the EEOC and AT&T involving $2.5 million back pay.	AT&T judged in non-compliance.	NOW files suit against Sears, Martin Marietta, and other companies.
1979	Termination of AT&T consent decree.		

INDEX